IMAGES
of America

REEDSBURG

On the Cover: After burning to the ground in 1900, the Bates House needed to be rebuilt. Around 5,000 loads of sandstone were hauled away in order to build the house at street level. The building operated as a hotel until 1911, when it was purchased by Dr. T.R. Hastings and opened as a sanitarium. (Courtesy of Reedsburg Public Library.)

IMAGES
of America

REEDSBURG

Craig Braunschweig, Kali Hentges,
and David Moon

ARCADIA
PUBLISHING

ISBN 978-0-7385-9864-2

Published by Arcadia Publishing
Charleston, South Carolina

Printed in the United States of America

Library of Congress Control Number: 2012950248

For all general information, please contact Arcadia Publishing:
Telephone 843-853-2070
Fax 843-853-0044
E-mail sales@arcadiapublishing.com
For customer service and orders:
Toll-Free 1-888-313-2665

Visit us on the Internet at www.arcadiapublishing.com

This book is dedicated to the city of Reedsburg,
for all who have lived in this great city and all who will live here.

Contents

ACKNOWLEDGMENTS

This book project began when Craig went to a meeting of the University of Oshkosh history club, where he was an officer. The meeting was about how to be published. Craig's personal friend and fellow history club officer, Austin Fredrick, was a guest speaker and talked about the book he had written and his experience writing an Images of America book about his hometown, Markesan.

After the meeting, Craig got on the phone and called Kali to see if she was interested in coauthoring the book with him. She must have thought he was nuts and pulling her leg. Kali told Craig that she would have to think it over and do some research to see if there would be enough history and information available to do a book about our hometown. After a few days, Kali let Craig know that she would come on board to coauthor the book. The problem was that they both were still in school and, though interested in and studying history at the time, neither had yet received a degree. While such an academic certification was not a requirement for writing a book about the history of Reedsburg, Craig and Kali agreed that they would benefit from the insights of a social studies teacher or someone in the community with a background in history. The person uppermost in their minds was David Moon, who had been Craig and Kali's history teacher in high school. Having a huge amount of respect for David, they scheduled a meeting with him and told him the idea about the book. Luckily, he signed on to the project right away.

With David on board, Craig and Kali started working on the book proposal and began setting up information and reference contacts. These people would end up being very helpful in the production of the book. Among them are Peggy Albert, of Lorraine's Mini Mall; Marisa and Dale Thomson; and Barb Steinhorst. When Craig meet with Barb Steinhorst at the Reedsburg Area Historical Society, she told him how happy she was to help out with anything the coauthors would need. Without the support and help from Barb and the Reedsburg Area Historical Society, it would have been very hard to complete the book and make it a fun and exciting adventure. Lastly, we would like to thank Craig's mom, Beth Braunschweig, for her work on this book. In a way, working as Craig's secretary, she was also a coauthor. She helped set up meetings, got information on subjects that Craig was stuck on, and ran errands, picking up photographs and information while Craig was in school. She was more important to the completion of this book than she gives herself credit for.

Finally, we would like to thank Jeff Seering for help with information and photographs, Alissa Witt for text editing, Alex Beld for photographic editing, and Kelsey Jernander for quality editing and photographs. A special thanks goes to the *Reedsburg Times Press* for their kind donation of photos, and to the many people who gave Craig, David, or Kali photographs. Without you and your help and information, this book would never have been done. Thank you!

INTRODUCTION

Upon being told of the prospects of a book about Reedsburg, many people responded with, "Why? Why write about Reedsburg? There is not anything remarkable about the town." For the longest time, the authors' answer was simply, "Why not?" Convincing folks that the authors were not crazy was not always easy. However, through research and writing, the authors found many good answers to the original questions and have changed the opinions of skeptics. So, why Reedsburg?

From Reedsburg's early days as a milling village on the banks of the Baraboo River, it has experienced growth and change. Established as a community in the pioneer era of the 1850s, the city of Reedsburg is now home to nearly 10,000 residents and a variety of thriving industries. Throughout Reedsburg's history, its people have been innovative in creating conditions for economic success and have shown the ability to overcome setbacks. This book's chapter on the town's floods and fires describes the community's ability to bounce back from such disasters. Many notable hotels and businesses were completely destroyed in various disasters, yet in many cases, the businesses were rebuilt. The Big Store fire is one of the most well-known disasters, but the building remains and serves as a home to many local businesses. While the Woolen Mill was a complete loss, the office building remains, home to the Wormfarm Institute and the Woolen Mill Gallery.

Today, visitors are drawn to Reedsburg's historic downtown, home to specialty shops and restaurants. Once a railroad stop on the Chicago & Northwestern Line, Reedsburg is now the trailhead for the 400 State Trail bike route. The Baraboo River runs through Reedsburg, providing a great opportunity for canoeing, especially during the annual Lazy Beaver Canoe Race. One of the largest baseball tournaments in the area takes place at Nishan Park. Freda Meyers Nishan, who is remembered for her philanthropic spirit, donated money to build a community building and purchased and donated land for the old hospital on Park Street. Nishan Park has five baseball/softball fields. Next to these fields is the Lions/Jaycees building and the RACA building, which houses an ice rink in the winter. This facility allowed the city to develop a good hockey program. Both structures are important in June during Butterfest, an annual weeklong festival that arose from Reedsburg's high rate of butter production. The festival, including the food court and craft fair, takes place in Nishan Park.

Two points of pride for the city of Reedsburg are sports and military service. Barney Klecker, a graduate of Webb High School, is the US record-holder for the 50 mile run, finishing with a time of 4 hours, 51 minutes, and 25 seconds on October 5, 1980. The high school regularly sends exemplary athletes to state-level competitions in many sporting events, including, but not limited to, track, Special Olympics, basketball, and football. In the case of the latter sport, the school made back-to-back appearances at the state championship. Reedsburg High School also strongly supports the military. Each year on Veteran's Day, the school hosts an assembly, open to the public, honoring local veterans. An assembly was recently held as a sendoff to the Red Arrows upon their deployment. A Veterans of Foreign Wars memorial was also recently completed in Nishan

Park, and the local chapter hosts a breakfast one weekend a month at the VFW hall. This book covers Reedsburg's veterans and the town's involvement in the nation's wars, along with some great history of the local police and fire departments.

What people often hear about Reedsburg is that "it is just a bunch of churches and bars." While that is a serious overstatement, there is some truth to the idea. Reedsburg has a rich religious history in which community members bonded together to create places of worship based on need. As soon as a need was identified, people of like faith would work to organize a congregation, find a meeting place, and eventually build their own place of worship. The bars are just one category of the many local businesses that help to make Reedsburg what it is. Some of these businesses are well-established, recognizable names, and some of them are new but help to give fresh life to the buildings on downtown's Main Street. The Blue Heron, a fairly new business, has adapted an old bank to house the store, leaving the old vault intact. This vault is now part of the store and customers can walk inside while shopping. The store is mere miles down the road from Viking Village, which has been a part of Reedsburg since the 1970s. Farming, also a staple in the areas surrounding Reedsburg, is highlighted during the annual Farm Art D'tour, in which art pieces are created on many local farms to highlight the industry's impact on the area.

The city of Reedsburg's website has a small section devoted to local history, including information on notable people, places, wildlife, and architecture. Hopefully, this book will inspire more people to get interested in local history. No matter where someone ends up, their hometown will always be a part of their life, and knowing its history instills pride.

So, why Reedsburg? Because there is so much not known or barely known about Reedsburg yet to be explored. The photographs in the following pages show the evolution of life through a perspective not everyone has access to. This book explores the history of the library, notable community members, businesses, churches, schools, the military, the police and fire departments, disasters, sports, and all that is generally interesting and good about Reedsburg.

The authors hope that readers of this book enjoy learning about Reedsburg, Wisconsin, and discover the importance of keeping history alive.

One

Life in Reedsburg

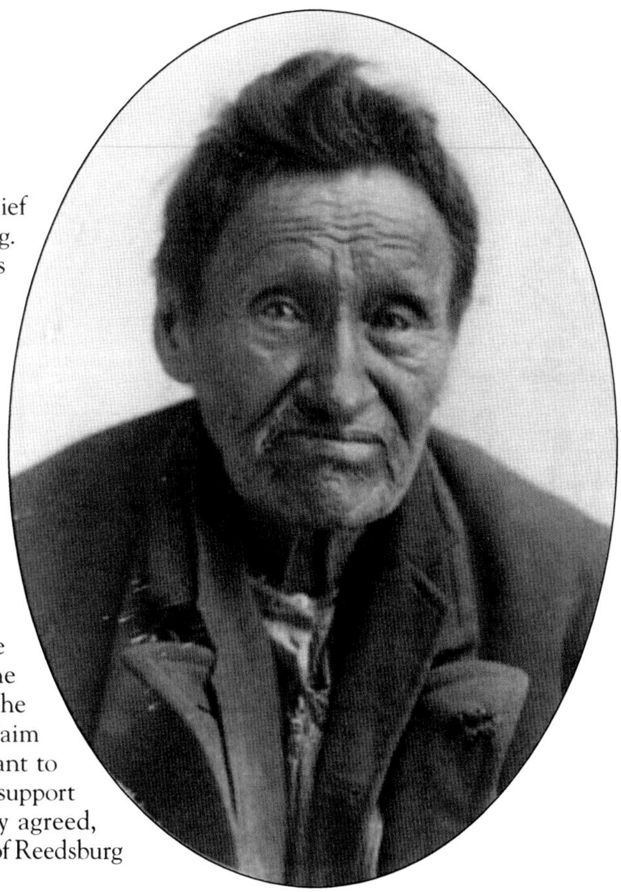

Ah-ha-cho-ka was a Ho-Chunk chief living in a village near Reedsburg. On December 26, 1873, US soldiers were sent from Sparta, Wisconsin, to forcibly relocate his family and other tribe members to a reservation in Nebraska. Many residents of Reedsburg showed up at the train depot to protest the deportation, and by 6:00 p.m., obtained a writ of habeas corpus sworn out before the court commissioner. This was given to Sheriff Buel, who, after initial reluctance, released a large number of the Ho-Chunk people, allowing them to remain in the Reedsburg area. In April 1874, the US Indian commissioner came to the area to investigate Ah-ha-cho-ka's claim to citizenship. The chief was reluctant to hand over his papers, but with the support of community members, he finally agreed, securing his right to stay. (Courtesy of Reedsburg Public Library.)

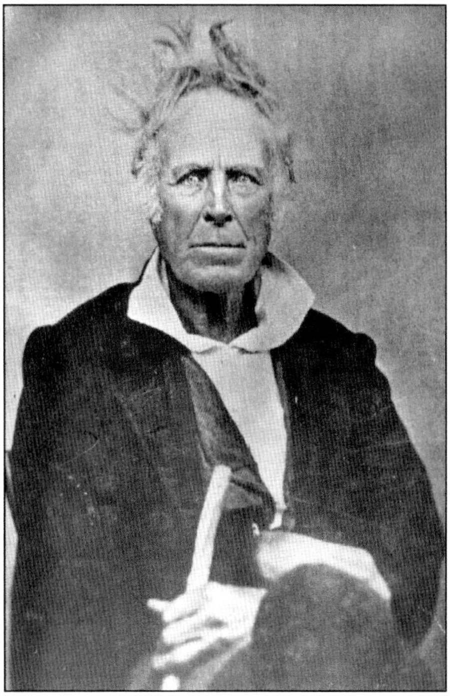

James Wilson Babb (September 26, 1789–May 20, 1875) was the first white settler in the Reedsburg area, originally naming it "Babb's Woods." Born in Frederick County, Virginia, he moved to Greene County, Ohio, in 1810 with his father. A few years later, he married Rebecca Scarff of Virginia and brought her to Ohio. Shortly thereafter, he inherited his father's 400 acres. In 1845, the couple moved to Wisconsin. Babb was a highly respected member of the community, as evidenced in his obituary. His monument is pictured below. (Both, courtesy of Reedsburg Public Library.)

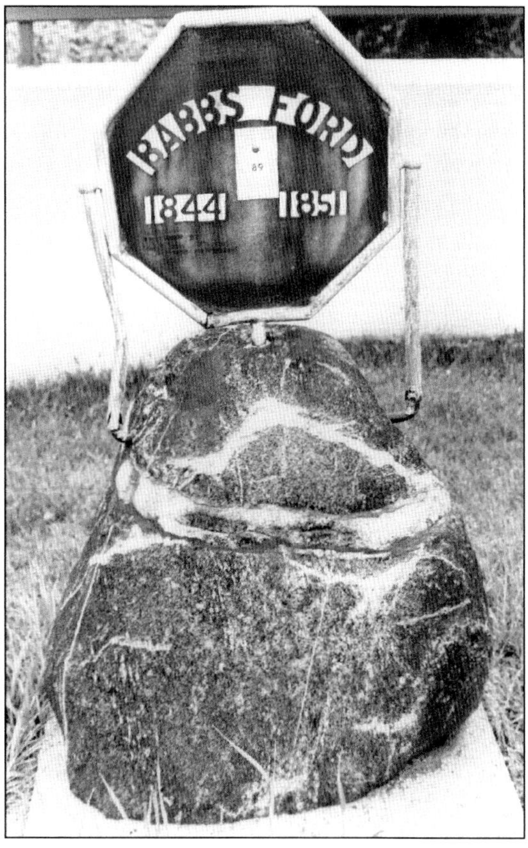

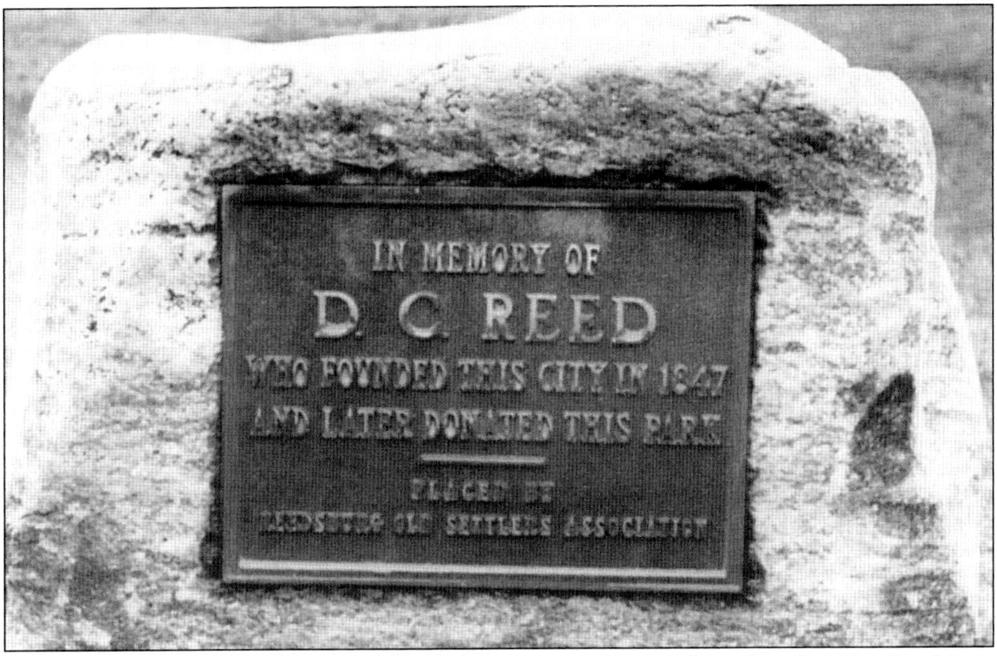

David Reed was the man who started the settlement as a village, and it is from him that Reedsburg takes its name. He founded the city in 1847. (Courtesy of Reedsburg Historical Society.)

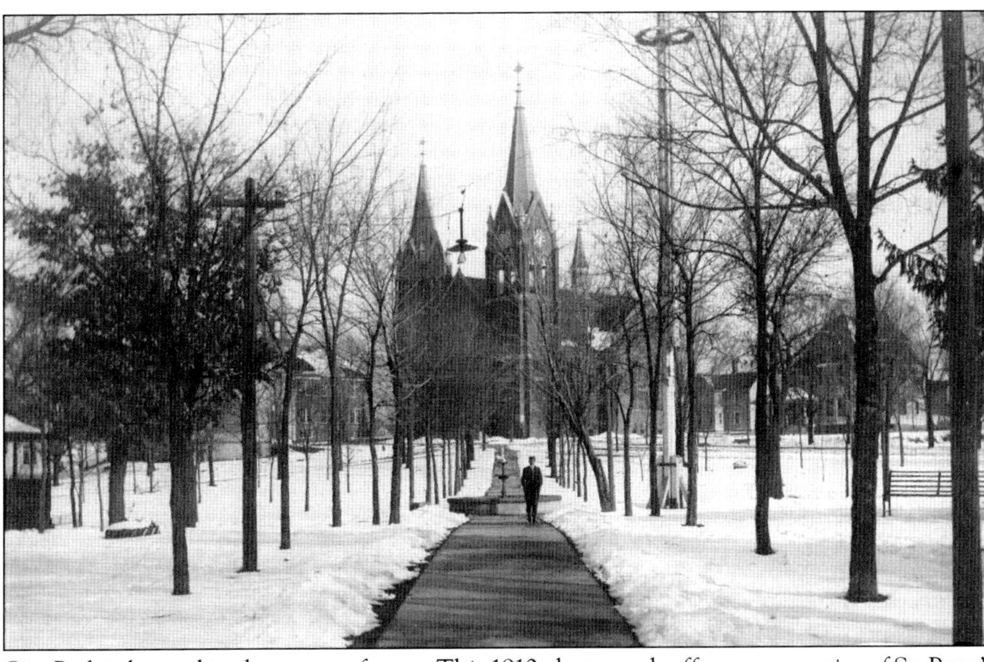

City Park is located in the center of town. This 1910 photograph offers a perspective of St. Peter's Church. (Courtesy of *Reedsburg Times Press.*)

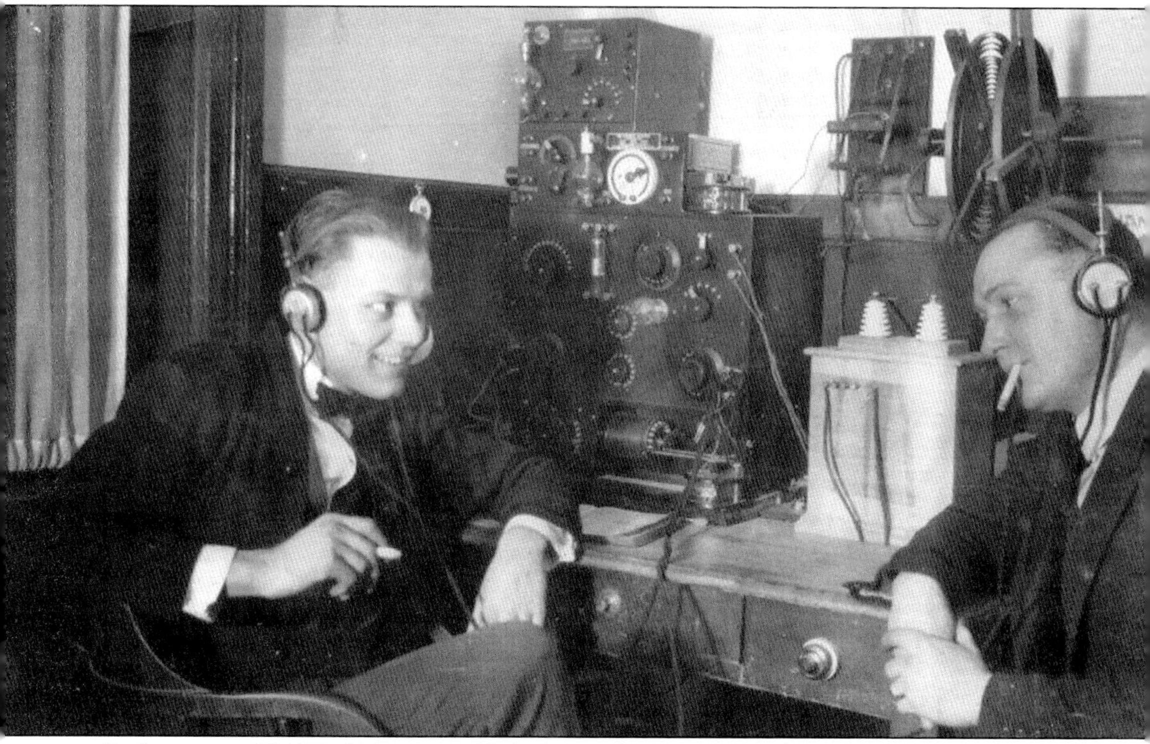

Radio station WRDB-AM was established on February 6, 1953, by its owner, W.C. Forrest. In 1964, he sold the station to the Schuetze, Stuart, and Swygart Corporation of Monroe, which then sold it to the Sauk Broadcasting Corporation in March 1971. WRDB-FM (104.9) was added in June 1967 and WBDL-FM (102.9) in October 1996. WRDB-FM's call letters were changed to the current WNFM in 1983, when the station changed its format to country music. (Courtesy of *Reedsburg Times Press.*)

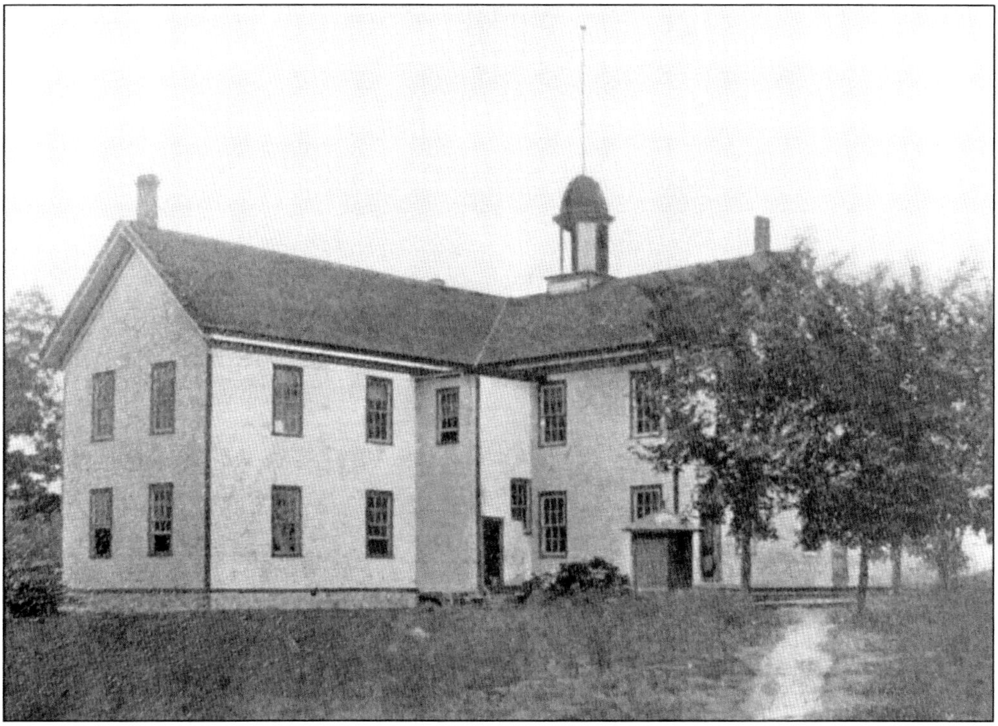

Reedsburg's old high school (above), built in 1905, accommodated 256 students. By the 1950s, over 600 students were enrolled, and it was deemed necessary to build a new school to house the students and to better suit the changing educational system. After much debate, it was decided that the new high school (below) would be built next to Webb Park to honor the large donation Herbert Webb had given for the school's construction. (Both, courtesy of Reedsburg Public Library.)

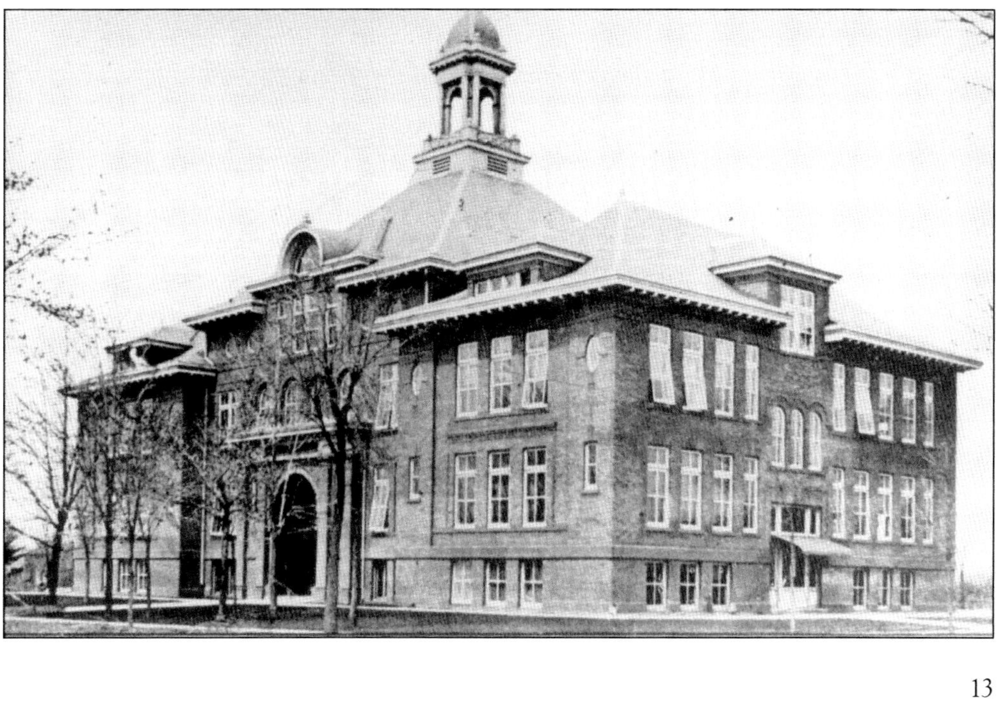

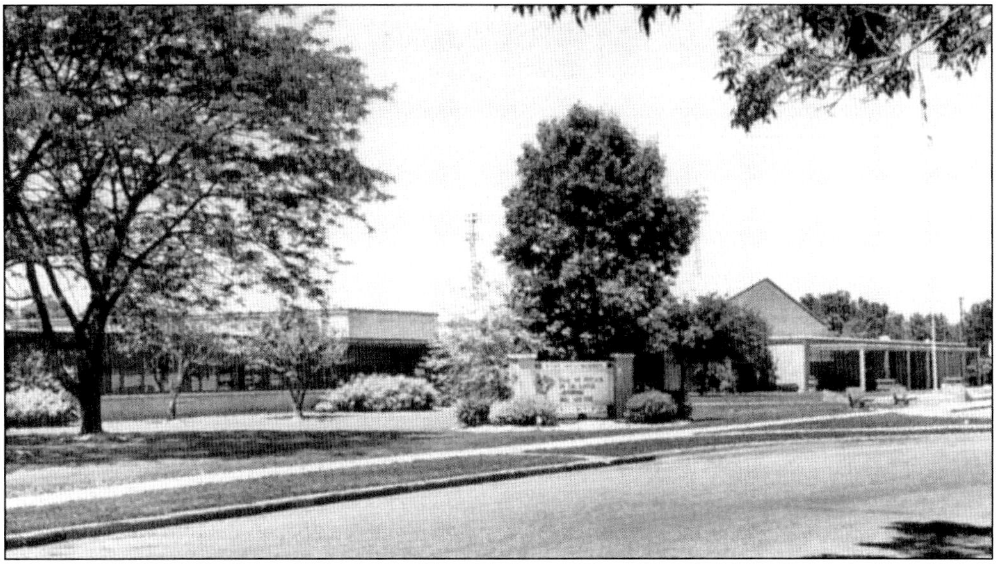

Webb High School (above) was dedicated on December 15, 1957, and served the community for four decades. By 1990, student enrollment was outgrowing the school, and a referendum was passed to build a new high school and convert Webb into a middle school. The current high school (below) opened in 1998. (Both, courtesy of Reedsburg Public Library.)

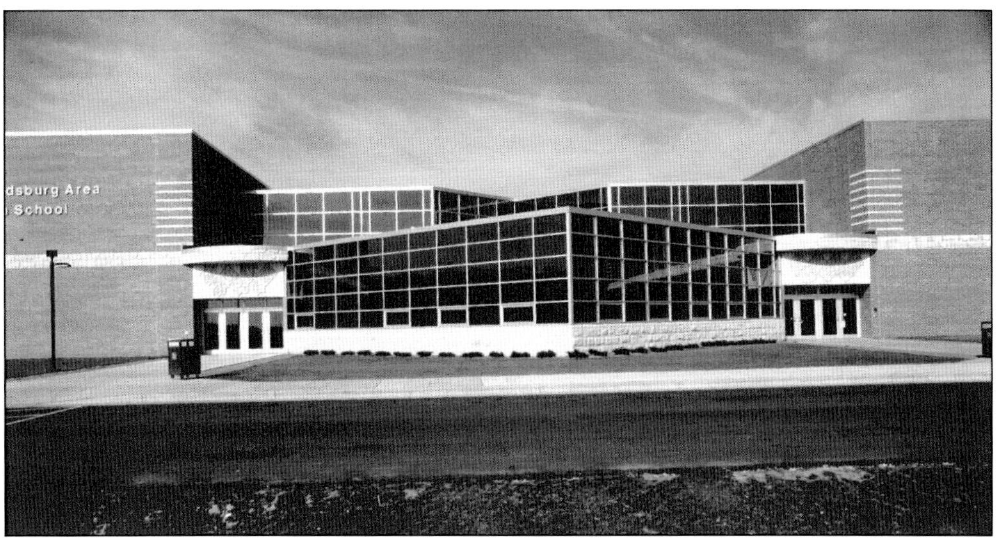

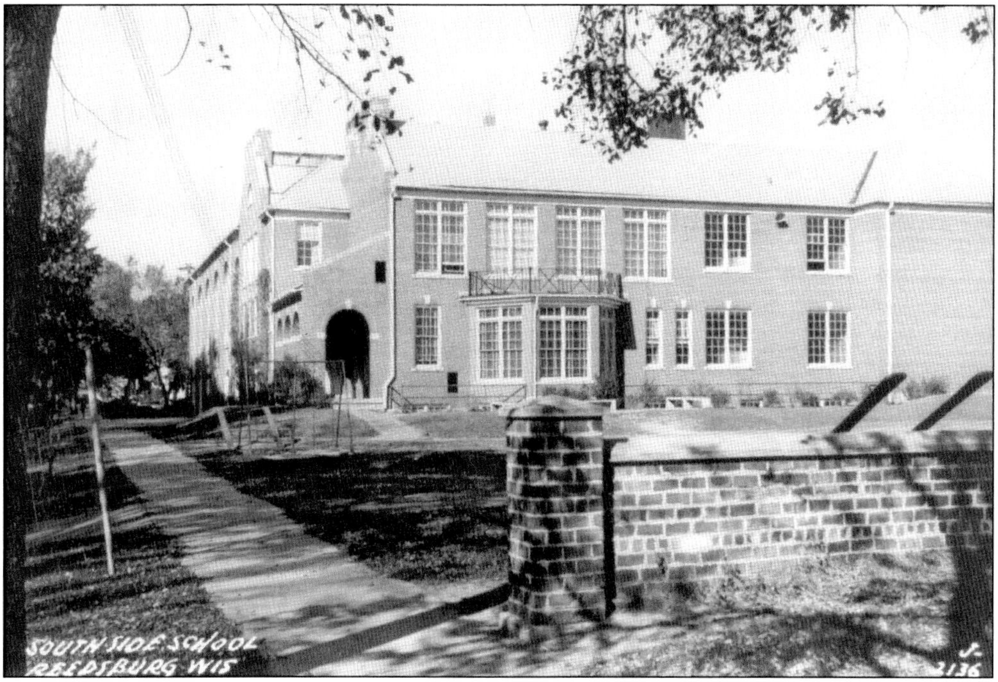

The original South School was built in 1889 and had two classrooms. A second story containing two more classrooms was added in 1895. The building served the community until 1936, when the modern South School (pictured) was built. Today, the building is a K–3 elementary school. (Courtesy of Reedsburg Public Library.)

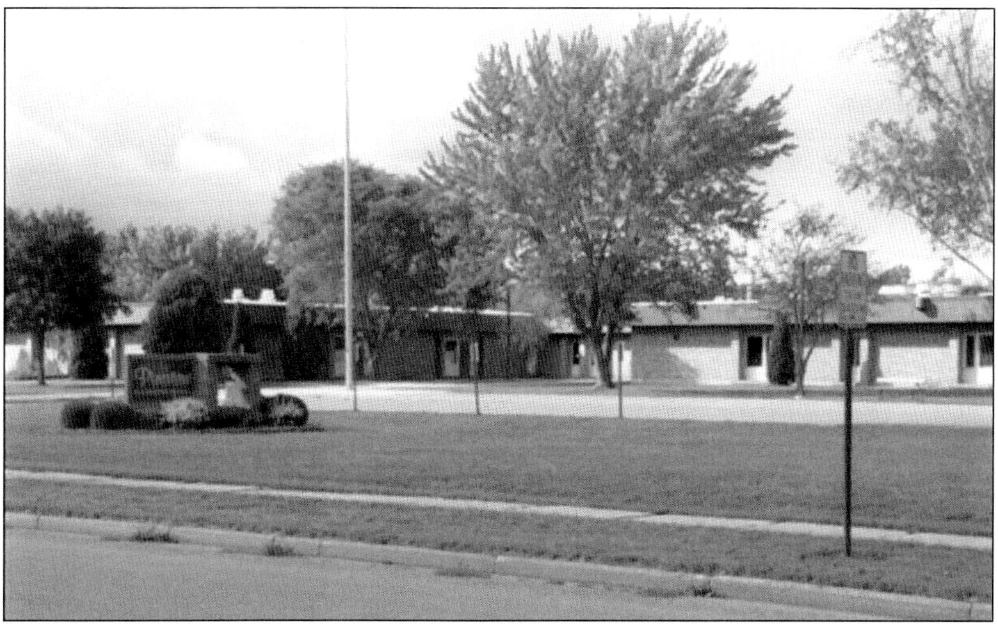

Pineview Elementary is located in the old middle school building. It made the move after the new high school was built to accommodate the growing school district. Now the largest elementary school in the Reedsburg School District, Pineview opened in 1998 and serves students from early childhood to fifth grade. (Courtesy of Steve Braunschweig.)

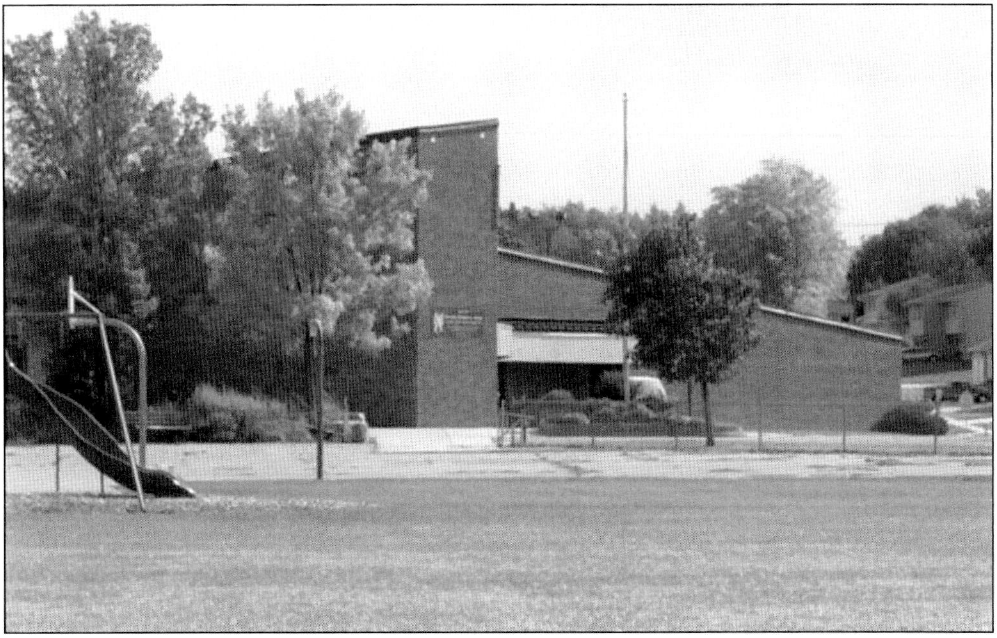

The first Westside Elementary School was set up in the Teacher's College building after it closed in 1969. In 1971, 10 acres of land were purchased, and construction on a new building began in 1977. The school was dedicated on November 11, 1979. In 1990, Westside underwent a renovation to better suit the needs of the growing number of students. (Courtesy of Steve Braunschweig.)

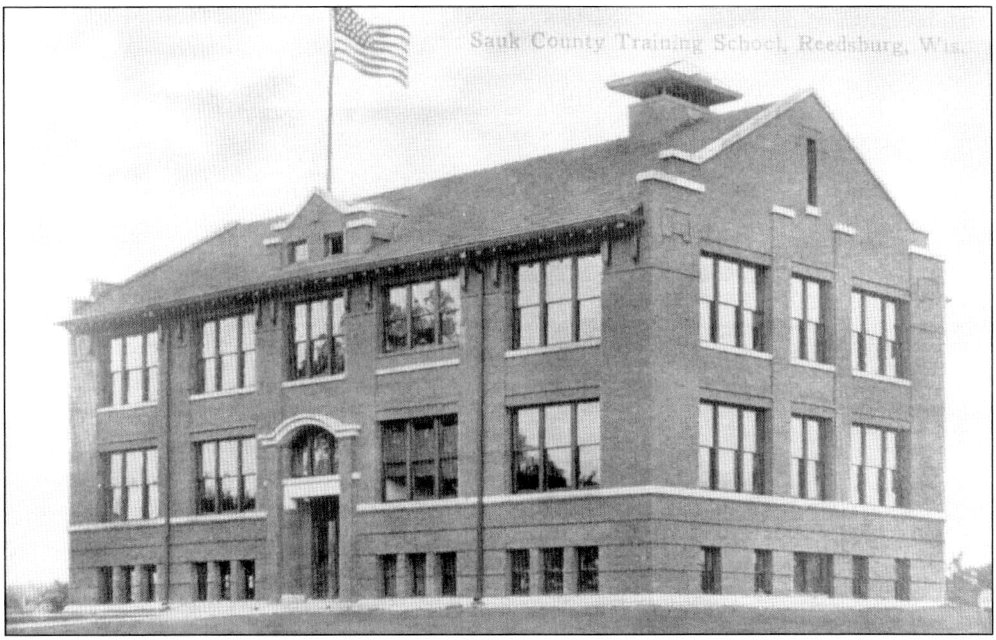

The Sauk County Teachers College was originally located on the top floor of the high school. As the school's popularity increased, a larger space was deemed necessary in 1910. The new building, shown here, opened in the fall of 1911. The school continued to train teachers even after the legislature instituted a law requiring all teachers to have a four-year degree. The county board decided to phase out the school in the spring of 1969. (Courtesy of Reedsburg Public Library.)

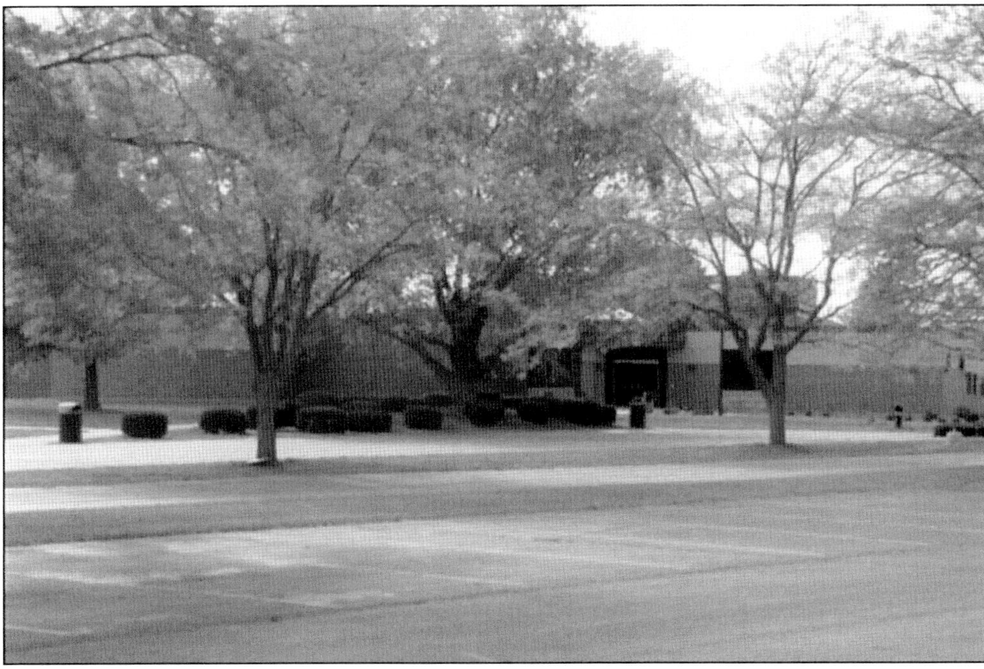

Madison College–Reedsburg (formerly Madison Area Technical College) began as The Reedsburg Vocation School in 1959. It merged with the Area Vocational Technical and Adult Education District No. 4 on July 1, 1967. Construction of the current building began in 1977. Since that time, the campus has undergone renovations to continue to meet the needs of its students. (Courtesy of Steve Braunschweig.)

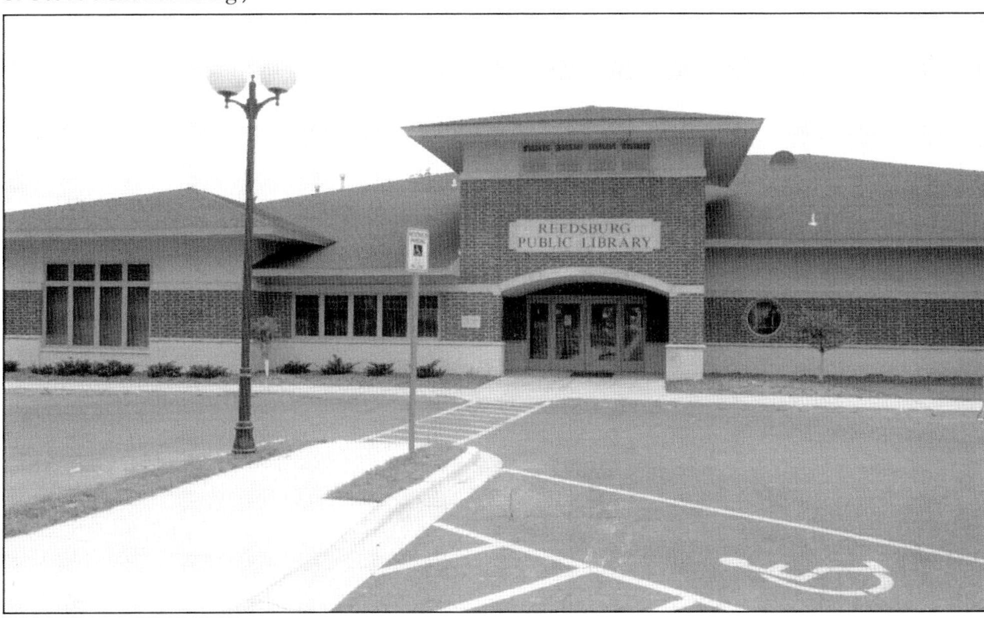

The current library building opened in January 1998. The building has a conference room and a community room that can be rented out for meetings, a fantastic children's section, quiet study rooms, a plethora of computers, and many other resources to serve the community. (Courtesy of Reedsburg Public Library.)

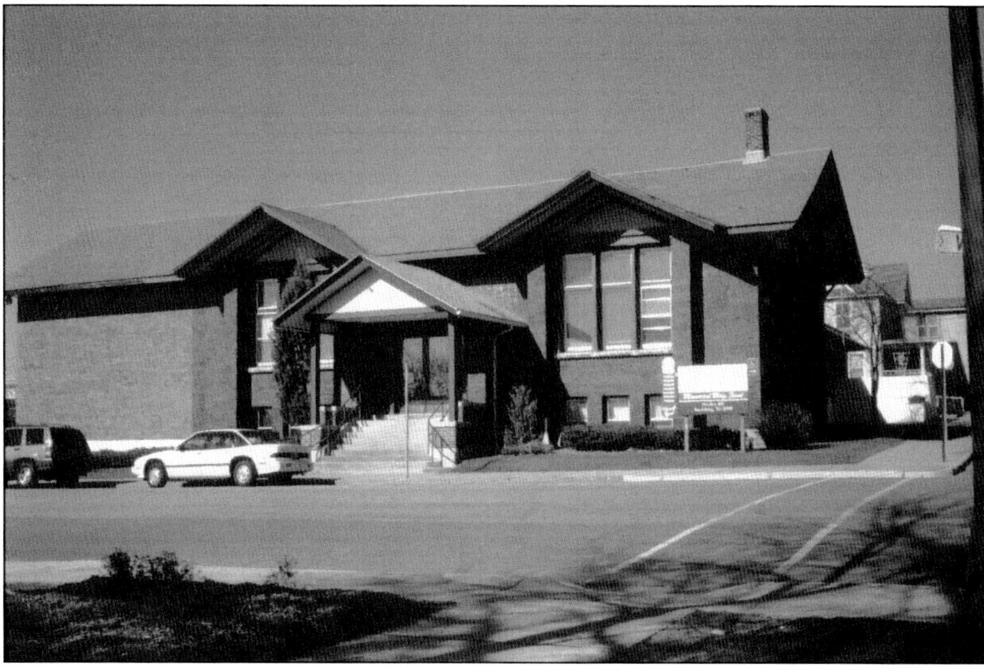

Reedsburg's first library opened on May 8, 1899. The library has expanded greatly over the years, outgrowing its space three times. The Carnegie library, pictured here, was opened on January 1, 1912, and served the city until the mid-1990s, when expansion and technology began to limit the space for tables and working. (Both, courtesy of Reedsburg Public Library.)

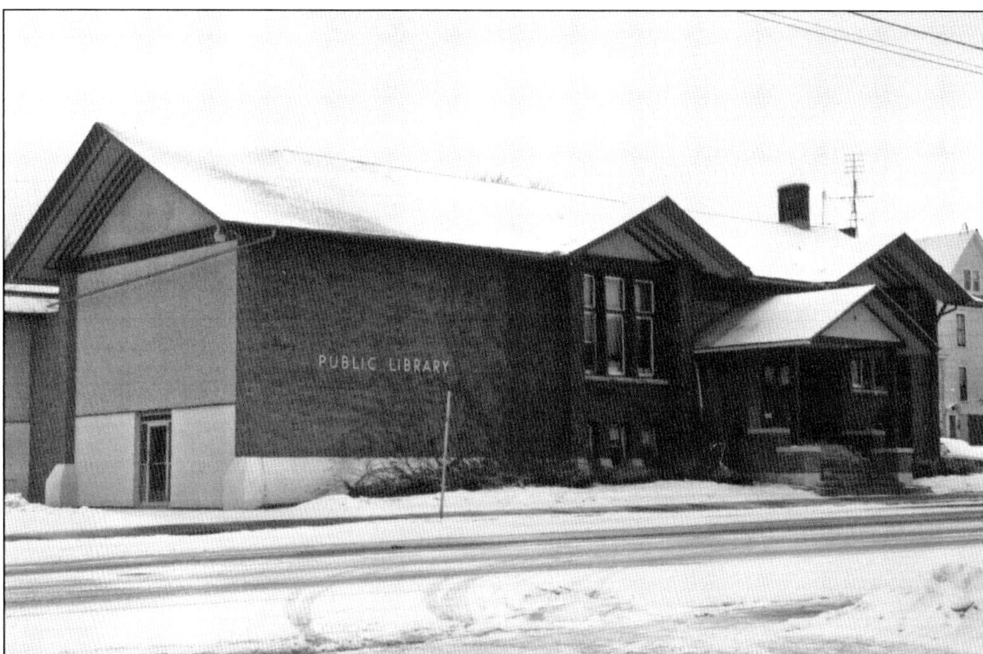

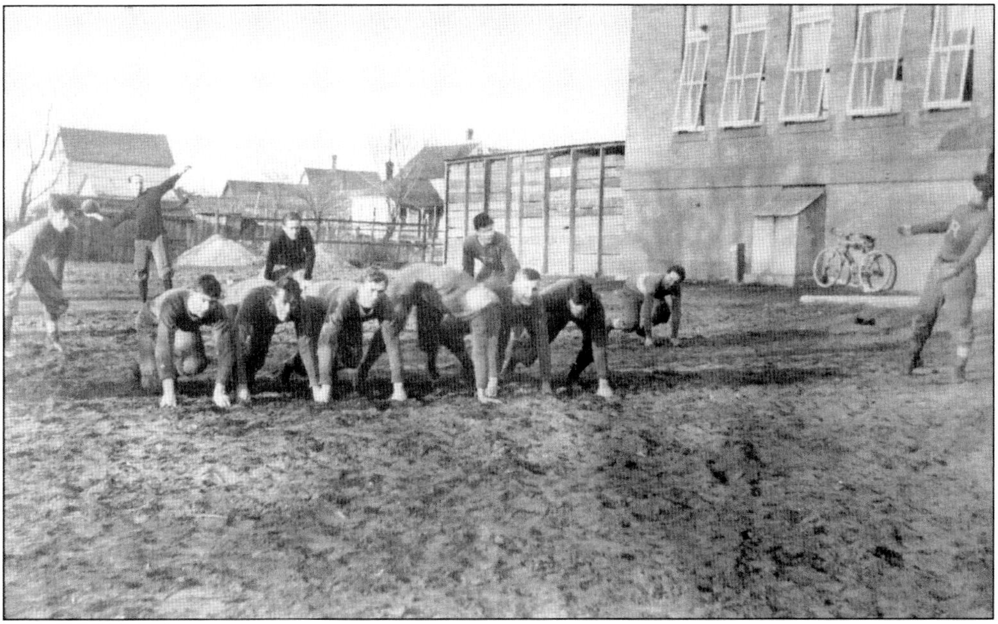

Among those pictured above are Harold Kleeber, Reg Myer, and Joe Carrol. Reedsburg football was first played where the city dump is now located. The team's field was then moved to Webb High School. In 2000, after the New Reedsburg Area High School was constructed, Millennium Field was built. In 2008, coach Brian Pottinger (at right, holding trophy) led his football team to their first state finals, in which they lost to Waupaca High 21-20. The following year, Pottinger led his team back to the state championship game, this time beating West De Prere 34-27. (Above, courtesy of Reedsburg Public Library; right, courtesy of Noah Hofrichter.)

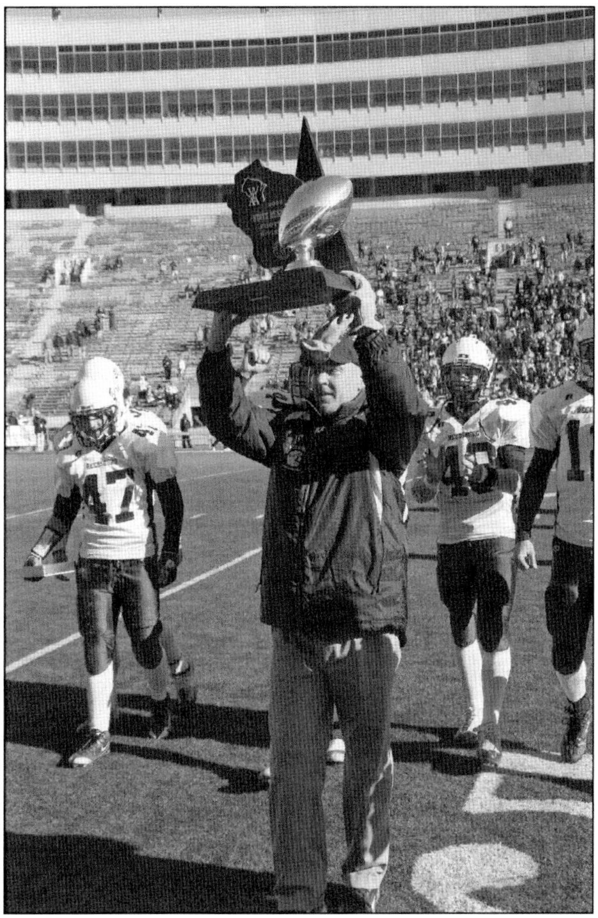

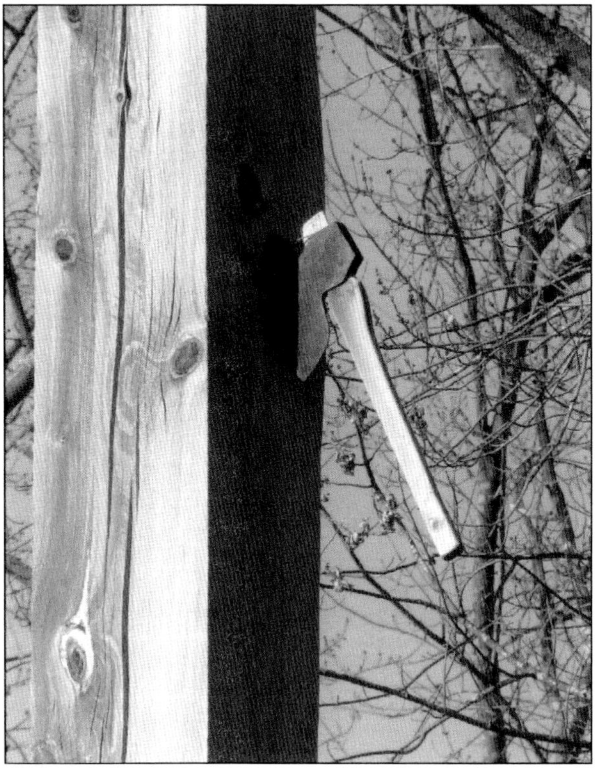

The Bicentennial Monument was dedicated on July 5, 1976. It consists of a timber spire, representing the logs used in settlers' homes, and an axe from the Kleeber family, symbolizing the tools used in settling the area. The marker's concrete base calls to mind the rocky river bottom, and the entire monument sits atop a mound to honor the Native Americans who inhabited the area. A time capsule was placed inside the base and will be opened at the nation's tercentennial. (Left, courtesy of Craig Braunschweig; below, courtesy of Steve Braunschweig.)

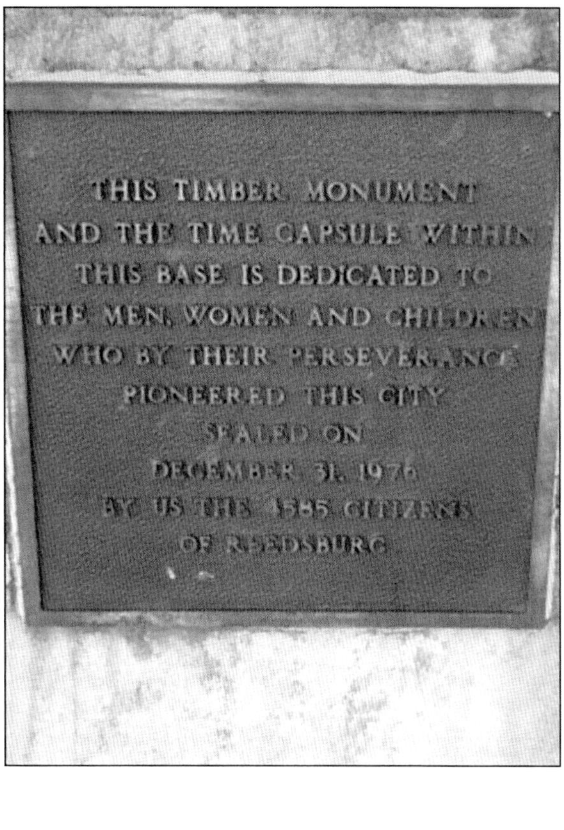

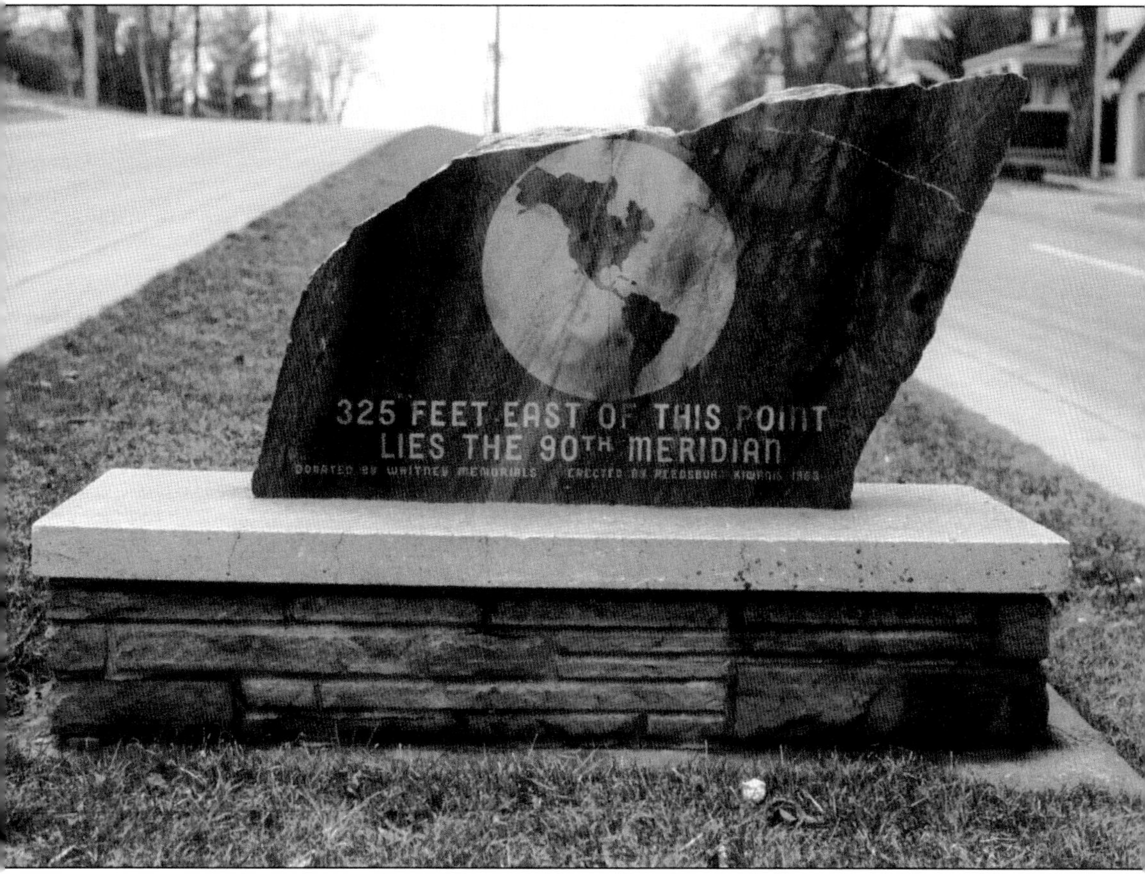

Reedsburg is located on the 90th meridian, the baseline for the Central Time Zone, and this fact is marked with a stone on Main Street. The marker, dedicated on October 14, 1963, was donated by Whitney Memorials and erected by the Kiwanis. Reedsburg's special location means that clocks here are exactly in sync with Central Standard Time. (Courtesy of Reedsburg Public Library.)

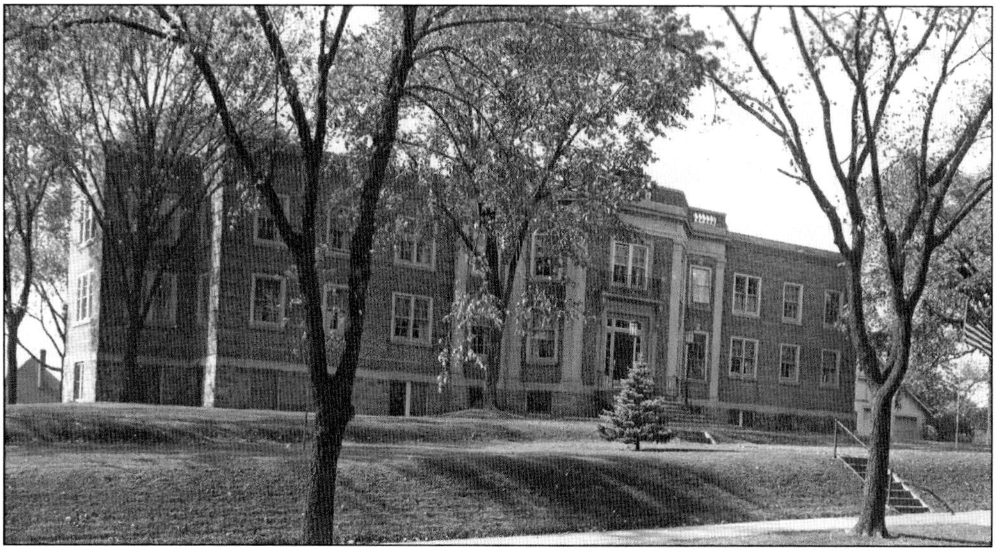

Reedsburg Area Medical Center (RAMC) was built in 1976 (above), and the first patients were transferred from the Park Street Hospital in February of that year. The special care unit was added in September 1982. Over the years, RAMC has undergone several renovations and additions, including the most recent addition of the specialty center (below). (Both, courtesy of Steve Braunschweig.)

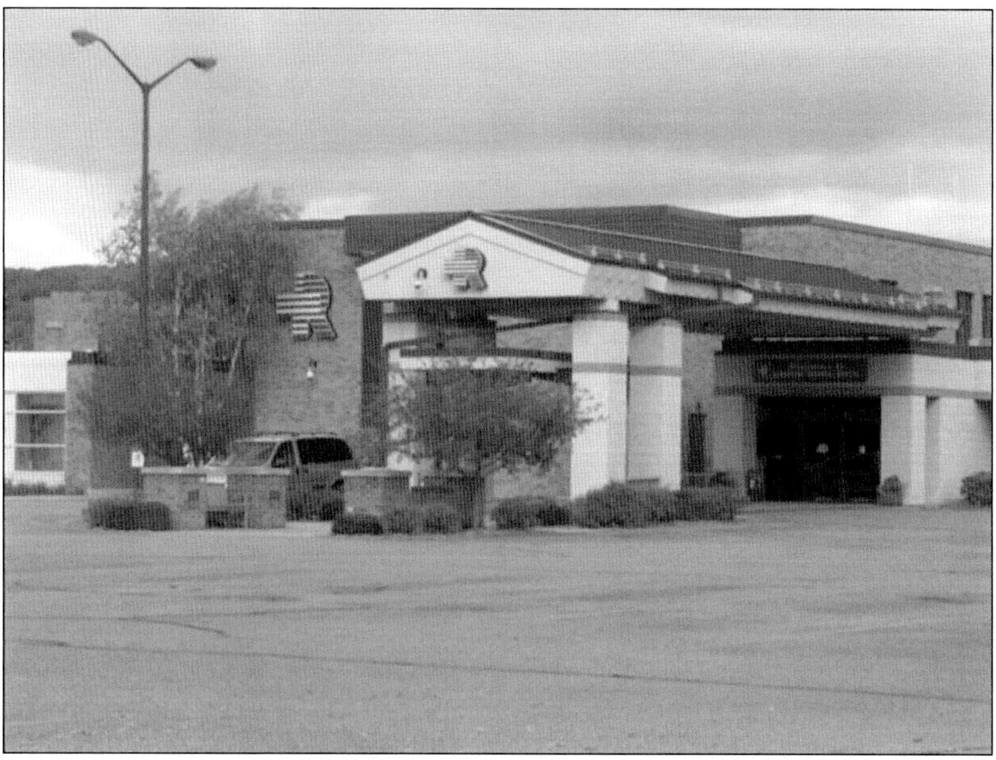

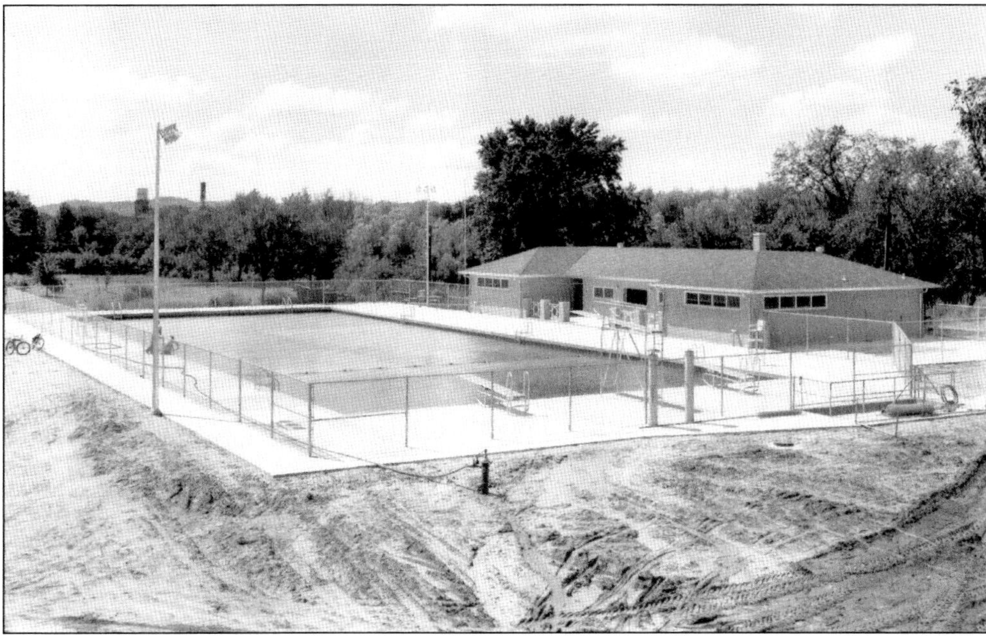

Reedsburg's first cement pool, built in 1923, was located near the South Webb Bridge. The pool worked well for 35 years until the community outgrew it. A new pool was built and dedicated in July 1957 and was renovated and updated in 1998. It continues to serve the community. (Courtesy of Reedsburg Public Library.)

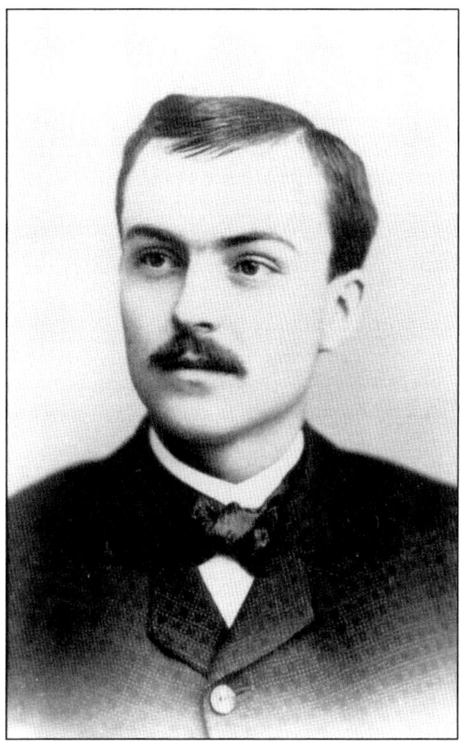

Herbert H. Webb (1858–1954) was born in New York. He and his family came to Reedsburg in 1869, but the majority of them passed away soon after, leaving Webb and his brother to tend to the farm. At 21, Webb enrolled in high school, but dropped out after one semester. Webb did not care for farming and, after saving his money, was able to attend Valparaiso Business School for a short-term business education. In 1881, he returned to Reedsburg and joined Harris & Holster as a bookkeeper and retail operator. On December 1, 1883, Webb partnered with D.G. Schweke and G.C. Schweke to open the Boy's Store department store. It was so prosperous that, three years later, they moved locations and opened Big Store. Webb dissolved his partnership and left Reedsburg in 1908. In 1944, he set up a $300,000 trust to be used by the city for a project deemed appropriate by the city fathers. Development of Webb Park began in 1945, and its dedication took place on July 6, 1952. In February of that year, Webb donated funds to build a high school next to the park, citing the importance he placed on education. (Courtesy of Reedsburg Public Library.)

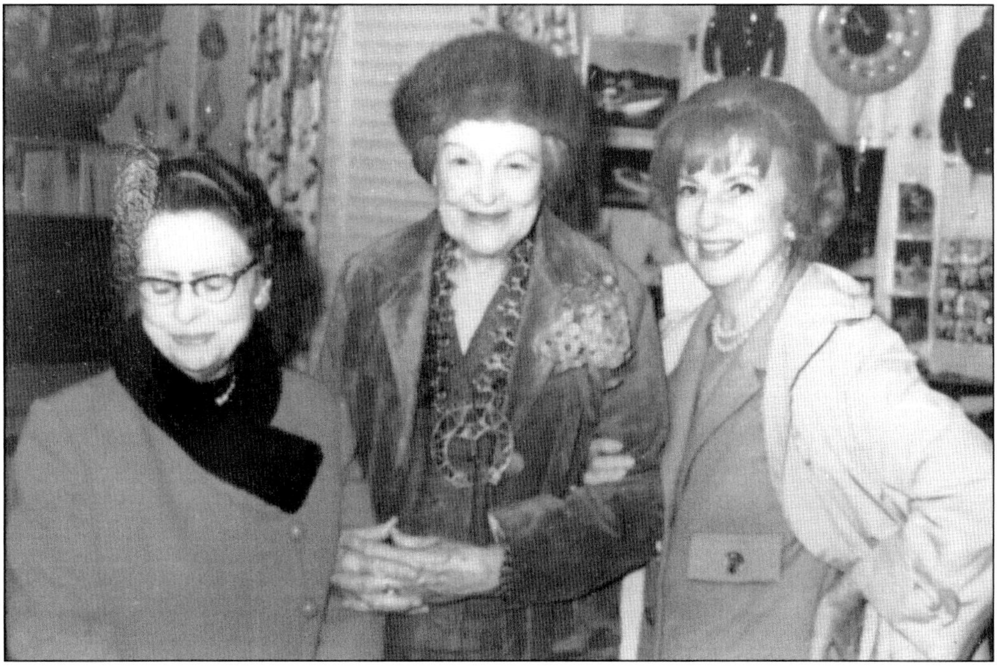

Agnes Moorhead (December 6, 1900–April 30, 1974), pictured at far right above, famous for her role as Endora on the television series *Bewitched*, was born to John and Mary (Mollie) in Clinton, Massachusetts. In 1919, her family moved to Reedsburg, where her father worked as a minister and her mother as organist, choir director, and vocalist at First Presbyterian Church. The family left in the 1920s, but Mary did move back after John passed away. Moorhead earned her MA in public speaking and drama from the University of Wisconsin–Madison. Upon her passing, her old manuscripts were bequeathed to the library. She visited Reedsburg often and said that the city brought out nostalgic sentiments. Below, on October 3, 1971, Moorhead returned to Reedsburg as a guest speaker at the dedication of the new municipal complex. (Both, courtesy of Reedsburg Historical Society.)

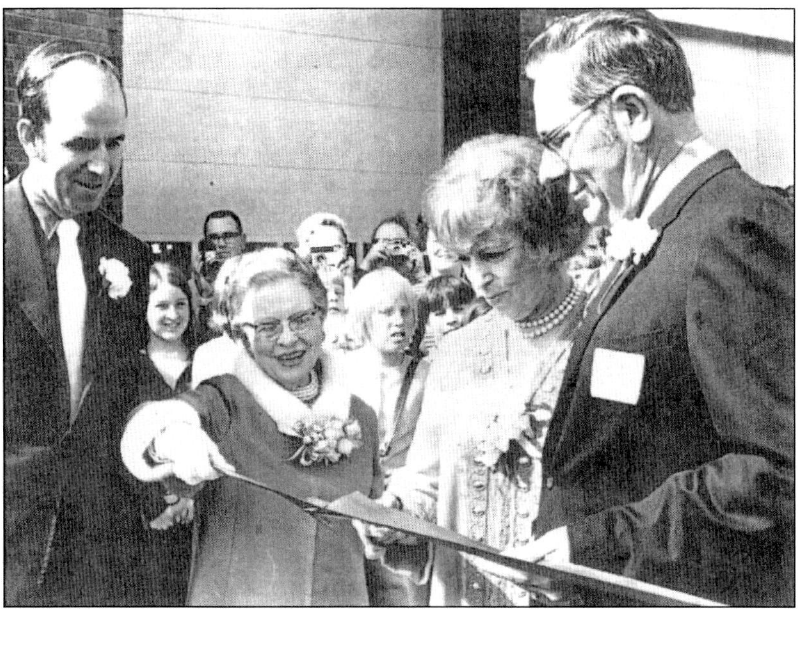

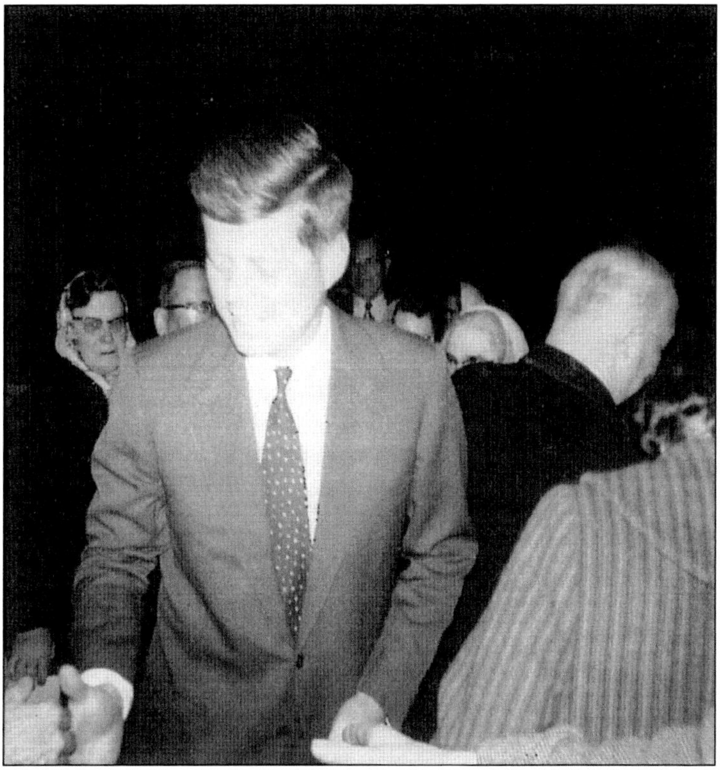

John F. Kennedy (right) and Jackie Kennedy (below) stopped at the Badger Theater on March 9, 1960, during his campaign to secure the Democratic presidential nomination. Kennedy spoke about the decline in income for dairy farmers and expressed alarm at the situation. He also praised the primary system, noting that it allowed candidates to become more in tune to each state's specific issues. (Both, courtesy of Tom Seamonson.)

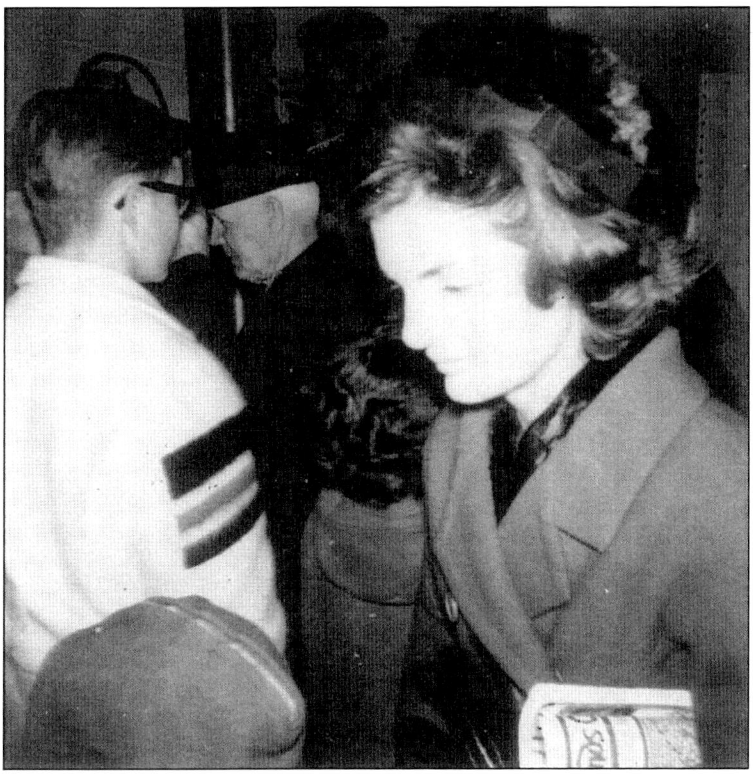

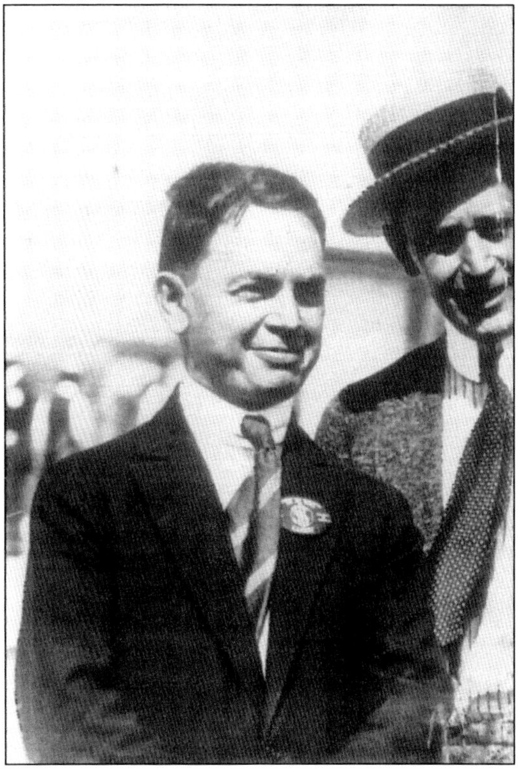

Clare Briggs (1875–1930) was born in Reedsburg and lived there until age nine, when his family moved to Dixon, Illinois. He attended the University of Nebraska and found success as a cartoonist. His works include political cartoons and two sketches about his time in Reedsburg, "Ole Swimming Hole" and "Skin-nay." (Both, courtesy of Reedsburg Historical Society.)

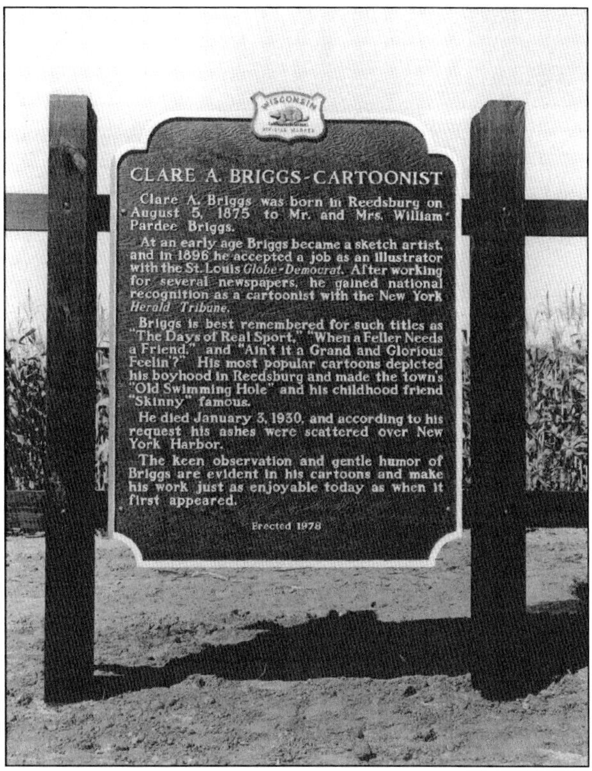

Arthur Colby (1909–1996) grew up just outside of Reedsburg. Becoming blind by the time he was 11 months old, Colby developed an amazing ear for music and great technical skill. His talent progressed rapidly, and he graduated from college with the intention of becoming a music teacher. He was unable to find a job, but he and his wife contributed greatly to the Janesville School for the Blind, including writing a dictionary in Braille. (Courtesy of Reedsburg Public Library.)

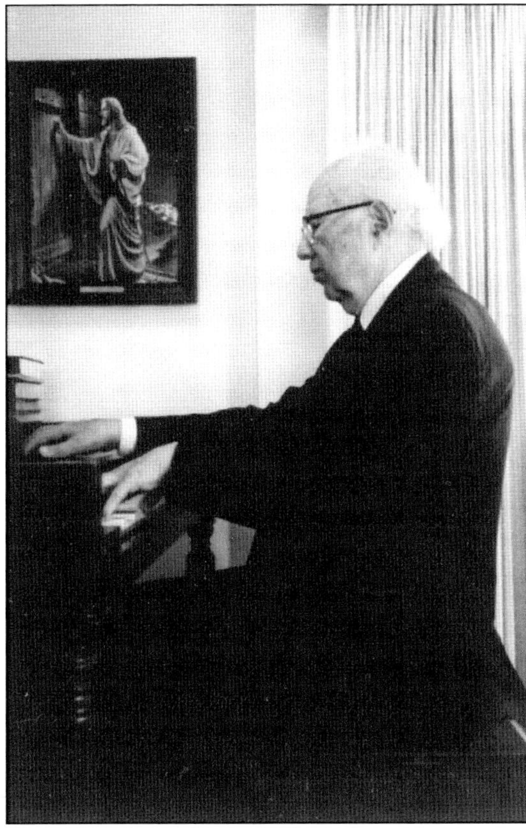

Freda Meyers Nishan (1875–1938) generously donated money to various community and charitable causes. She provided money to erect a community building with an auditorium and to provide for its maintenance. Nishan also purchased and donated land for the old hospital on Park Street and had the Presbyterian Manse built and provided money for its maintenance. A scholarship fund she established still helps many Reedsburg High School graduates. (Courtesy of Reedsburg Public Library.)

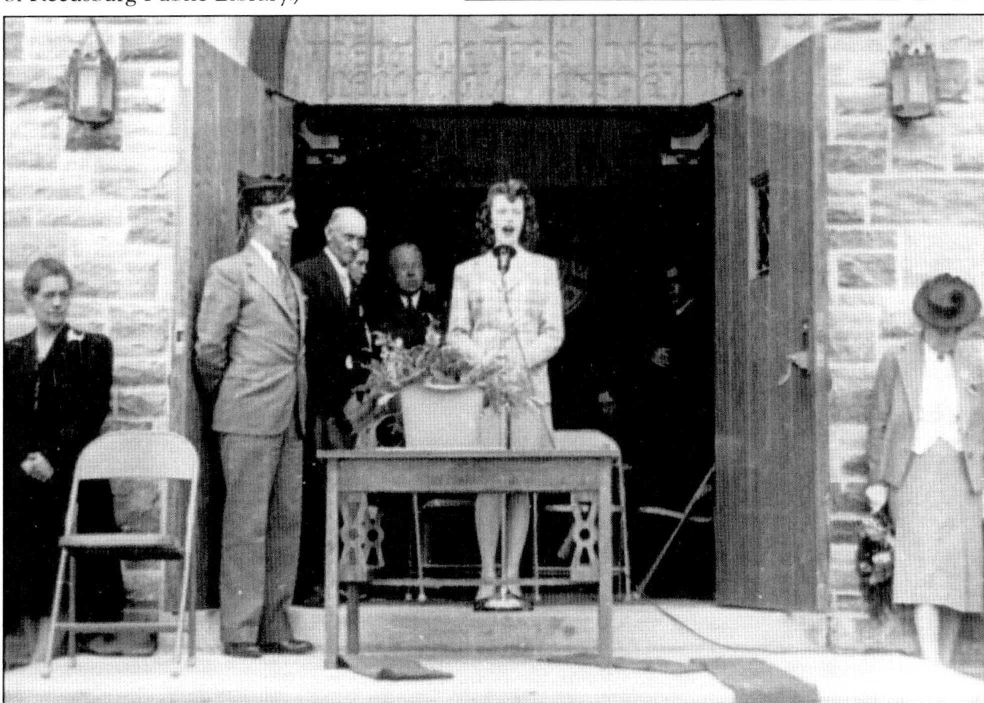

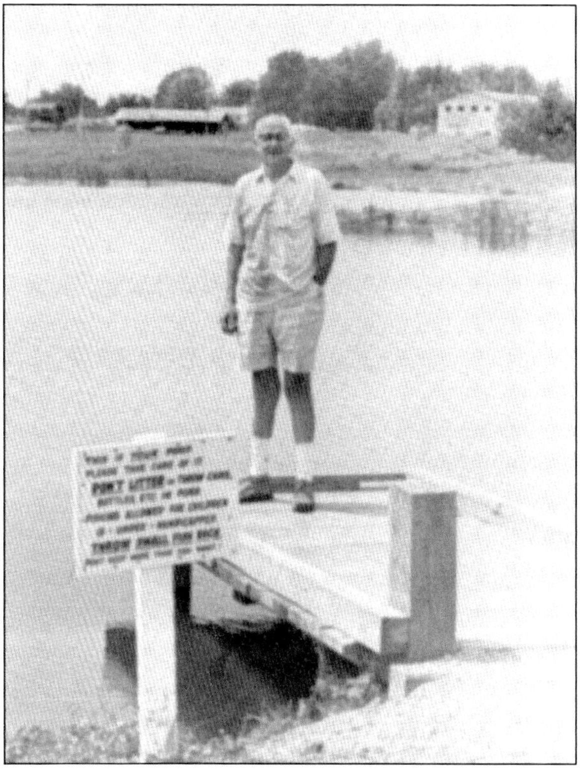

Kenneth Plenke (1912–1995) was an avid outdoorsman. The majority of local fishing holes dried up after the Woolen Mill dam was torn out, so Plenke decided to build a pond dedicated to children under the age of 15 and the disabled. The U-shaped pond ranges in depth from 10 to 13 feet, is stocked with crappie, largemouth bass, bluegill, walleye, and catfish, and is fed by three pumps supplying fresh springwater daily. (Courtesy of *Reedsburg Times Press*.)

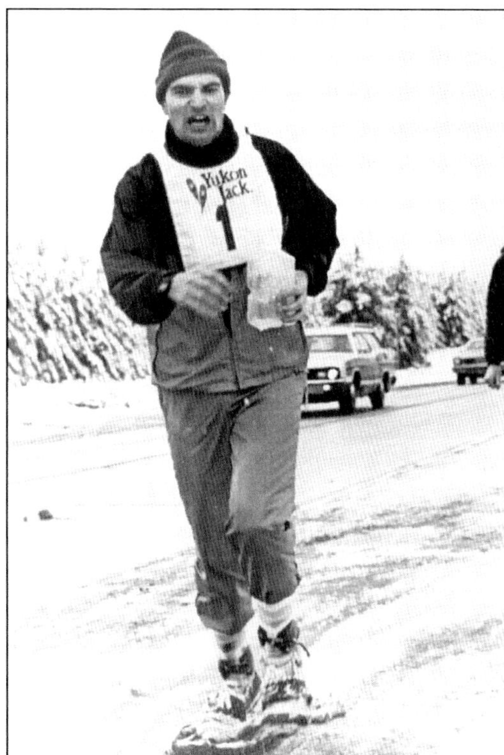

Barney Klecker, born in Ellsworth, Wisconsin, graduated from Webb High School in 1969. A lifelong runner, Klecker has set many records around the country, including an American mark for the fastest 50 miles. Klecker raced on snowshoes in races beginning in Superior and ending in Rice Lake, Wisconsin, in 1978 and 1979. (Courtesy of Reedsburg Public Library.)

When Reedsburg wanted to add an industrial park to the city, Mayor John Bernien went to Max Laukant (1907–1990) to acquire some land. Laukant, a farmer born in Germany, owned land outside of Reedsburg. Bernien and Laukant made a deal that allowed Reedsburg to establish the desired industrial park. (Courtesy of Alice Laukant.)

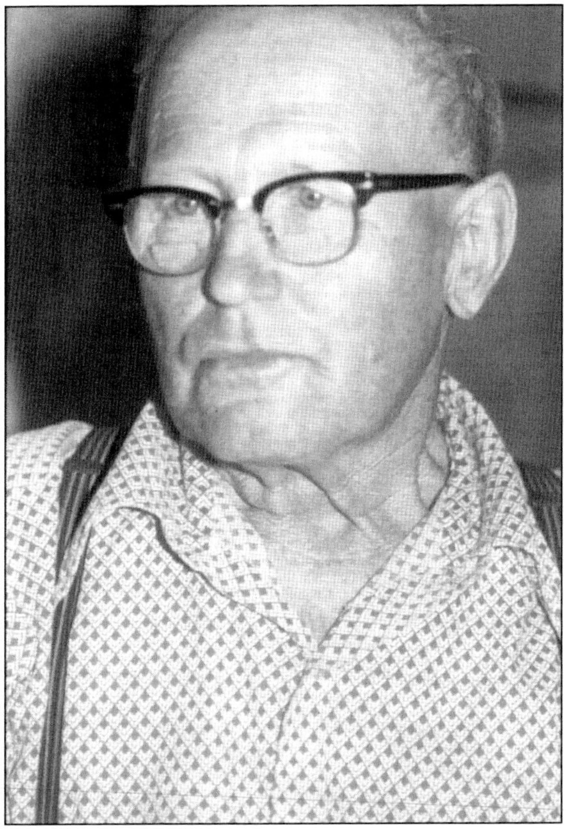

The resurfacing of Reedsburg's Main Street, shown here, took place in 1930. Many such infrastructure projects had taken place in the past. This time, the streets were being paved in brick. In later years, they would be resurfaced using concrete, which is the form the streets currently take. (Courtesy of *Reedsburg Times Press.*)

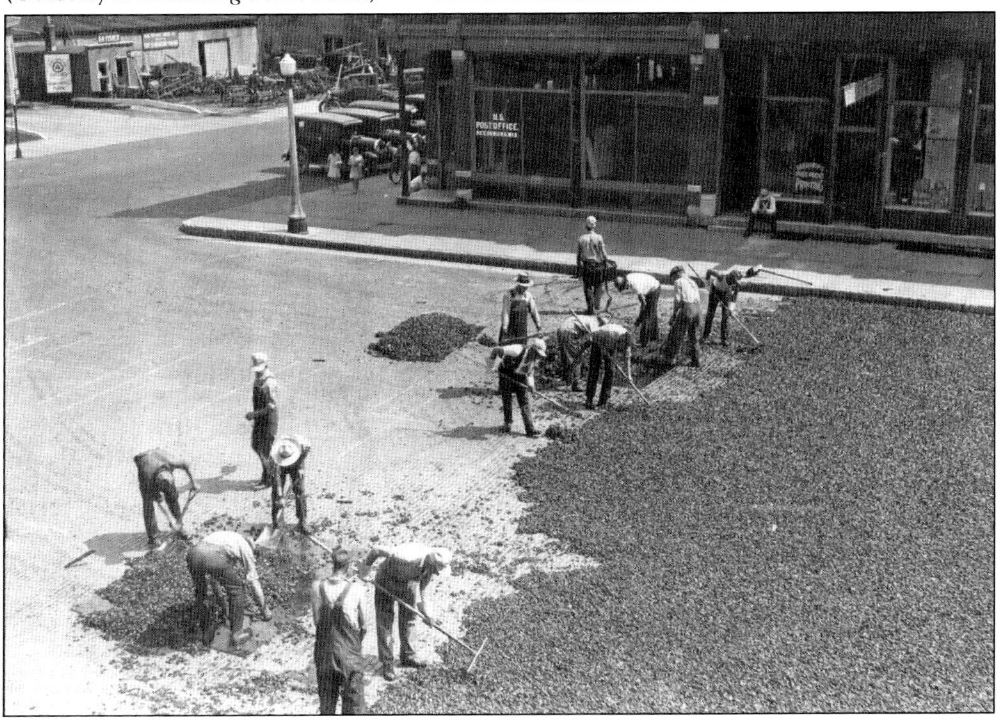

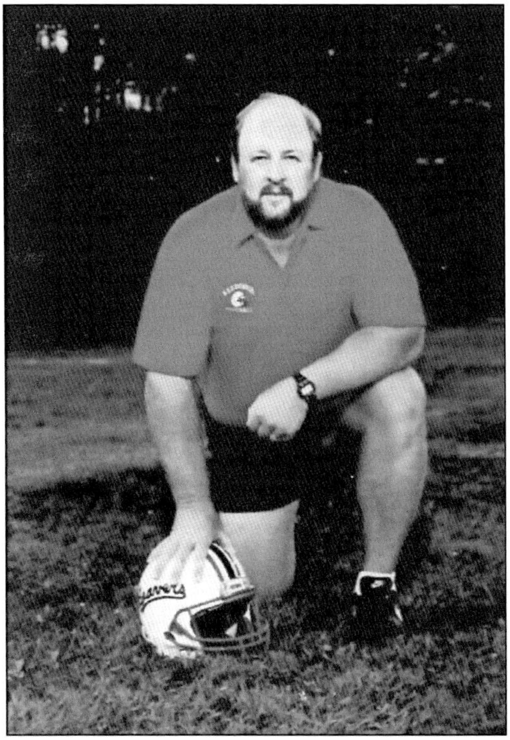

Paul Allen Rosholt (1952–1995) graduated in 1974 with a degree in elementary education from Luther College, where he was a standout athlete in football, rugby, and track. Rosholt married Debby Steinhorst on June 21, 1975, and the couple had three children, Erik, Gretchen, and Kristofer. He later completed his master's degree in educational administration at the University of Wisconsin–Madison. His teaching career included jobs at South, Westside, Loganville, the Middle School, and Ironton–La Valle. Rosholt was principal at Ironton–La Valle and Westside. Rosholt coached high school football, high school track, and youth hockey, and was a varsity football coach for 20 years in Reedsburg. Some of his hobbies included camping, traveling, hiking, hunting, playing sports, being a counselor at Upham Woods, and spending time with his family. He died on September 19, 1995, in Reedsburg after a second bout with cancer. (Courtesy of Gretchen Whitehurst.)

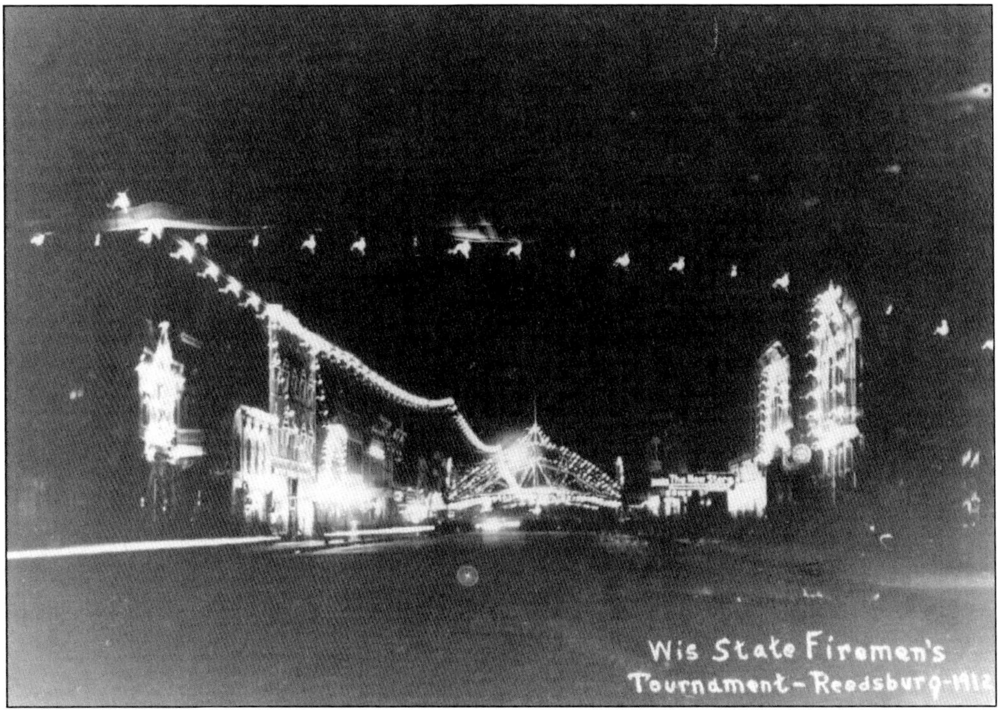

In 1912, Reedsburg hosted the Fireman's Tournament. The tournament was a major event in Reedsburg and included a carnival on Main Street in the historic downtown section. (Courtesy of *Reedsburg Times Press.*)

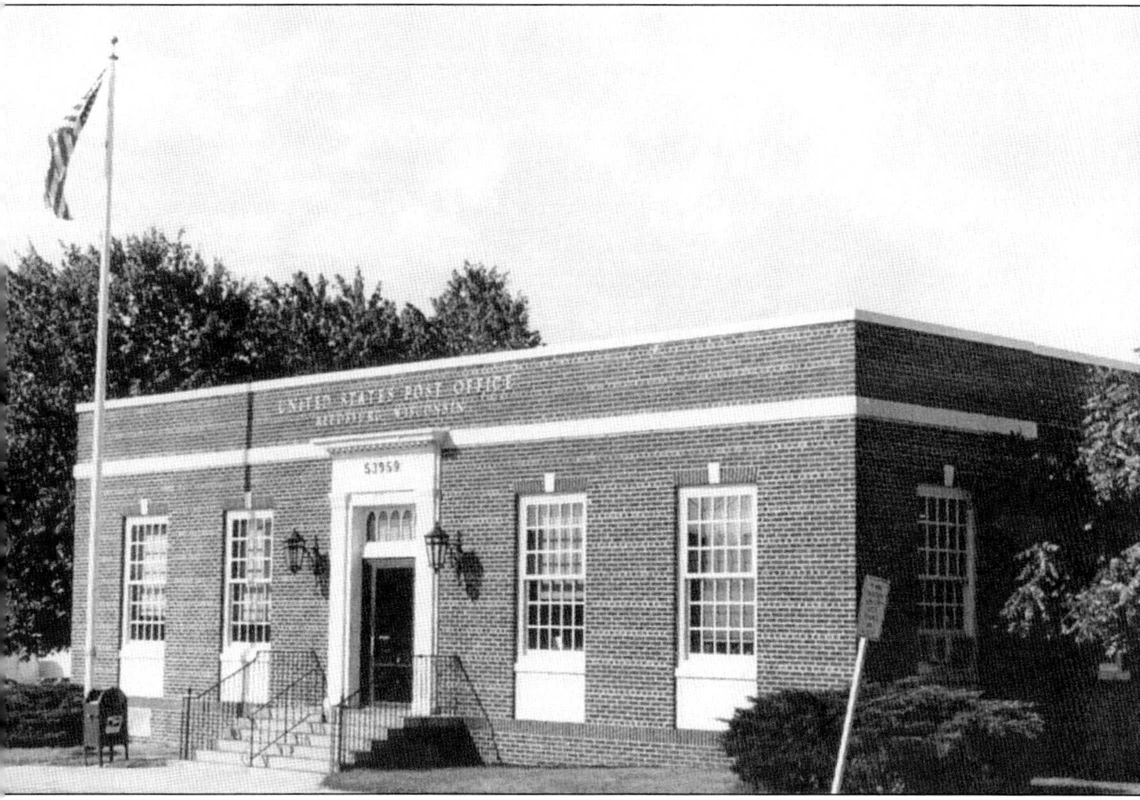

The Reedsburg Post Office was built in 1938 for $75,000. The building is still used today as the post office. Inside, there is still an old feel to the building, making it one of the town's most wonderful buildings to step inside. (Courtesy of Reedsburg Historical Society.)

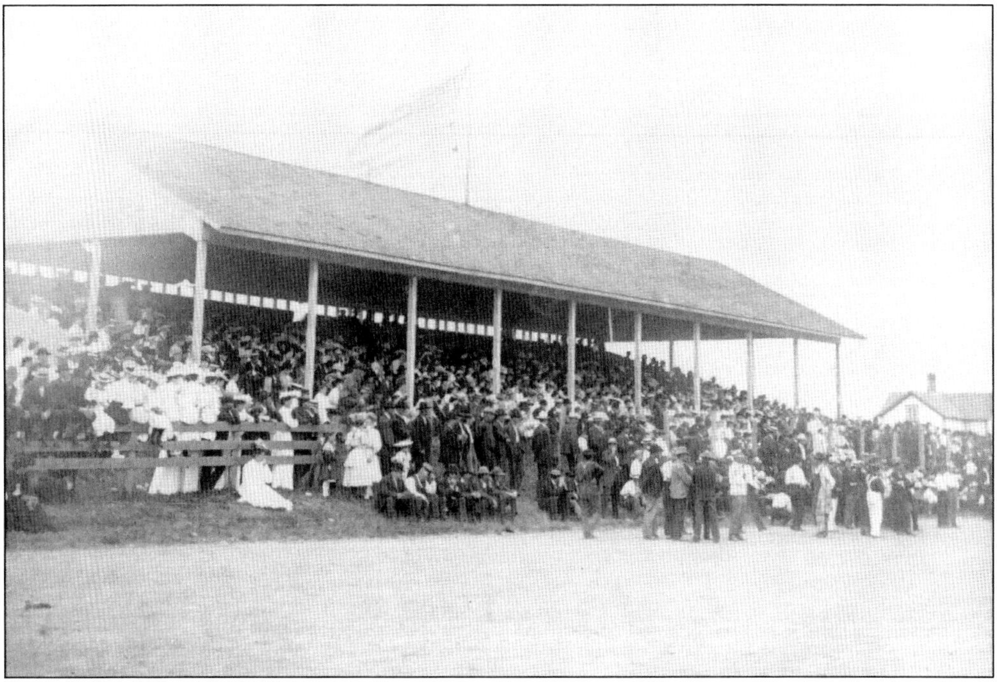

The Reedsburg Fair Grounds were located on the west side of Reedsburg, where Madison Area Technical College is located today. The fairgrounds, started by A.P. Ellinwood, hosted amusement rides and was the site of horse races during the celebration. (Both, courtesy of Reedsburg Public Library.)

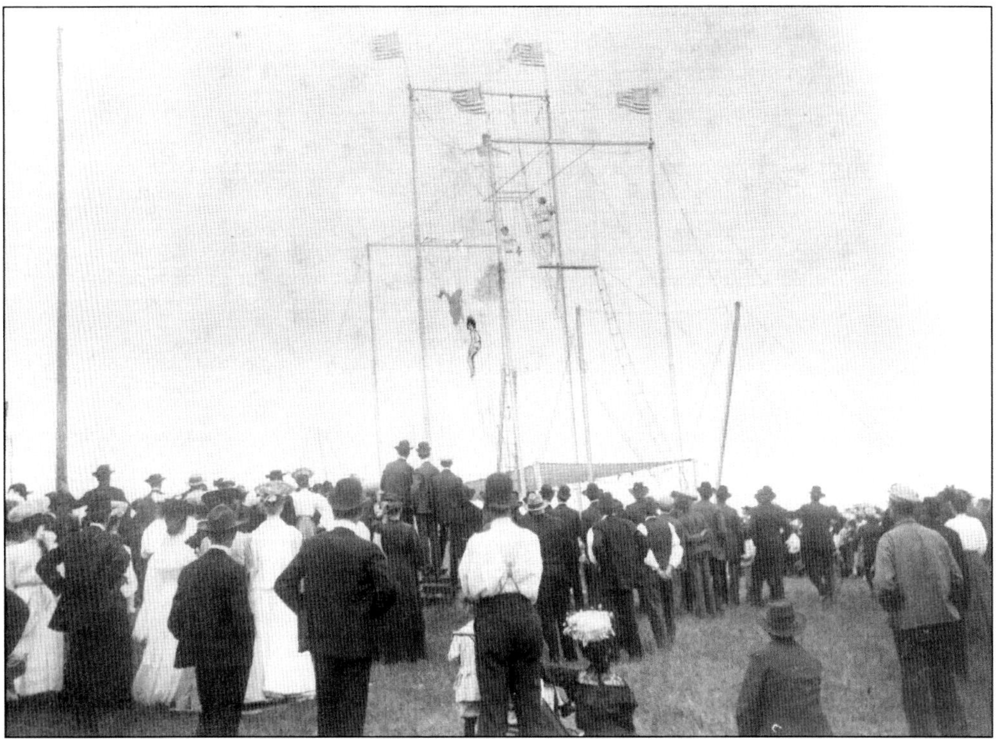

Two

TO PROTECT AND SERVE

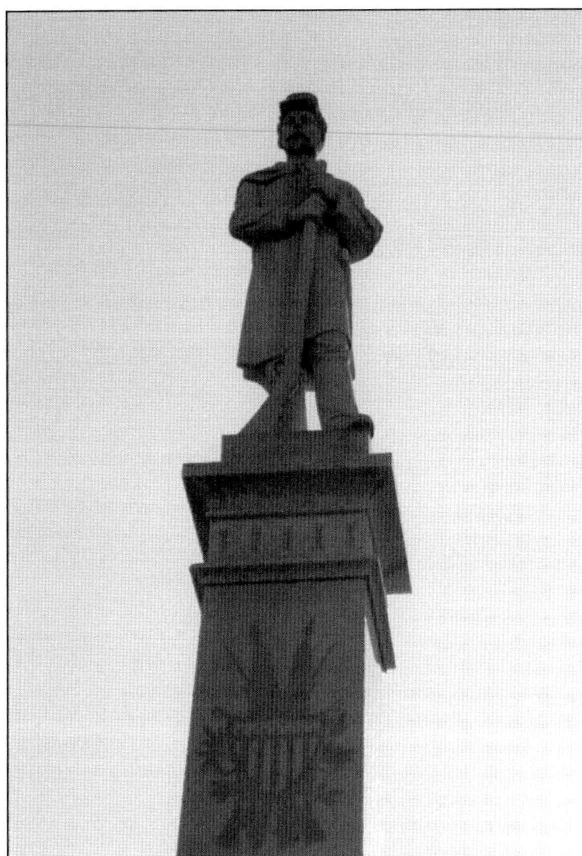

In the decades following the Civil War, villages and towns throughout the United States erected monuments to honor the local heroes who fought for the Union. Reedsburg was no exception. Spearheaded by the local chapter of the Grand Army of the Republic, a monument dedicated to the local "Defenders of the Flag" was erected in Greenwood Cemetery in 1892. Several thousand spectators turned out for its dedication. (Courtesy of Annabelle Moon.)

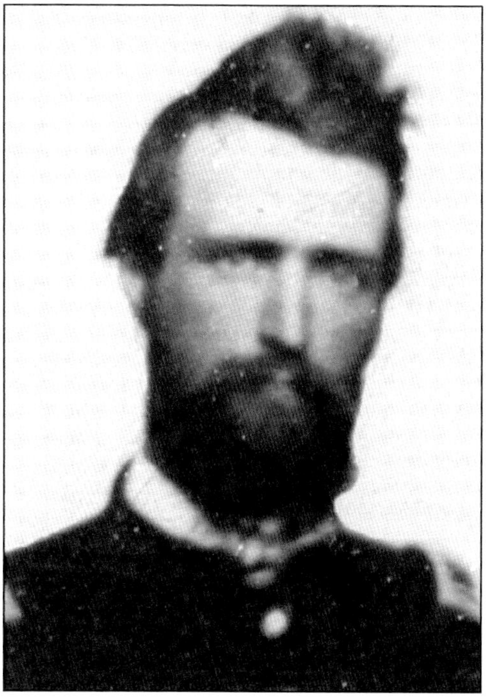

A.P. Ellinwood came to Reedsburg in 1858 to teach. In 1861, he signed up to fight for the Union Army, enlisting in Company A of the 19th Wisconsin Volunteer Infantry. Ellinwood served during the 1862 Peninsula campaign and throughout the war, rising to the rank of captain. Later, returning to Reedsburg, he joined the state legislature and became president of the Reedsburg Village Board. The fairgrounds he built on Reedsburg's west side hosted racing events and other entertainment throughout the late 19th and early 20th centuries. (Courtesy of Reedsburg Public Library.)

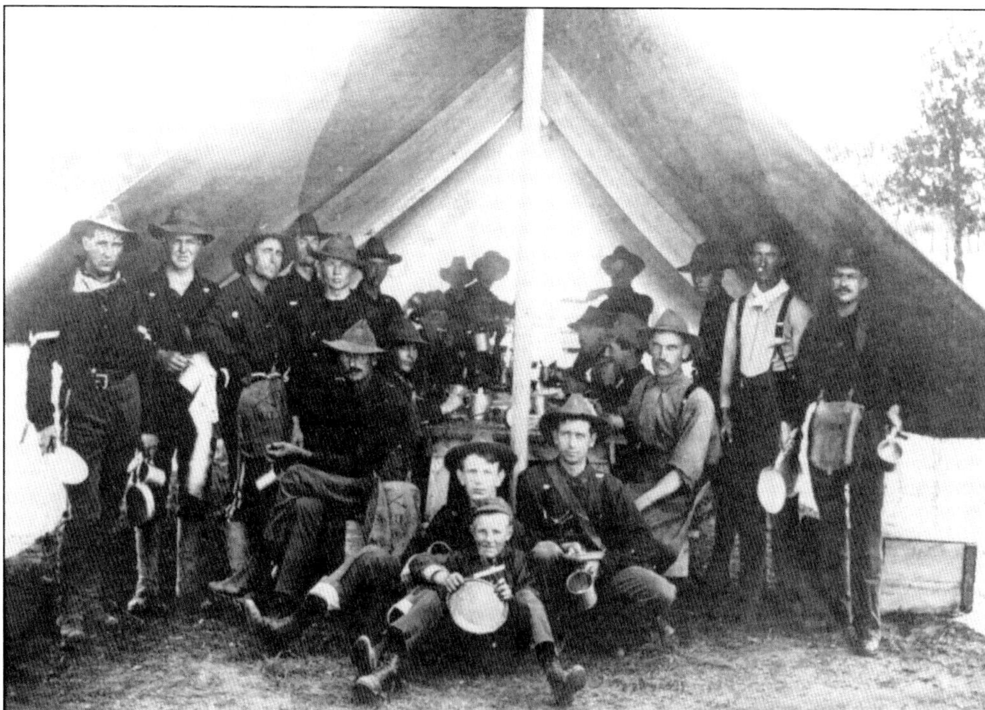

Just over three decades after the end of the Civil War, Reedsburg soldiers were again called to fight. Among the soldiers pictured here are several who were part of Reedsburg's Company F during the Spanish-American War in 1898. The war was over before Company F saw combat. (Courtesy of Reedsburg Public Library.)

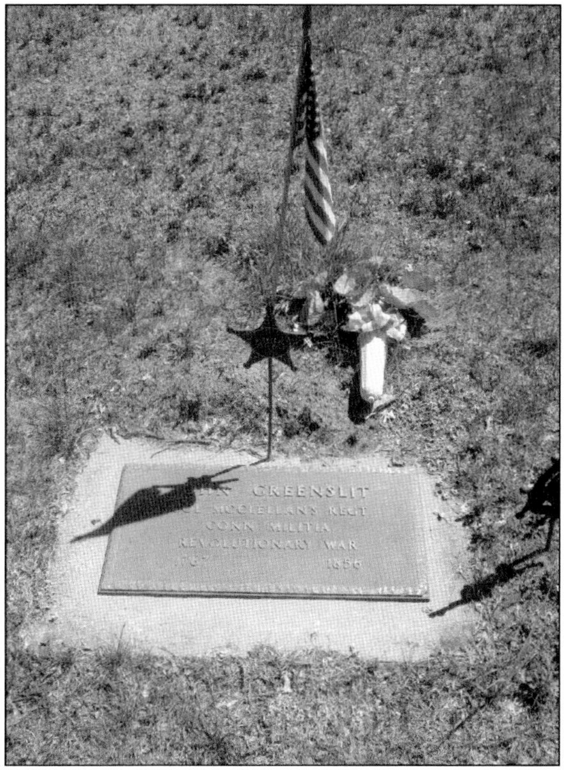

John Greenslit, laid to rest in the Dellona Center Cemetery, is the only known veteran of the American Revolution to be buried in Sauk County. At age 15, Greenslit served in the Connecticut militia with the Continental Army. He relocated to the Reedsburg area in 1855, shortly before his death the following year. (Right, courtesy of Calvin Moon; below, courtesy of Annabelle Moon.)

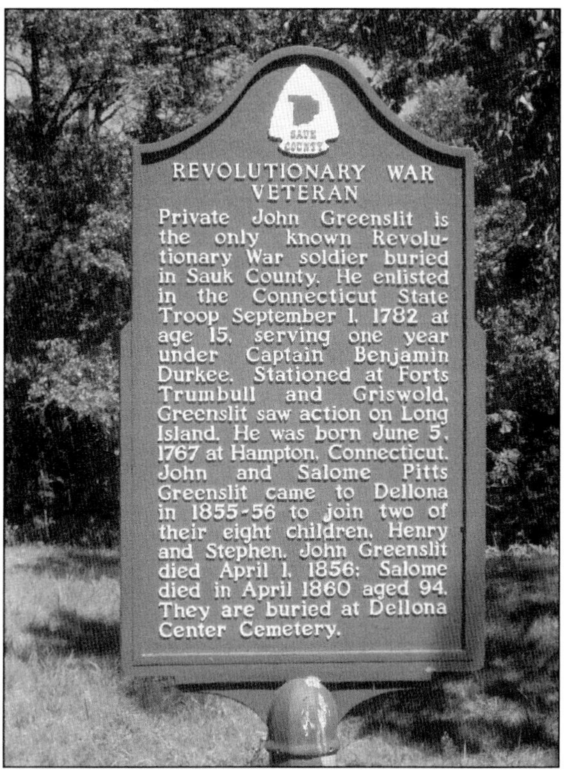

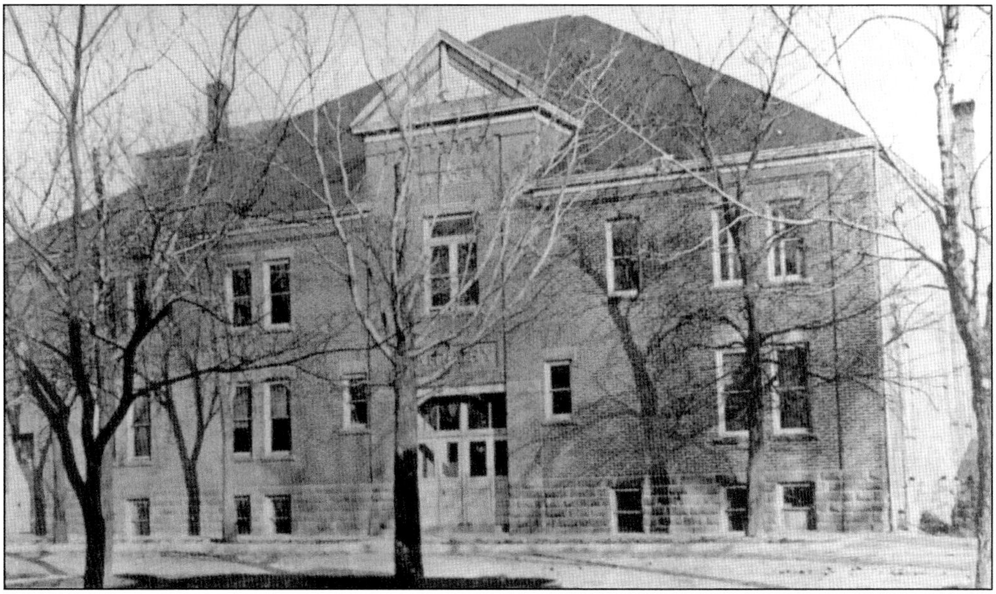

Reedsburg saw the construction of its first armory in 1903. The building, located on South Park Street, served the town's National Guard units until 1965, when the current armory was built on South Dewey Avenue. (Courtesy of Reedsburg Public Library.)

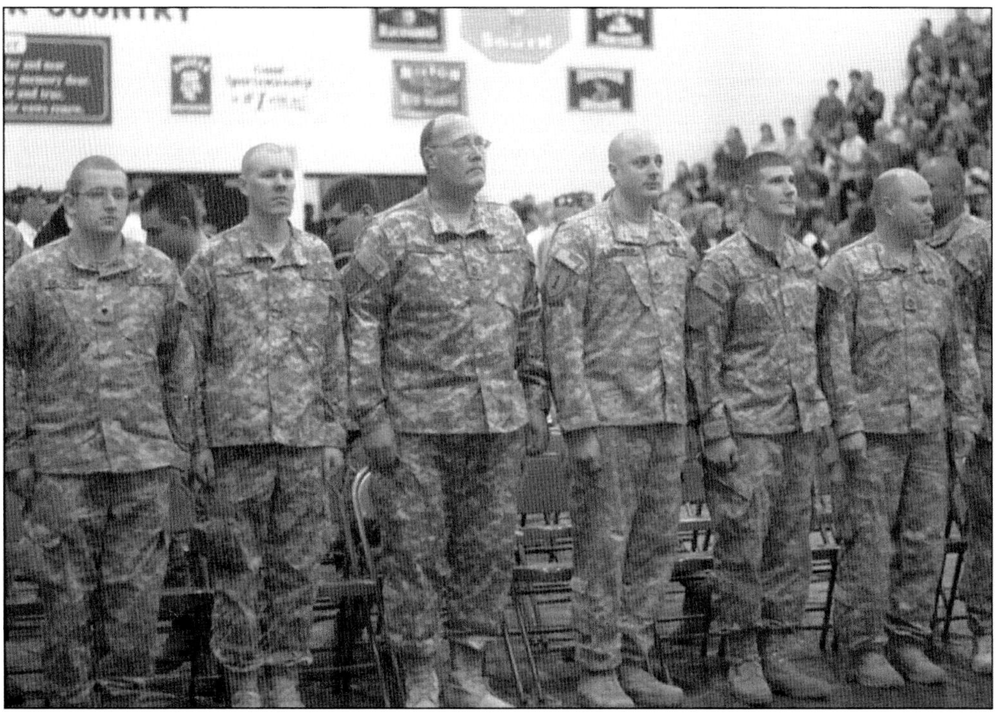

The 32nd Infantry holds a significant place in Wisconsin history. Due to its outstanding service in World War I, during which the unit successfully pierced every enemy line, the 32nd was dubbed the "Red Arrow" Division. Through all military conflicts of the United States in the 20th and 21st centuries—from World War I to the War on Terror—Reedsburg's Red Arrows have stood ready to answer the call to serve country and community. (Courtesy of Jeff Seering.)

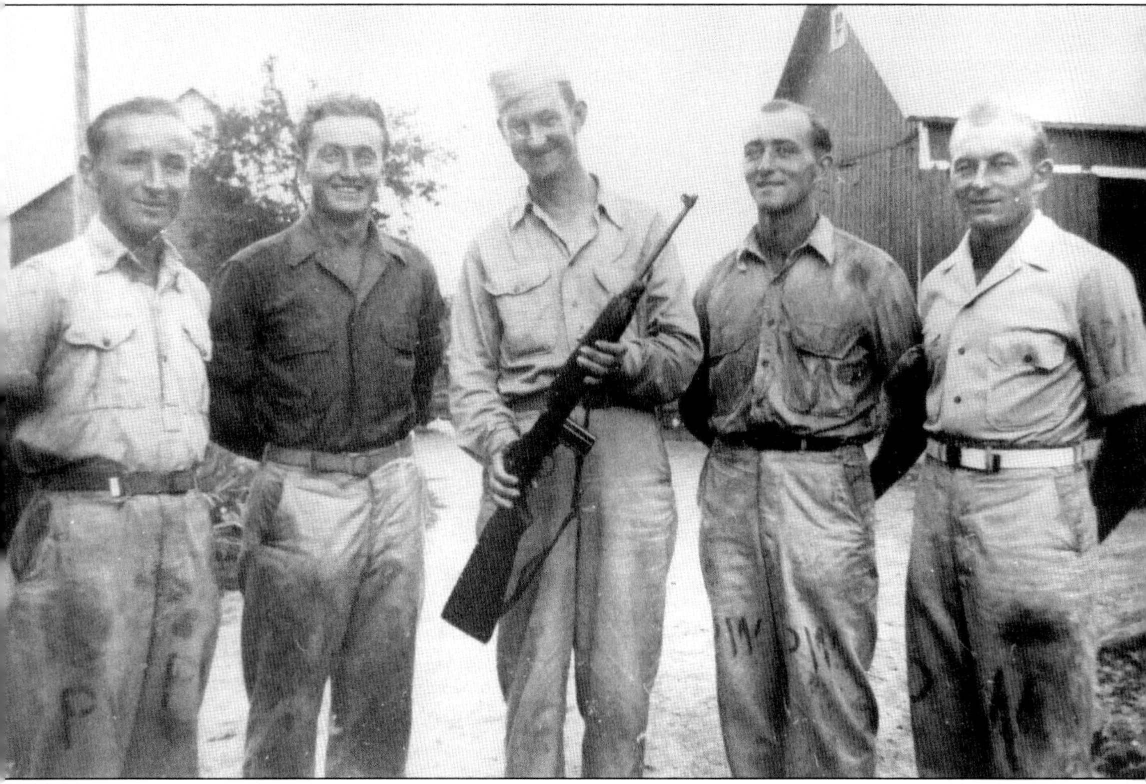

Beginning in June 1945, in a camp on the north end of Webb Avenue, 137 German prisoners of war were interned in Reedsburg. The prisoners were set to work for Reedsburg Food Corp. to help bring in the harvest because so many of the local men were fighting overseas. The POWs received 80 cents a day, working 12 hours a day, six days a week. (Courtesy of Reedsburg Public Library.)

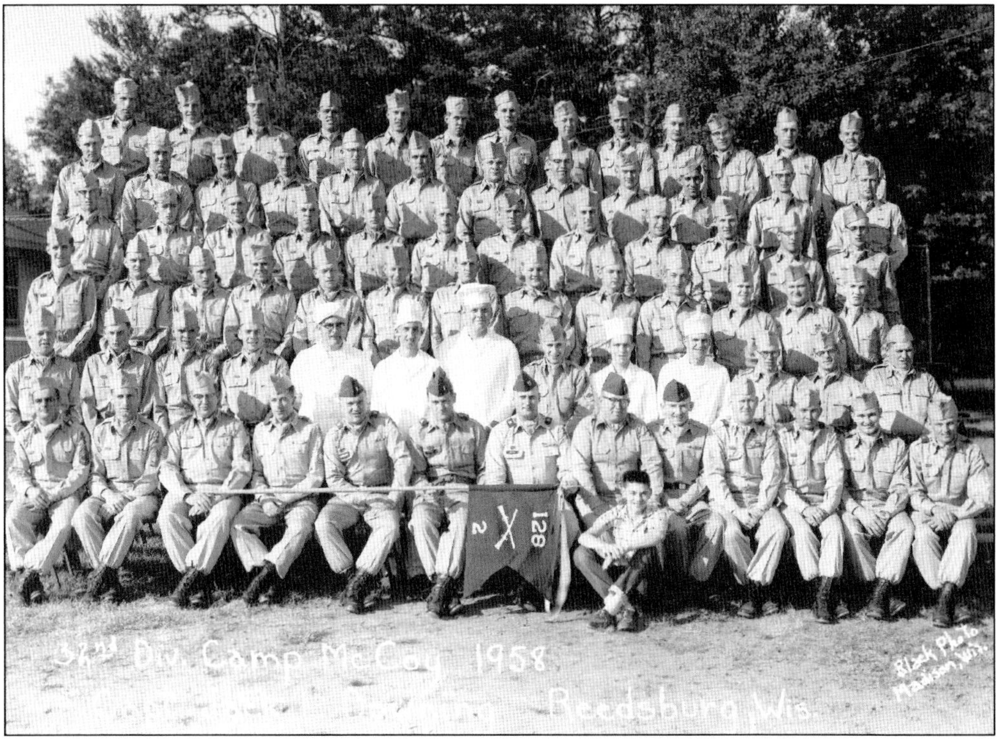

For nearly a century, soldiers from Reedsburg have served proudly in the 32nd Infantry Division. Throughout the Cold War era, National Guard soldiers from across America remained on alert. For Reedsburg's guardsmen, this meant regular training at Fort McCoy, as shown in these photographs from 1958. Pictured are soldiers from Reedsburg, serving along with others who made up the famous Red Arrow Division. In 1961, the 32nd was mobilized for service during the Berlin Crisis. (Both, courtesy of Jason McDonough and the Reedsburg National Guard Armory.)

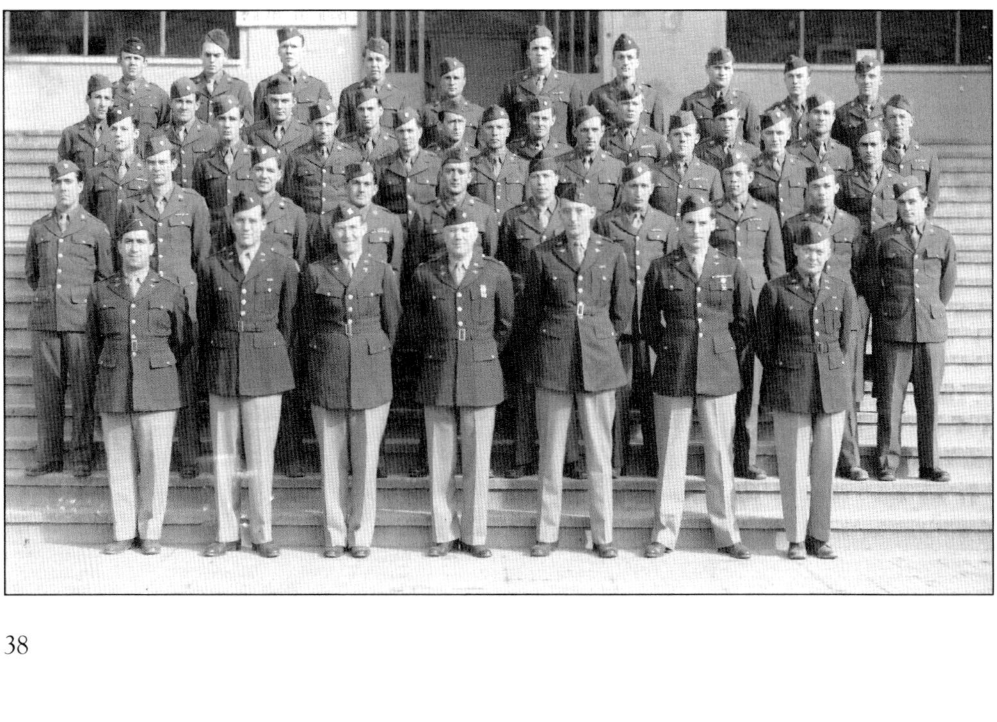

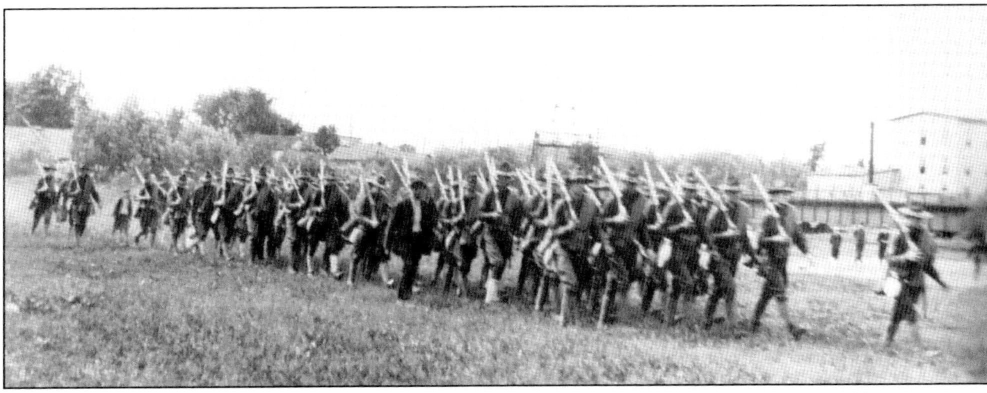

Reedsburg soldiers from Company A were called to duty in April 1917 during World War I. Seen here are troops drilling in Reedsburg at the old athletic grounds (where the City Shop now stands). At Camp McArthur in Texas, soldiers from Reedsburg joined others from Wisconsin and Michigan to form the 32nd Division. The 32nd earned its insignia—a red arrow piercing a line—by fighting in four campaigns during the war. (Courtesy of Reedsburg Public Library.)

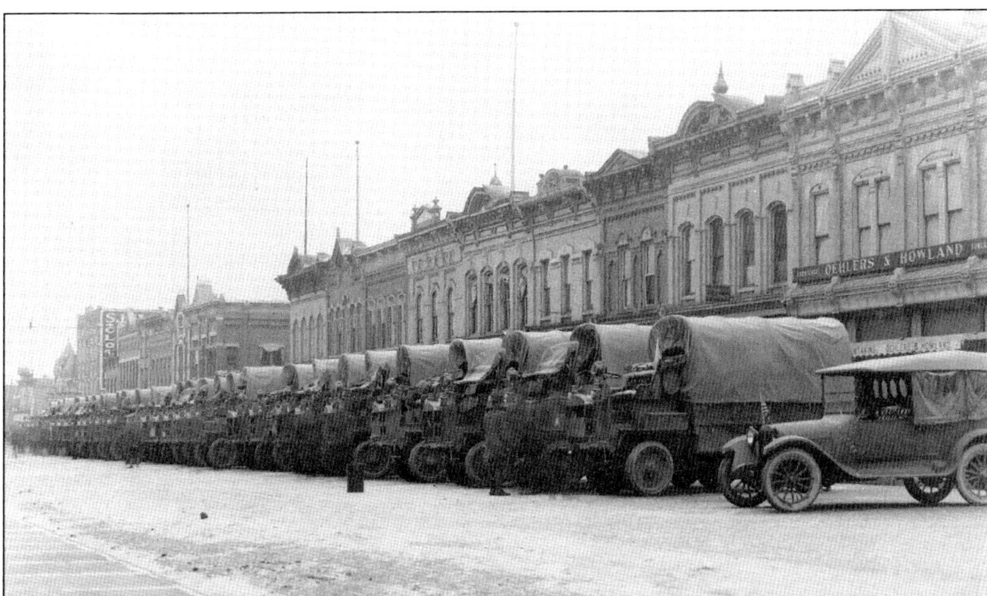

These US Army trucks have stopped on Main Street in Reedsburg while on a convoy. The trucks are believed to have been heading to Fort McCoy, which is located between Tomah and Sparta, Wisconsin. (Courtesy of *Reedsburg Times Press.*)

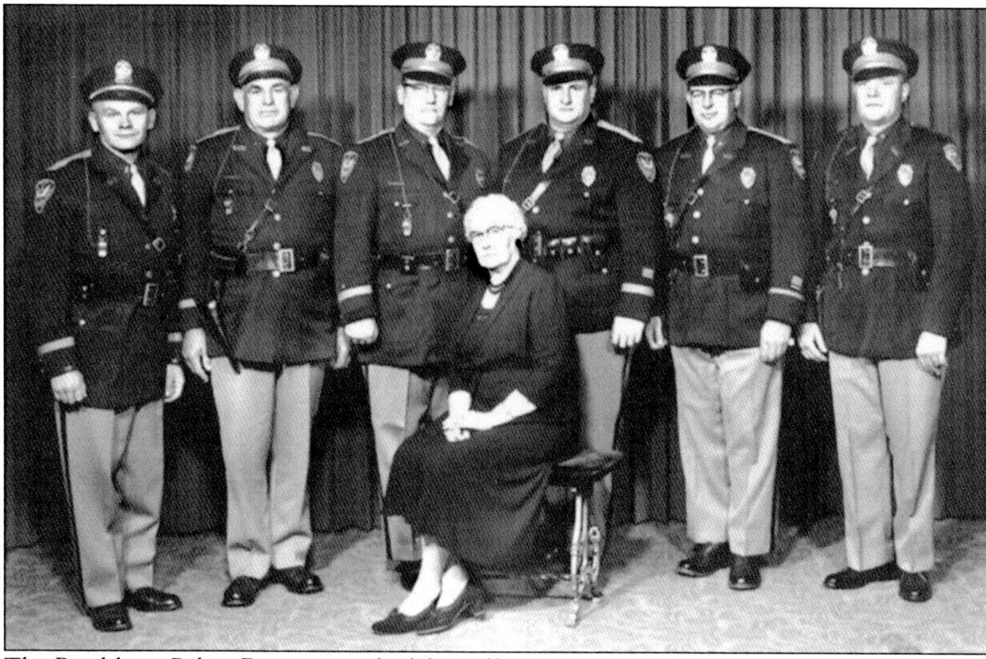

The Reedsburg Police Department had five officers serving under Chief David Dobson (third from left) in 1961. (Courtesy of Reedsburg Police Department.)

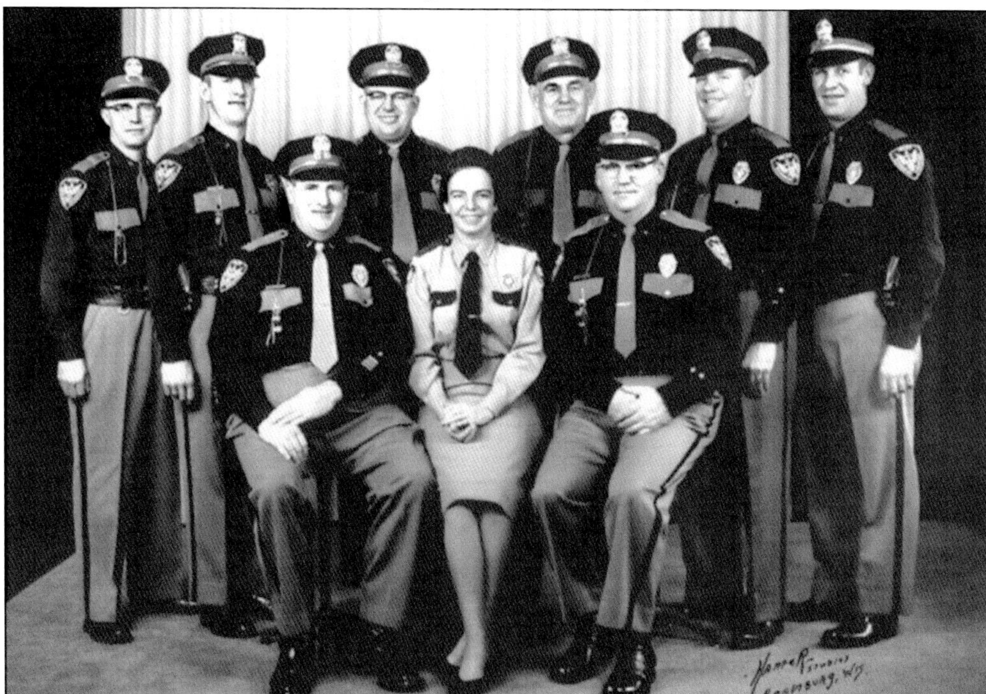

Two of Reedsburg's police officers were called up with the 32nd National Guard Division during the 1961 Berlin Crisis, necessitating the hiring of two replacements. The return of the two soldiers gave Reedsburg the eight-officer department shown in this 1963 photograph. (Courtesy of Reedsburg Police Department.)

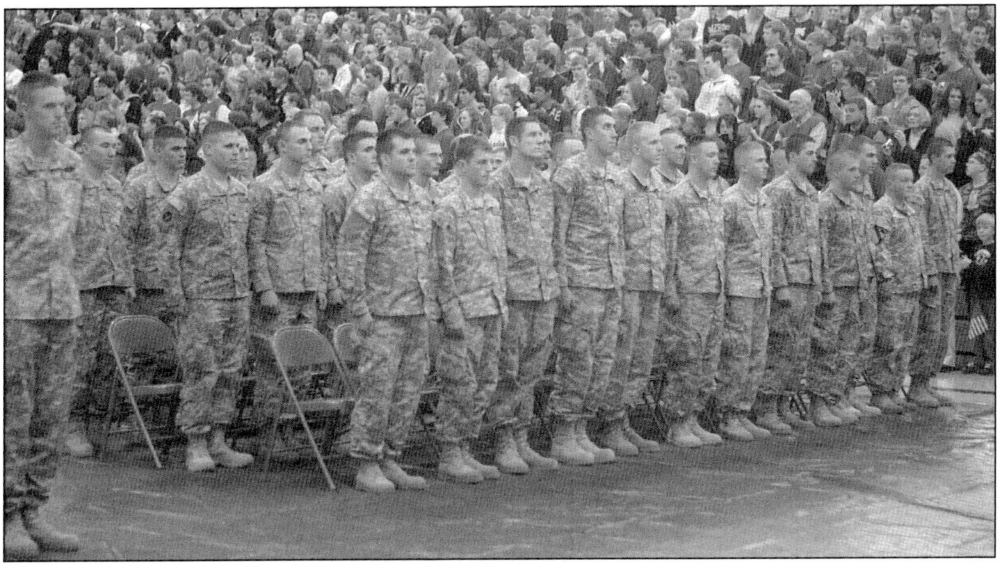

On February 1, 2009, the 32nd Infantry Brigade Combat Team, including many soldiers from the Reedsburg area, was mobilized for a deployment to Iraq. The students and staff of Reedsburg Area High School welcomed the community into the RAHS gymnasium to provide Charlie Troop with a proper send-off. (Courtesy of Jeff Seering.)

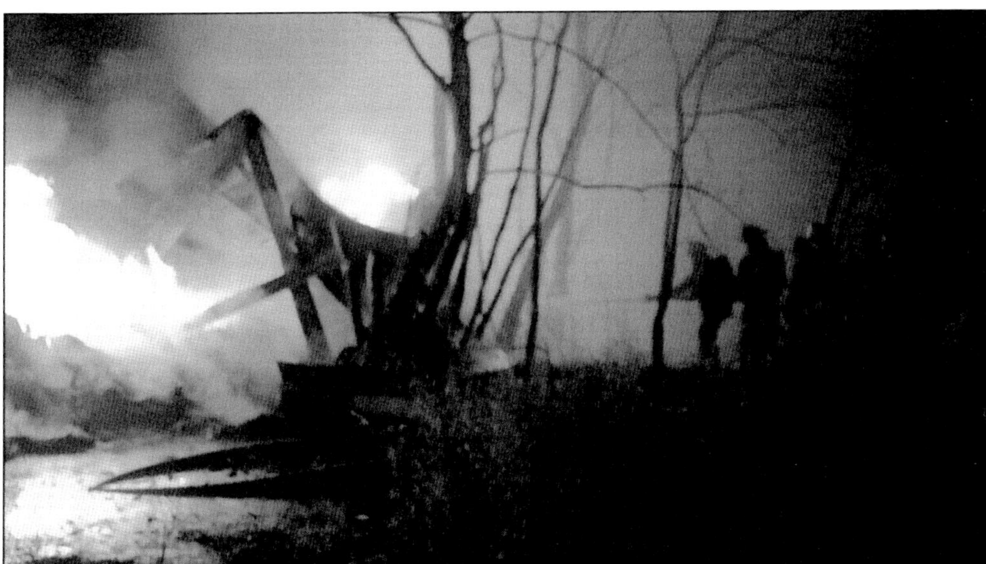

Since 1873, the citizens of the Reedsburg area have enjoyed the protection of the Reedsburg Fire Department. The department ranks among the most effective volunteer units in Wisconsin. In this photograph, firefighters battle a warehouse blaze in 2011. (Courtesy of Jeff Seering.)

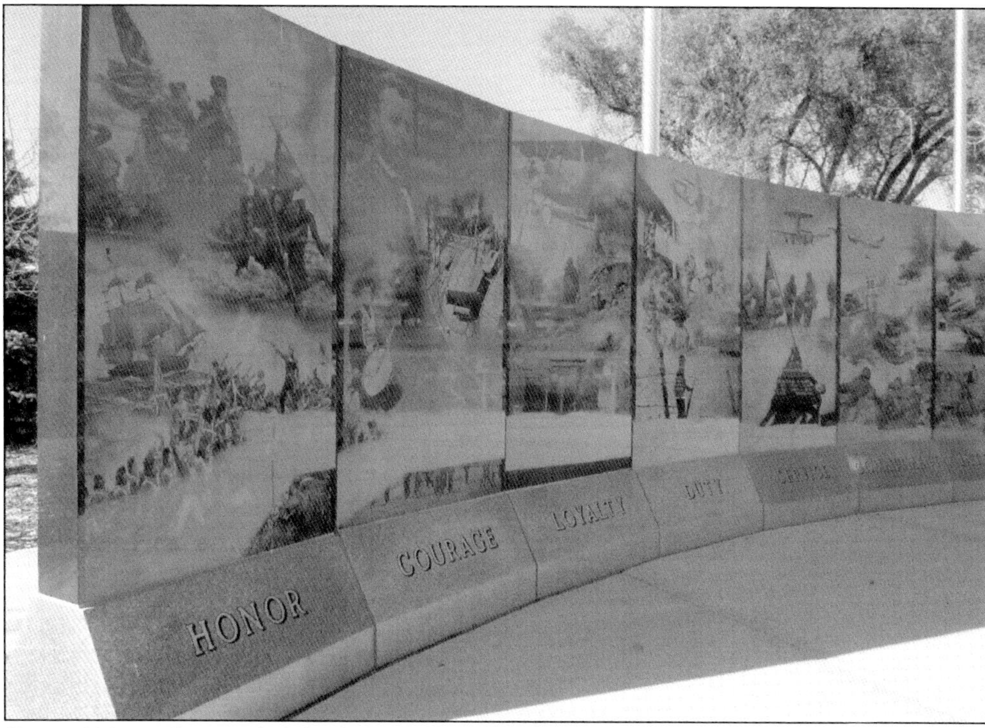

Over 1,000 people attended the dedication of the Reedsburg Area Veterans' Memorial on July 4, 2011, with S.Sgt. Jason McDonough serving as the master of ceremonies. The memorial, located near the south entrance to Nishan Park, displays images representing the full scope of America's military history. Members of the Thurber-Greenwood Veterans of Foreign Wars Post spearheaded the planning for the memorial in 2008, and the process of raising funds began soon after. (Both, courtesy of Annabelle Moon.)

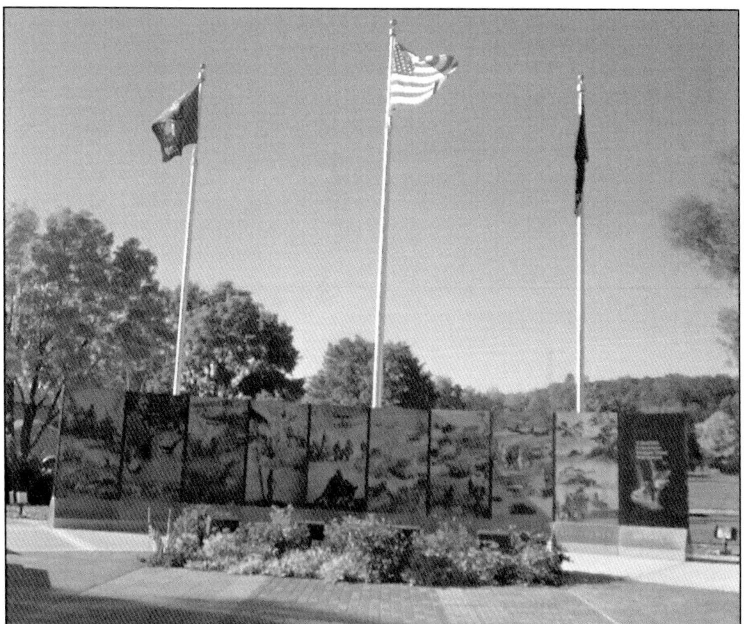

Three

Business in Reedsburg

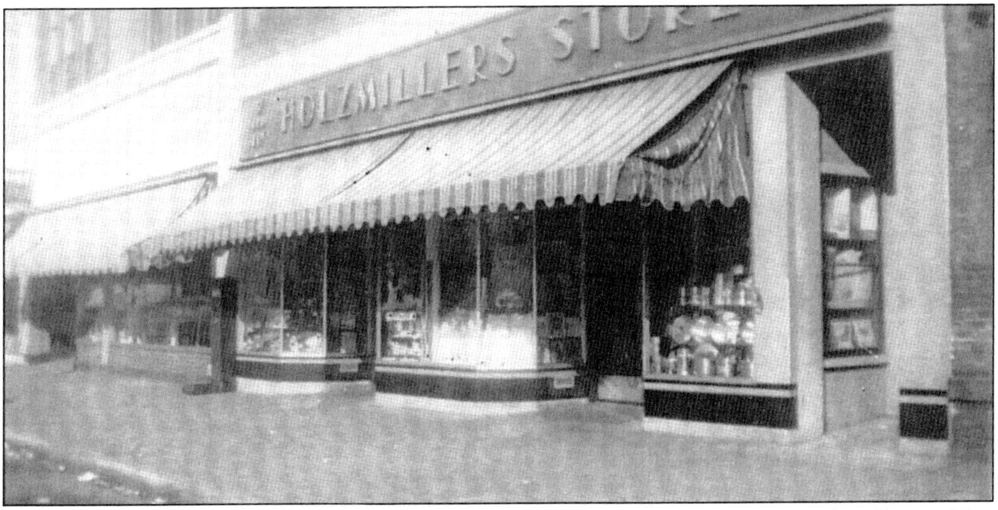

Pictured here is Holzmiller's Variety Store. In September 1933, William H. Holzmiller and his twin sons, Roy and Ralph, opened a Ben Franklin Store in the Conley Building on the corner. They moved to 283 East Main Street in 1939, which is today the home of Lorraine's Mini-Mall. (Courtesy of Peggy Albert.)

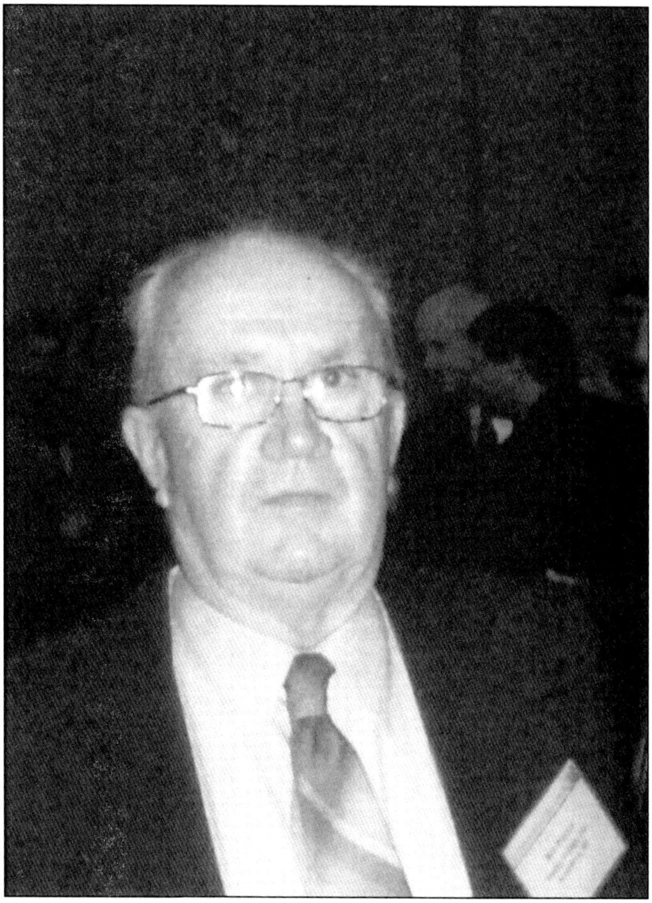

Bill Pierce, seen at left, grew up in Baraboo, Wisconsin, where he worked in his parents' grocery store alongside his brothers, Jim and Don. In 1974, he moved to Reedsburg with his wife, Phyllis, and two children, Brian and Pam. The family opened Viking Village Foods in 1975. Bill Pierce would continue to build and open businesses that he felt Reedsburg needed: Viking Liquor, Viking Family Restaurant, Viking Laundromat, Viking Express and Viking Express Mart convenience stores, Viking Bowl, and Viking Village Shopping Center. At right in the photograph below is the old Viking Village Store, which is now the Viking Liquor store. (Both, courtesy of Pam Coy.)

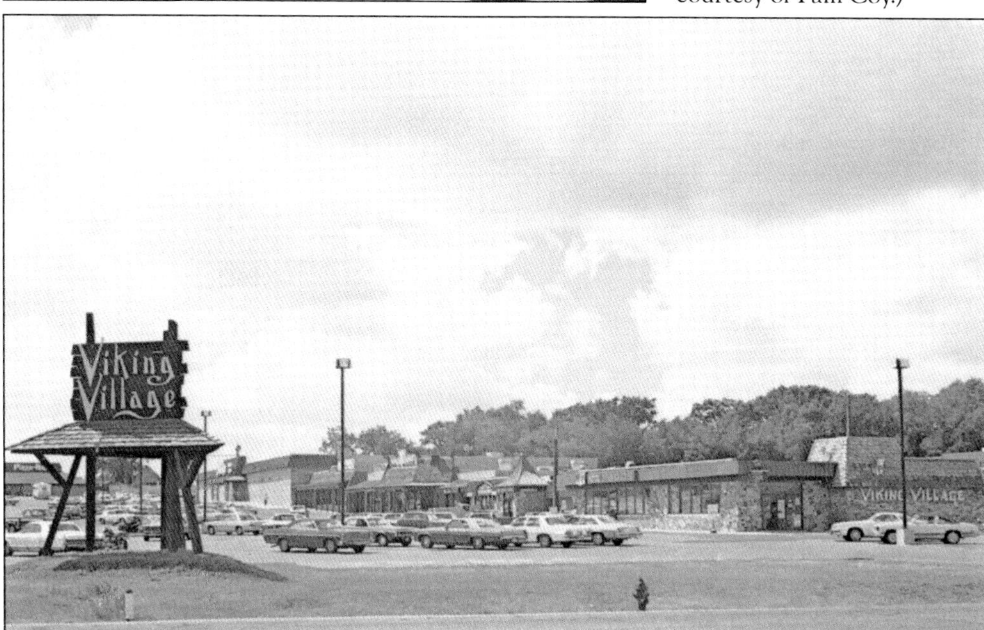

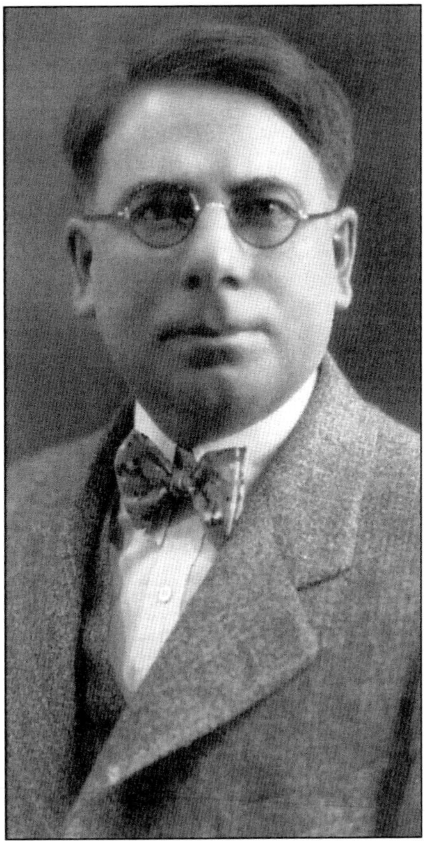

Alfred Bernien was born on May 20, 1891, in the town of Ironton, Wisconsin. Early on, he engaged in the sale of farm implements, in which business he became very successful. His two sons, Eldor (1918–1993) and John (1923–), worked for the Bernien Company. Alfred was mayor of Reedsburg from 1934 to 1939 and again from 1941 to 1949. He was active on many boards in town, including the hospital board. Bernien erected a building on Main Street where the corner pub is today. The inscription "Bernien" can still be seen at the top of the building. (Both, courtesy of Sherry Bernien.)

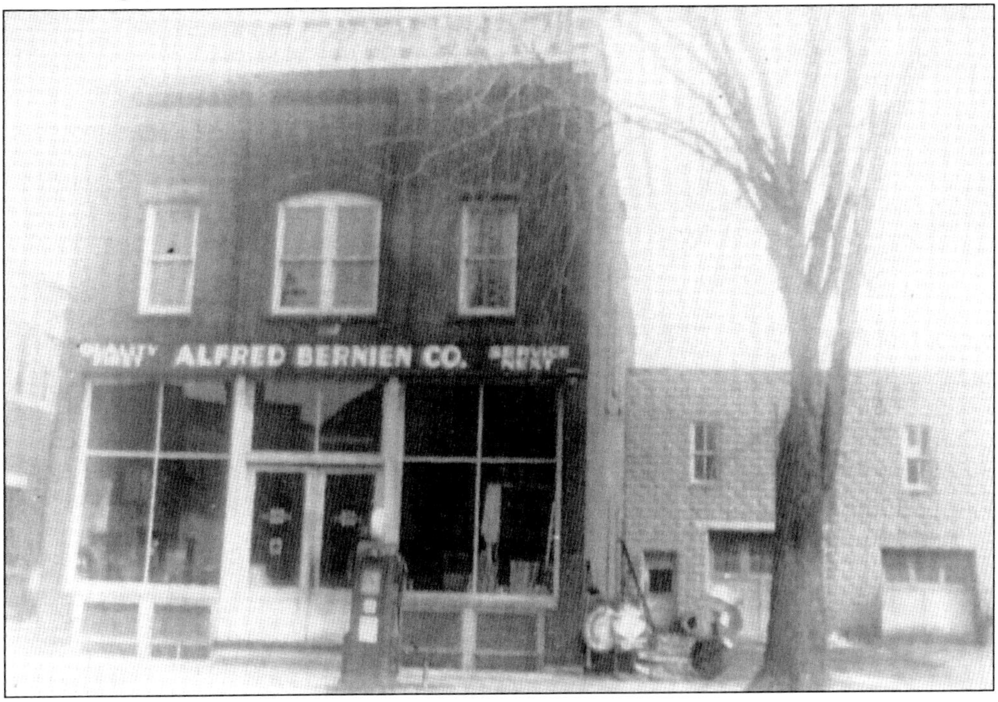

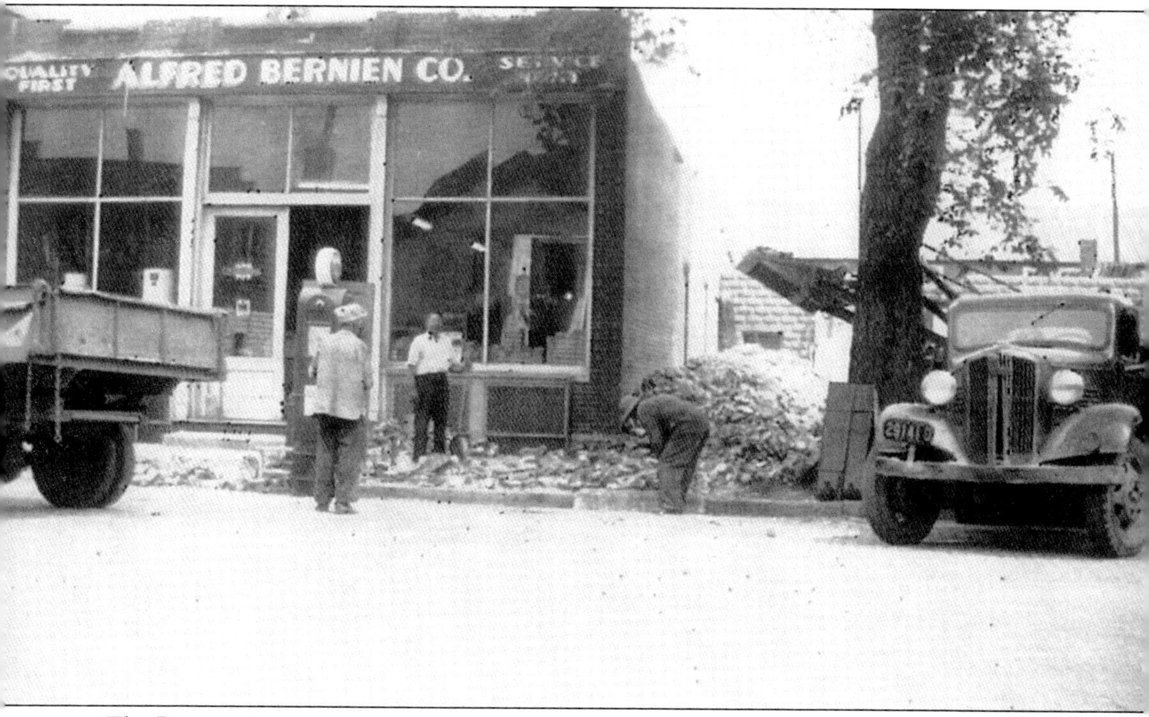

The Bernien Company was started by John Bernien Sr. and his son, John Bernien Jr. They ran the business from a two-story building that was constructed in 1906. Following John Sr.'s death in 1901 and John Jr.'s death in 1911, the business was taken over by the third generation, Alfred Bernien. The building was remodeled in 1948, as shown in this photograph taken during the work. After Alfred's death in 1965, his sons, John and Eldor, took over the business. The Bernien Company remained in business until 1986. (Courtesy of Sherry Bernien.)

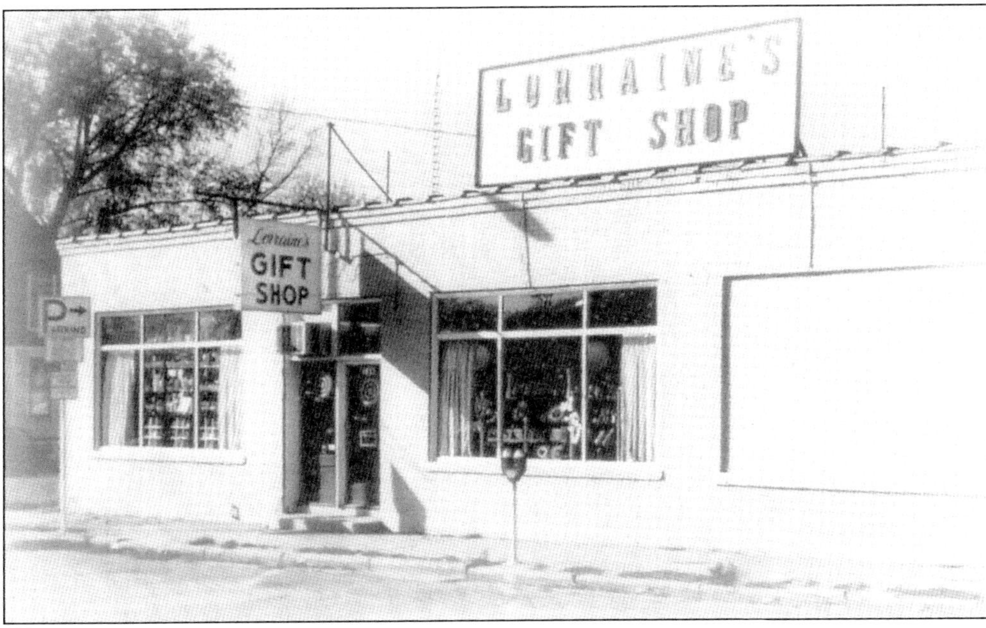

Lorraine's Gift Shop opened on April 1, 1972, on the corner of South Park and Vine Streets. It later moved to its current location on Main Street, taking over where the Holzmiller's Variety Store had been. During Lorraine's 40 years of existence, it has added more stores to downtown's Lorraine's Mini-Mall. The mall now consists of a fine jewelry store, Hallmark Gold Crown, US Cellular/UPS Shipping, and Radio Shack. Lorraine's is still owned and managed by Lorraine Traeder, with some assistance by her daughter, Peggy, and son-in-law, Blaine Albert. (Both, courtesy of Peggy Albert.)

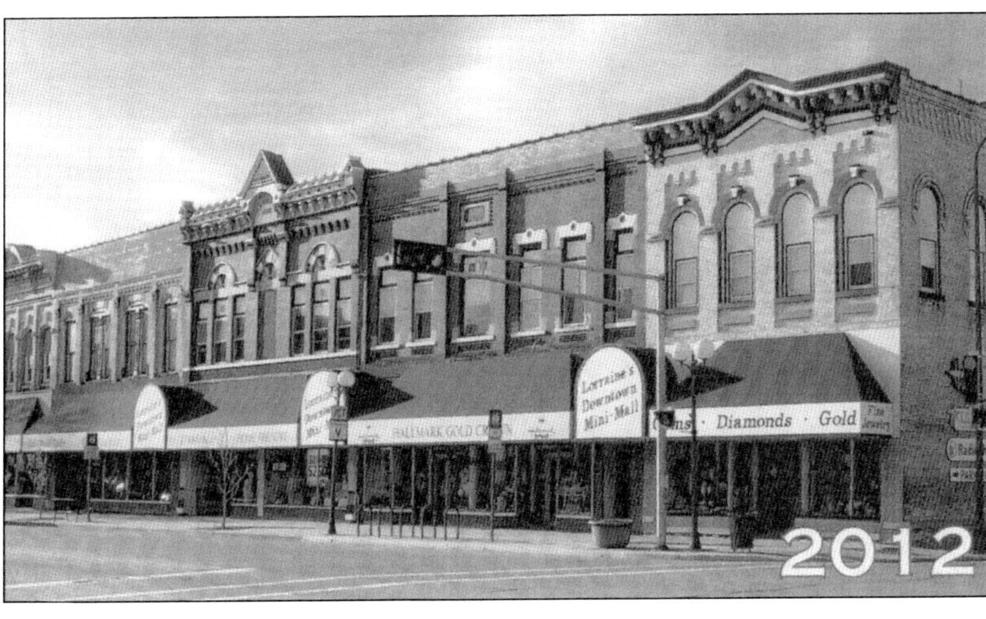

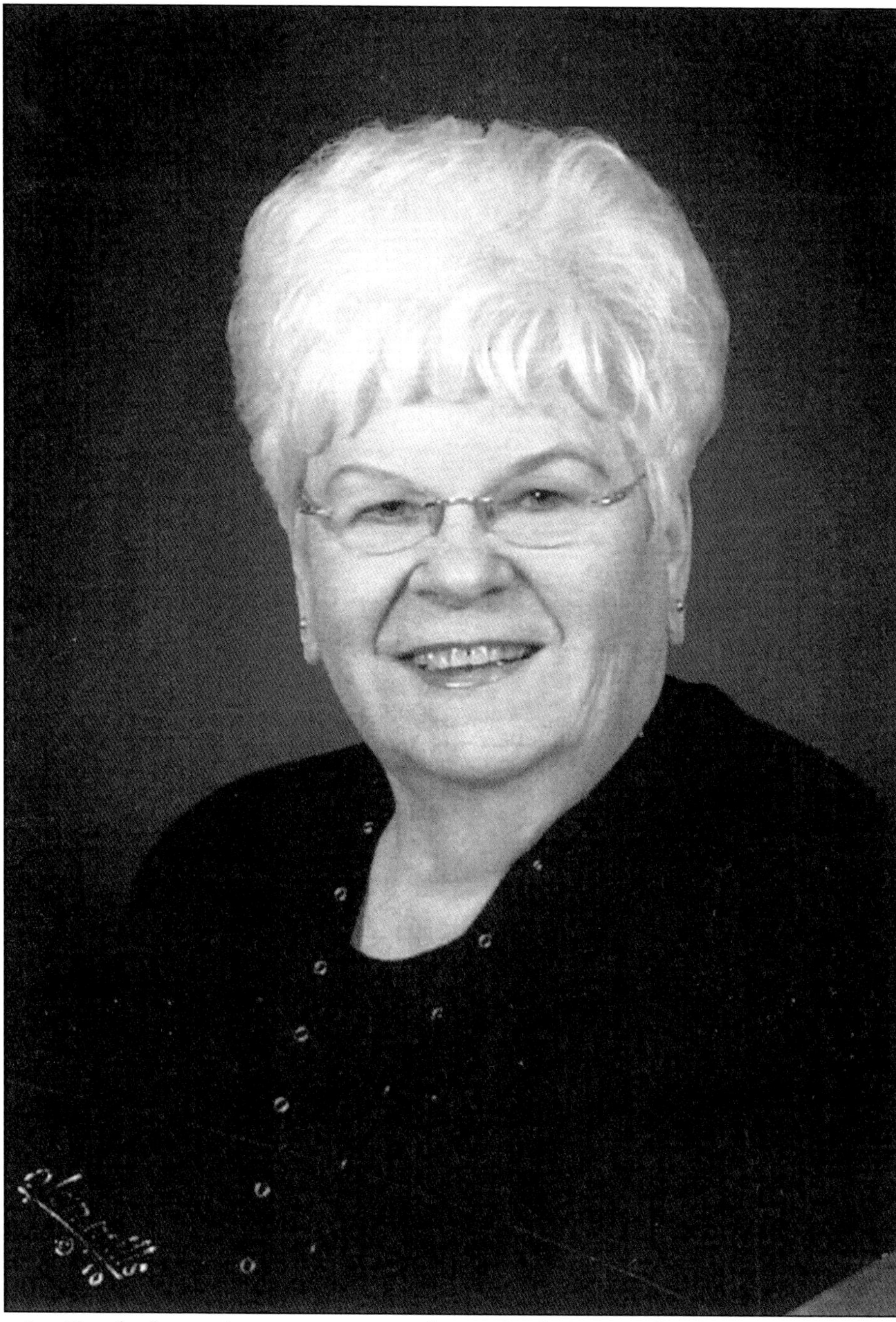

Lorraine Traeder began her career as a teacher in Sauk County, but later set out to begin a retail business in Reedsburg. Lorraine married Bill Traeder, who at the time was the manager of Hankscraft/Gerber. Bill supported her new career, which began in 1972. Lorraine continues her business with her daughter, Peggy, and son-in-law, Blain Albert. Lorraine enjoys participating in many activities in Reedsburg. Her greatest happiness is pleasing her customers. Offering good service and quality merchandise for the community and the visitors of Reedsburg is her goal. (Courtesy of Peggy Albert.)

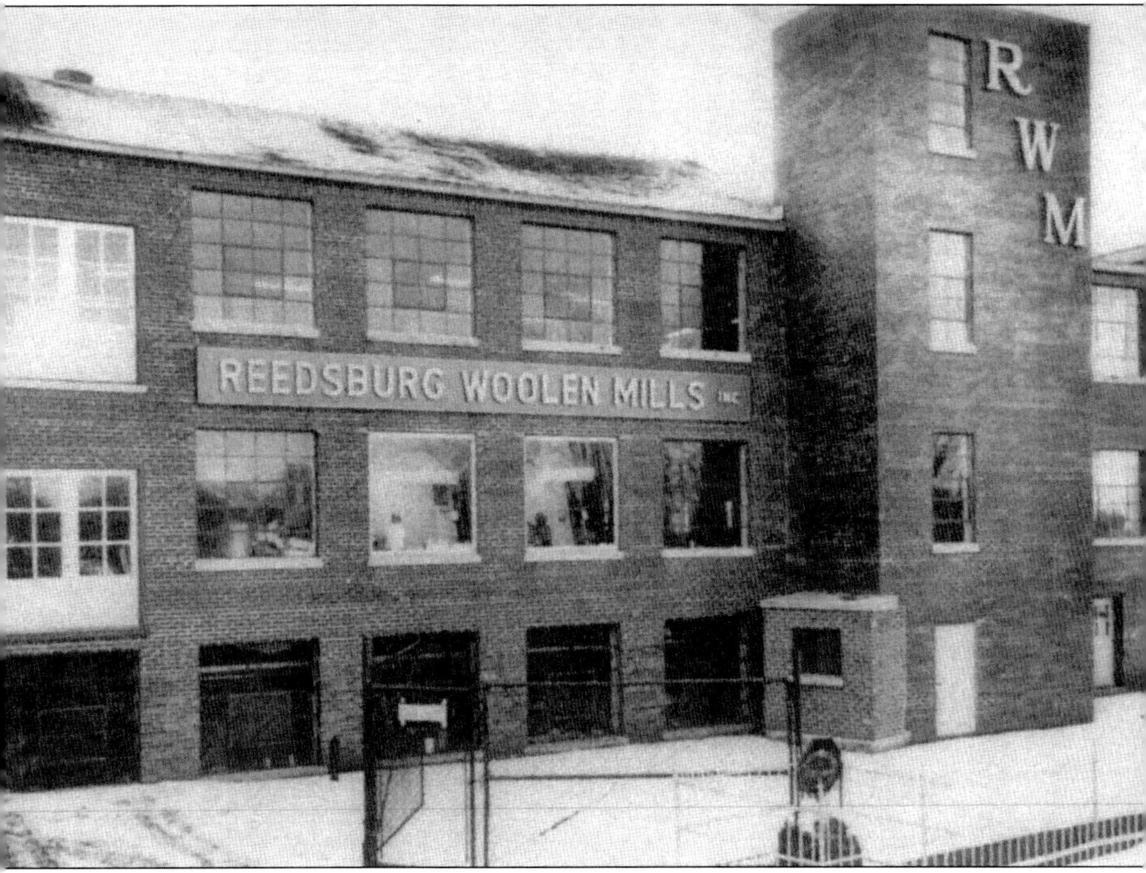

In the late 1800s, Reedsburg had a dam and a will to grow, so local businessmen met in the offices of Judge Luske to discuss the matter of a mill. Construction began on the Reedsburg Woolen Mill in 1879 and was completed in 1882. The mill shipped out $7,000 worth of goods to companies in Chicago by September of that year. It employed approximately 200 people during its 85 years of operation and was one of Reedsburg's longest-lived and most important industries. On April 9, 1968, the Reedsburg Woolen Mill burned to the ground, leaving only the mill office standing. Today, the office building remains on Main Street, and a monument with the picker device is located next to the Baraboo River on Main Street. The dam was torn down in 1973. (Courtesy of Reedsburg Historical Society.)

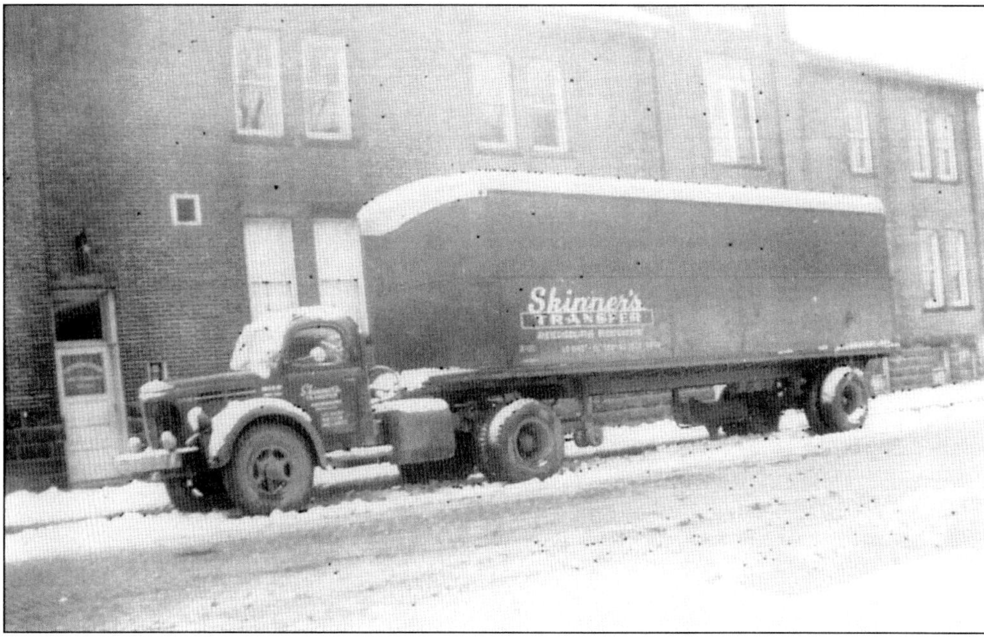

In 1960, Skinner Leasing Inc. was formed, and in 1970, Skinner Transfer Corporation was established. In 1973, Skinner had 34 employees, 69 trucks, and 81 trailers. While the business started small, it now transfers items throughout 48 states. In 1989, Bill Skinner was awarded Trucker of the Year in Wisconsin by the Wisconsin Motor Carriers Association. Also, in memorial to William Skinner, the Wisconsin Motor Carriers have established the William Skinner Humanitarian Award, given annually to an individual who has performed an act of heroism, extraordinary community service, or has made an unusual contribution toward improving public safety. (Both, courtesy of Evelyn Skinner.)

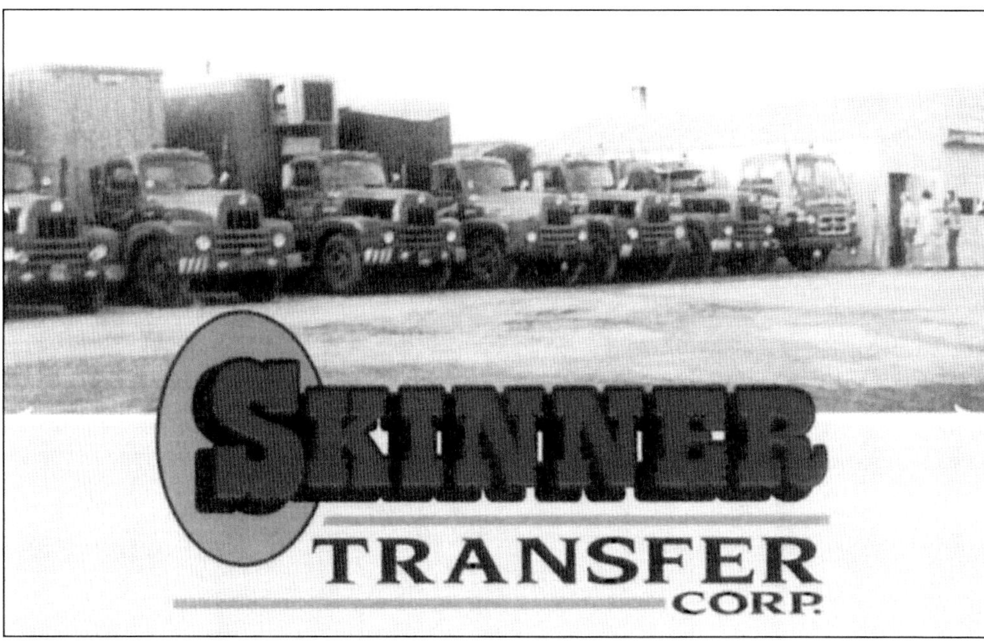

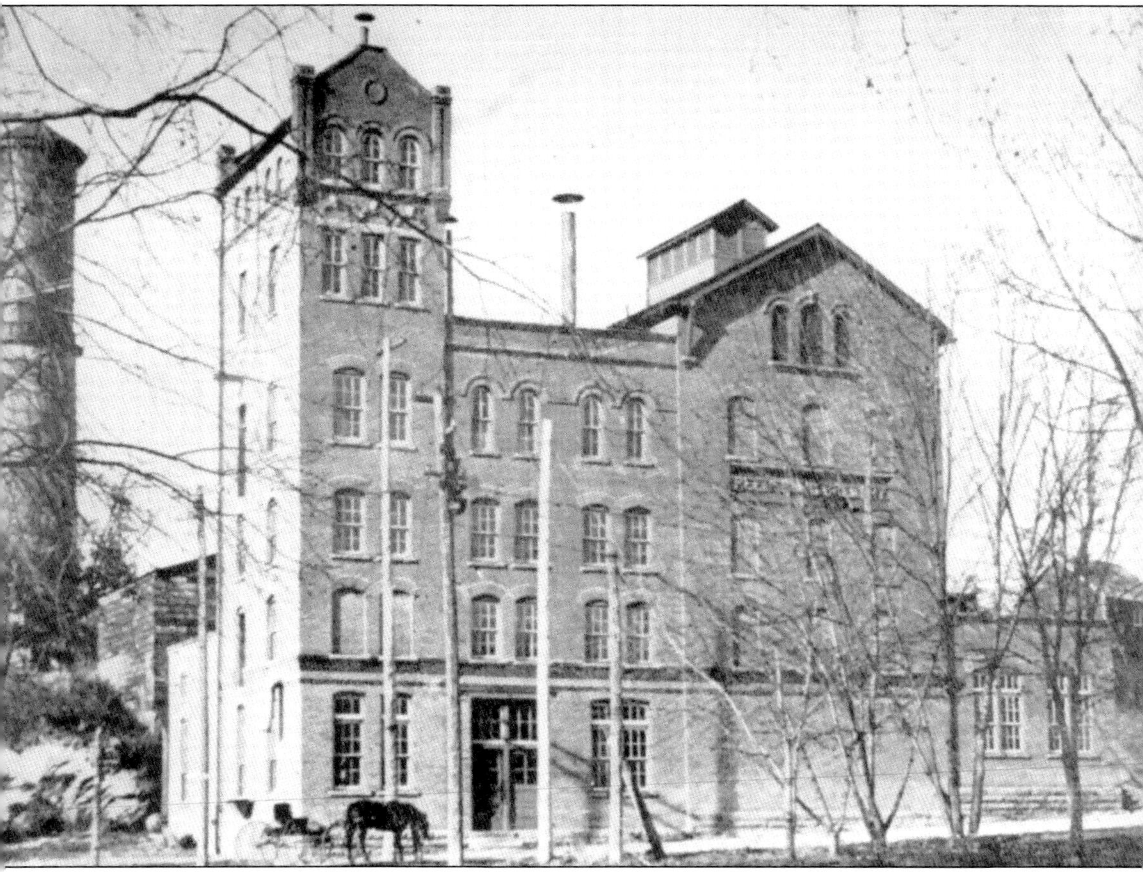

The Reedsburg Brewery faced challenges throughout its years of operation. Begun around 1872 by Frank and Florin Meckler, the brewery failed and a fire destroyed the building. Frank Meckler tried again, partnering with Fred Schroeder to rebuild on the same site. They operated the brewery from 1872 to 1879. After fires and financial struggles, Meckler and Schroeder sold out in 1879. John Hagenah and Henry Geffert, with partners William Dierks and Peter Hagenah, purchased the brewery in 1880. Now known as the Reedsburg Brewing Company, the brewery produced approximately 350 barrels of beer annually. Albert Fuhrman purchased the brewery in 1895 and ran it until Prohibition started in 1919. The current building was erected in 1905 with technologies to prevent further fire devastation. Following Prohibition, Hans B. Johnson reopened the brewery in 1933. P.H. Schweke purchased it in the late 1930s and ran it until 1947. L.C. Dobbert and K.P. Graber were the last to try their hand at operating the brewery, opening it in 1949. But the business closed in 1950. After years of vacancy and use as a storage site, the building was remolded into apartments in 1987 by Tom Elliot. (Courtesy of Reedsburg Public Library.)

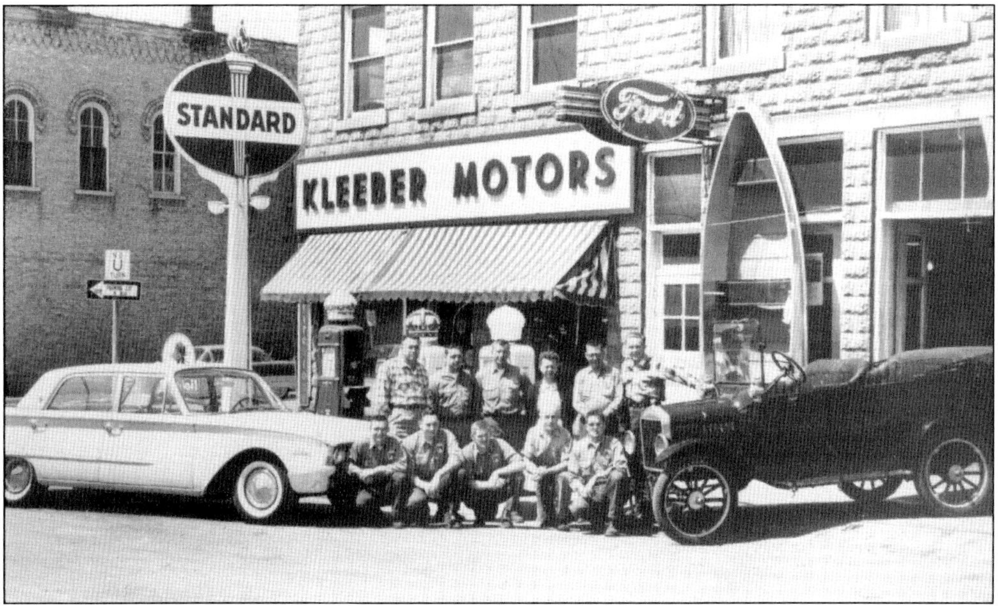

Kleeber Motors was owned by H.S. Kleeber and Willard Kleeber. The business ran from 1947 to 1981. Posing in the above photograph are, from left to right, (first row) Bob Hoege, Merve Jaech, Bob Luetkens, Ernest Selle, and Ron Cayse; (second row) Willard Kleeber, Buzz Scott, Ken Harder, Alice Burmester, John Kraemer, and Rueben Gade. (Above, courtesy of Reedsburg Public Library; below, courtesy of *Reedsburg Times Press*.)

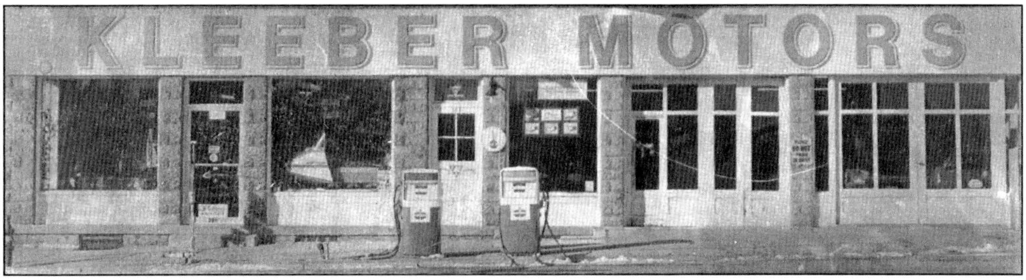

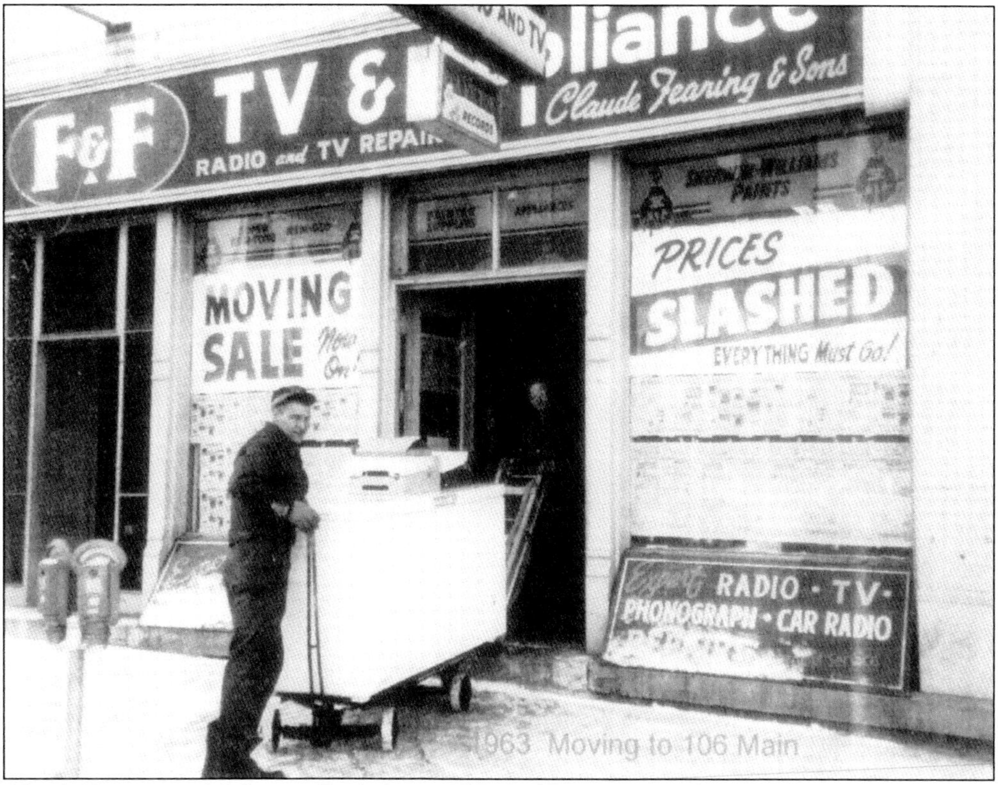

Claude Fearing and Sylvester Friebel started Fearing's TV & Appliance in 1953 at a root beer stand. Lester Fearing joined the business in 1954, and Friebel was bought out in 1955. Tom Fearing joined in 1956. The store was moved to its current location on March 15, 1963. A warehouse was built in 1970, and a service center was added to the warehouse in 1973. Grandsons Dan, Gary, and Steve Fearing have owned the business since 1994. (Both, courtesy of Fearings Store.)

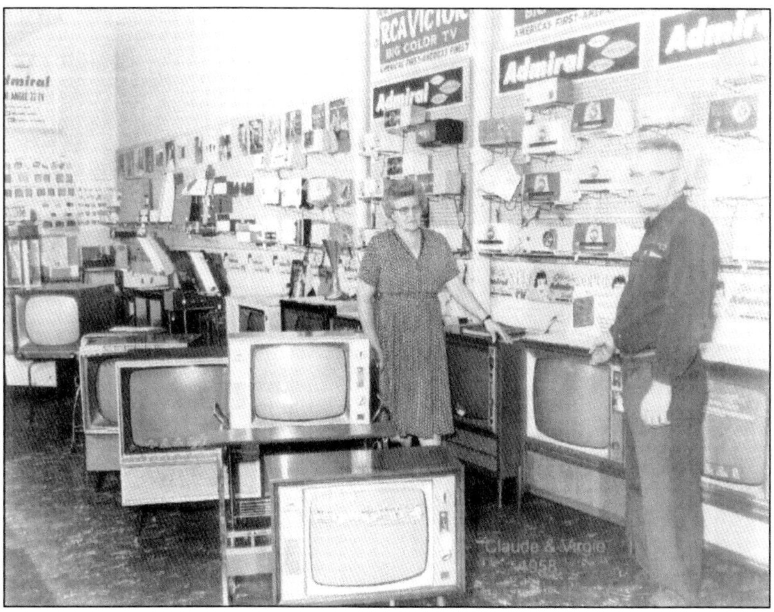

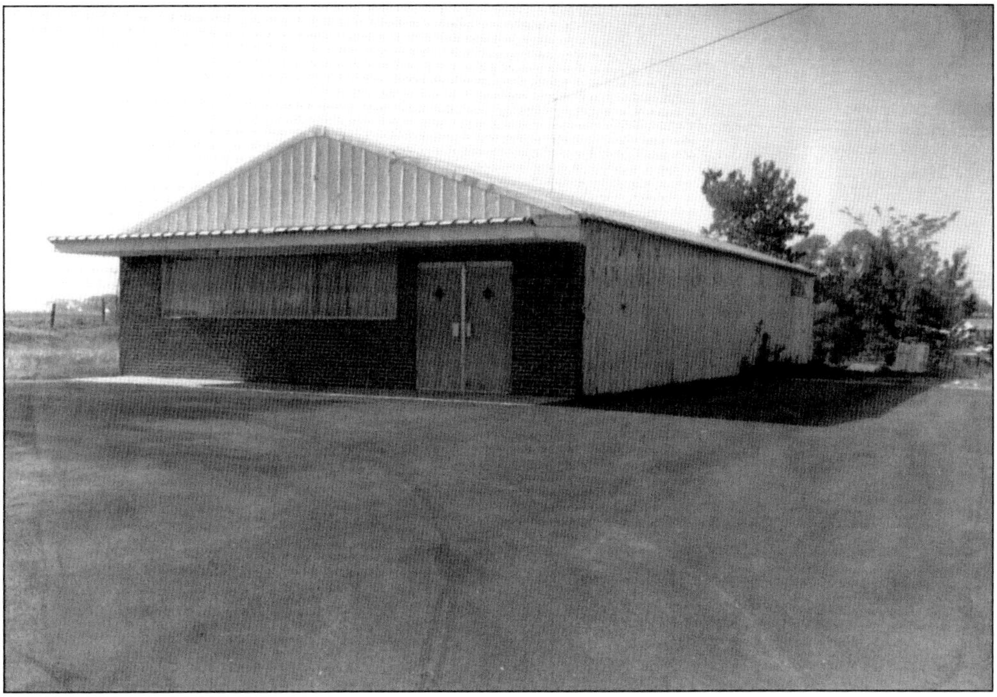

Krueger Printing & Office Supplies moved to its current location in 1967, when Jim and Virginia Krueger purchased the building. At the time, it was known as Krueger Duplicating Service Inc. and had previously been operating out of the Kruegers' basement. The building has undergone three expansions and now is 9,000 square feet. Krueger Printing is run by Jim Krueger, the son of Jim and Virginia. (Both, courtesy of Jim Krueger.)

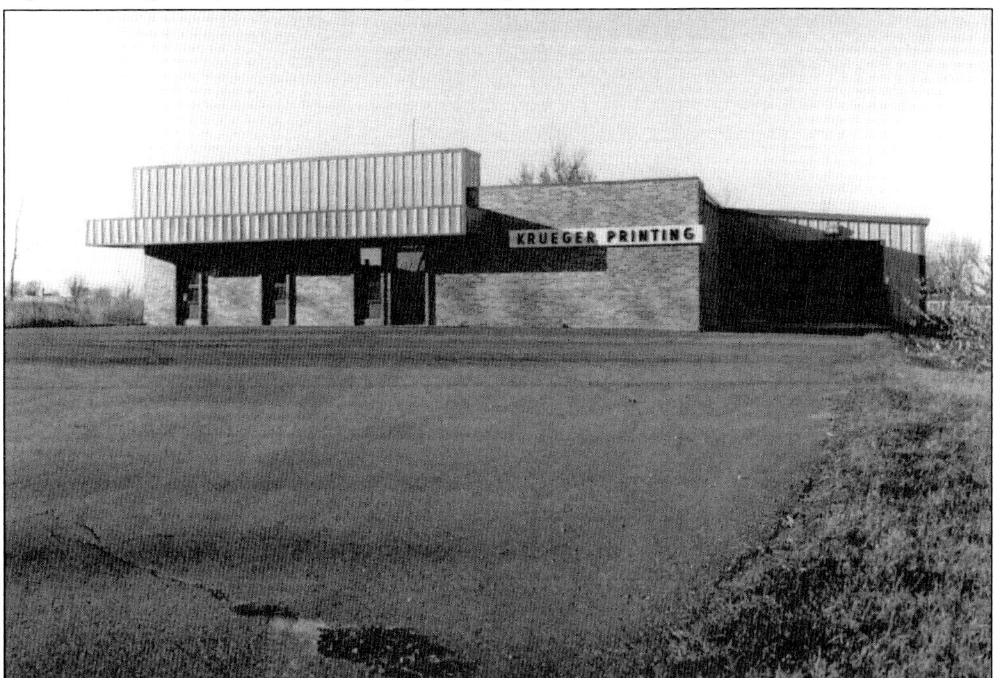

Otto and Hyacinth Schmitt purchased Big Store Shoes from Charles Utterbach in 1952 and started their own business, with assistance from their son Marvin. When the original building was destroyed in the Big Store fire of 1957, the Schmitts ran the business out of the Second Street building that had housed Emma Reed's business. The Schmitts ended up relocating to their current location in the spring of 1958 and then expanded. (Both, courtesy of John Schmitt.)

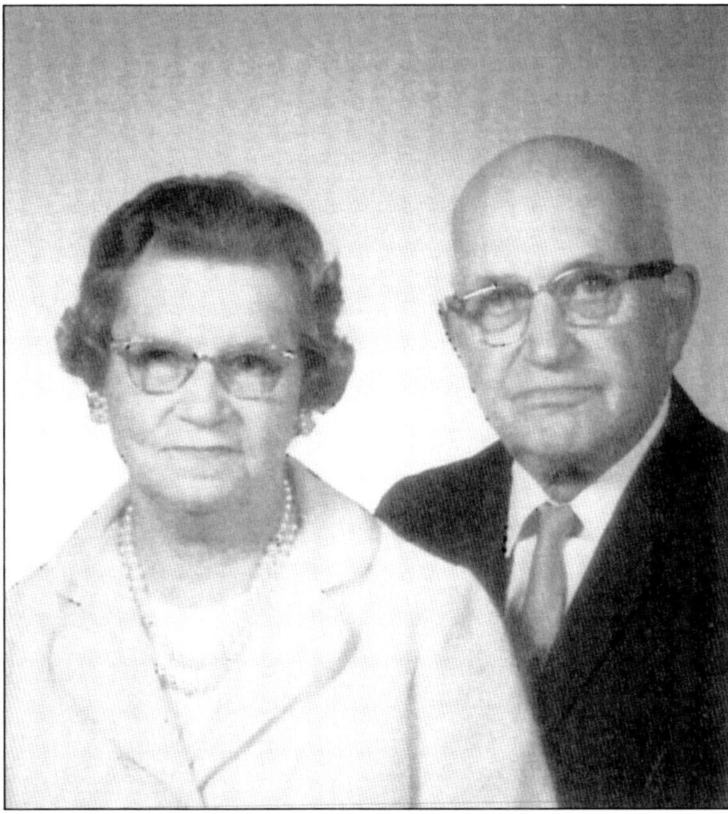

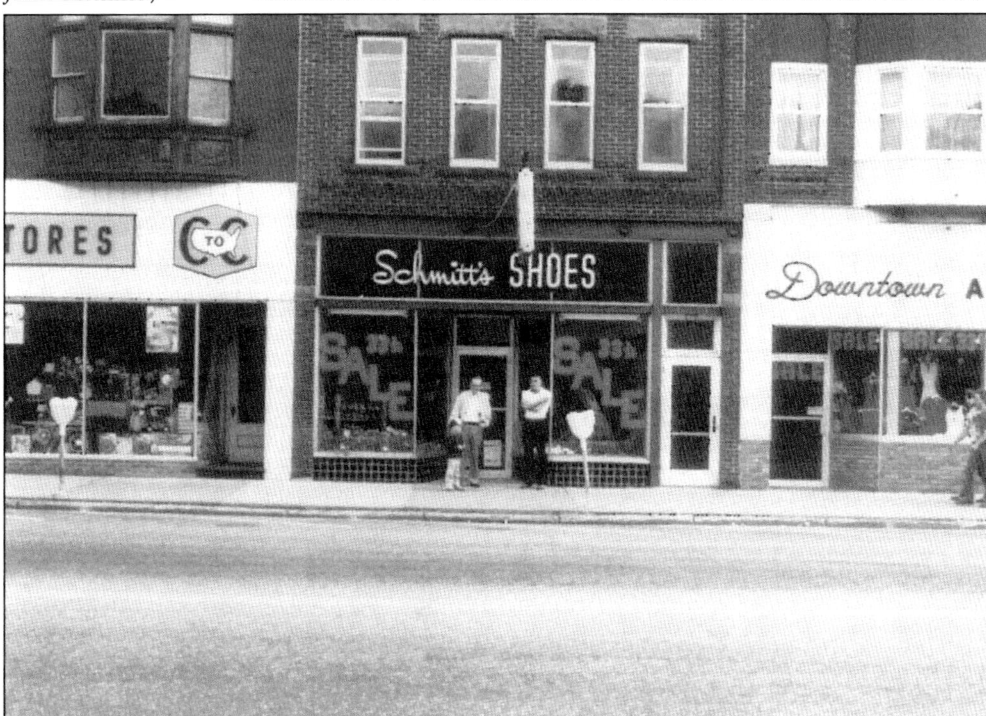

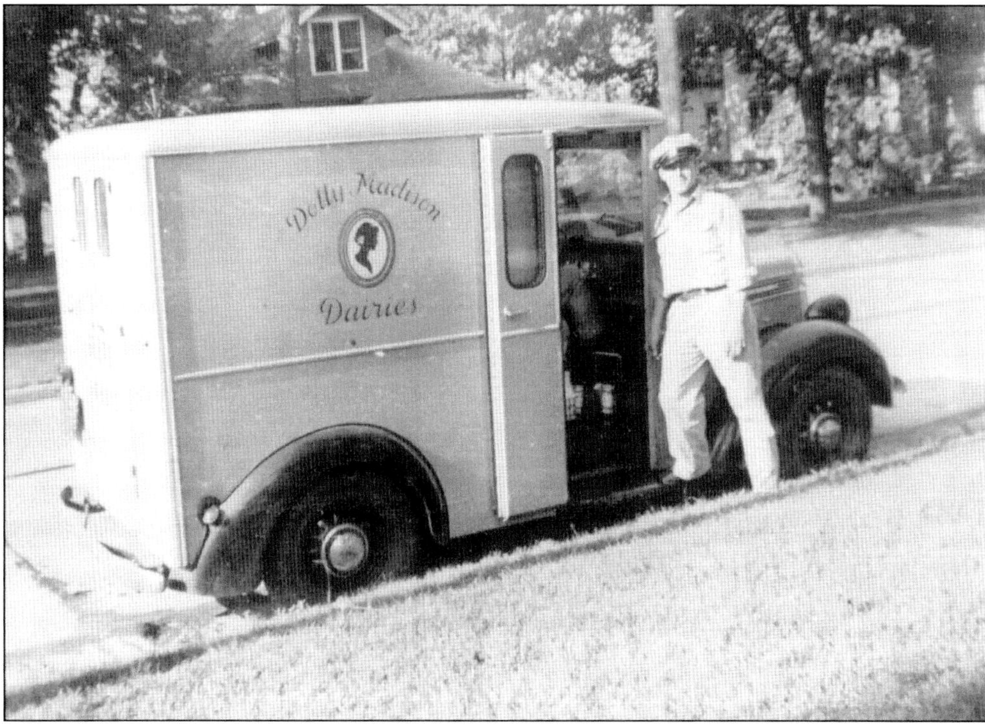

Dolly Madison Dairies delivered throughout the city. Patrons left a card requesting the milk products they needed in an insulated box on their porch. Even after the company changed hands multiple times and closed down production in Reedsburg, deliveries were still made until 1980. (Both, courtesy of Reedsburg Public Library.)

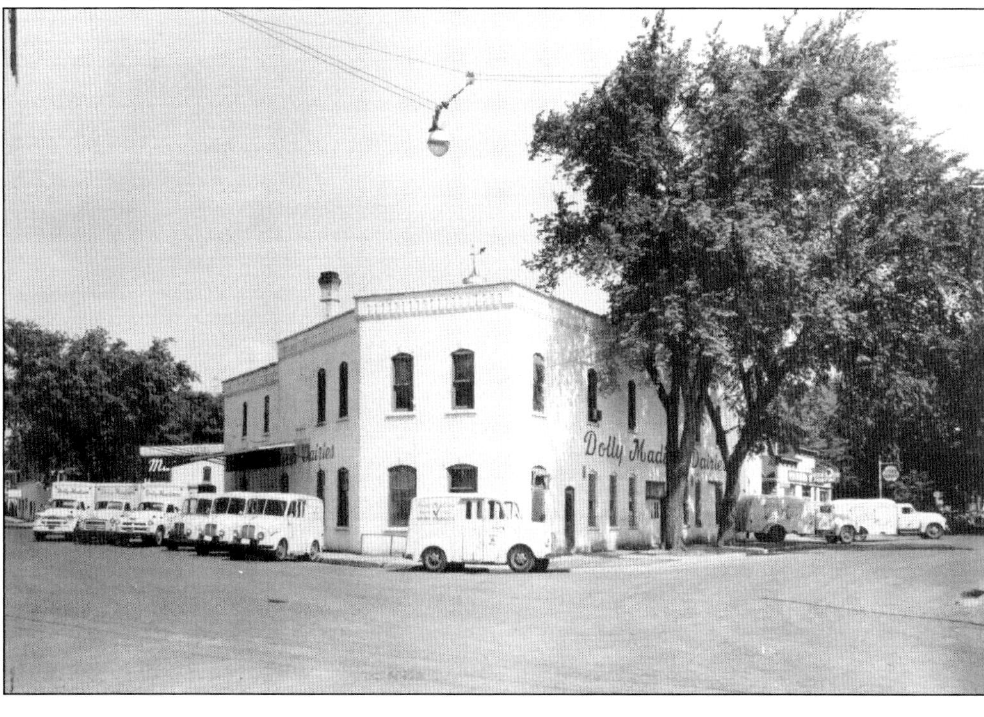

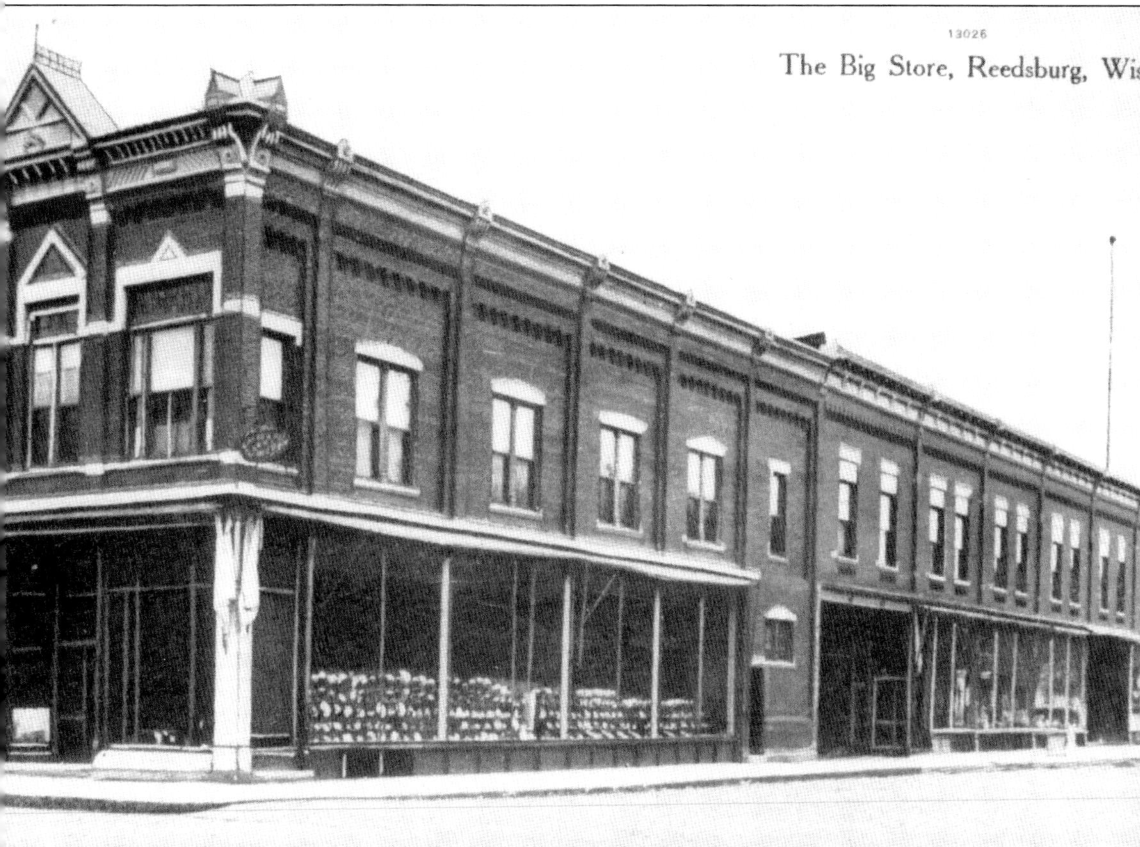

The Big Store burned down on Tuesday, August 27, 1957, resulting in the loss of nearly a block's worth of businesses. The fire resulted in nearly $2 million worth of damage, and many businesses did not rebuild. Those that did so constructed new buildings in a more modern style, on one level. Coincidentally, the Big Store had just passed fire inspection two days before the destructive blaze. (Courtesy of Reedsburg Public Library.)

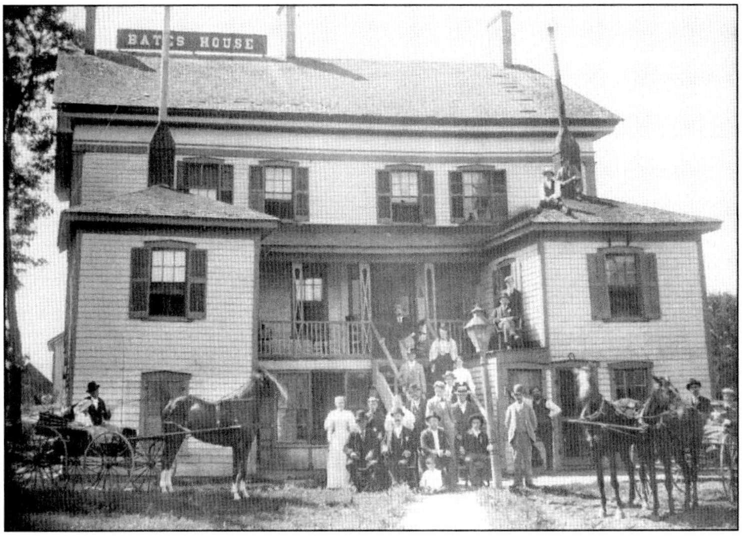

After burning to the ground in 1900, the Bates House needed to be rebuilt. Around 5,000 loads of sandstone were hauled away in order to build the house at street level. The building operated as a hotel until 1911, when it was purchased by Dr. T.R. Hastings and converted into a sanitarium. (Courtesy of Reedsburg Public Library.)

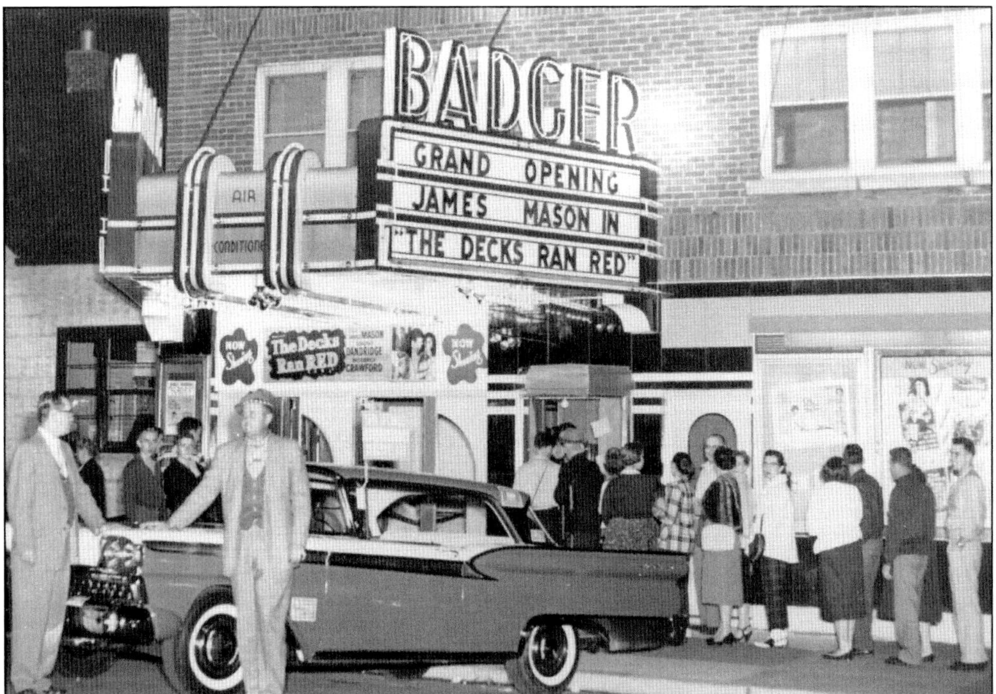

In 1924, the Badger Theater was moved to its current location. Formerly called the Majestic, Oscar V. and Mida Kelly moved the theater to the new building, which could accommodate 400 people and housed a pipe organ. A fire threatened the theater in 1927, but the building had been constructed with fireproof materials and automatic fire shutters, so the damage was minimal. The theater was one of the first in the area to show "talkies," and it served as a campaign stop for Sen. John F. Kennedy in 1960. (Courtesy of Reedsburg Public Library.)

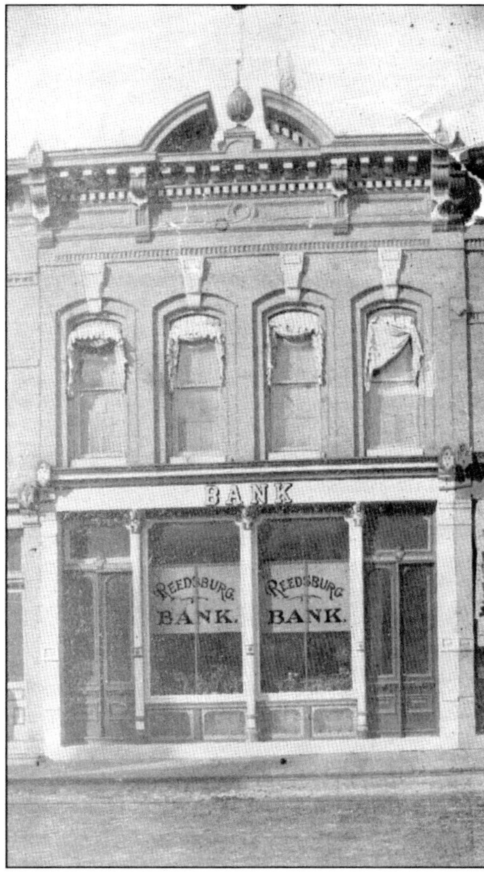

The Reedsburg Bank was started as a private bank in 1867 by Mackey, Rudd & Co. Located on the corner of Main and Locust Streets (below), this original bank was open for 10 years. It reopened in 1877 at 233 E. Main Street. In 1920, construction began at 201 Main Street, where Harris Bank Downtown stands today. In 2005, the Reedsburg Bank was sold to Community Bank Group. The Reedsburg Bank is now BMO Harris Bank, after the latter company took it over in 2007. (Both, courtesy of Reedsburg Public Library.)

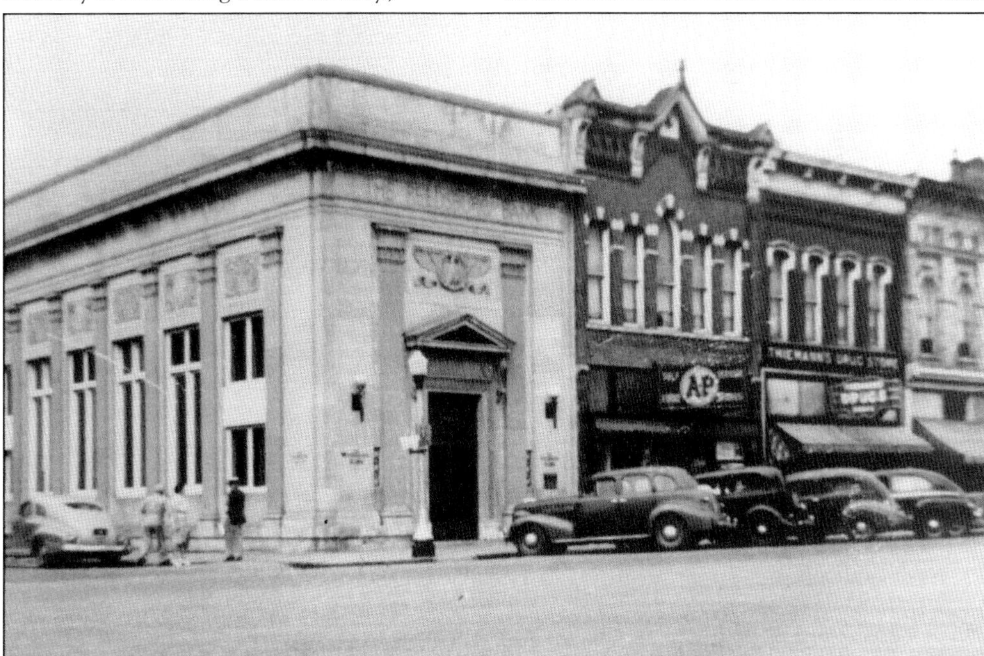

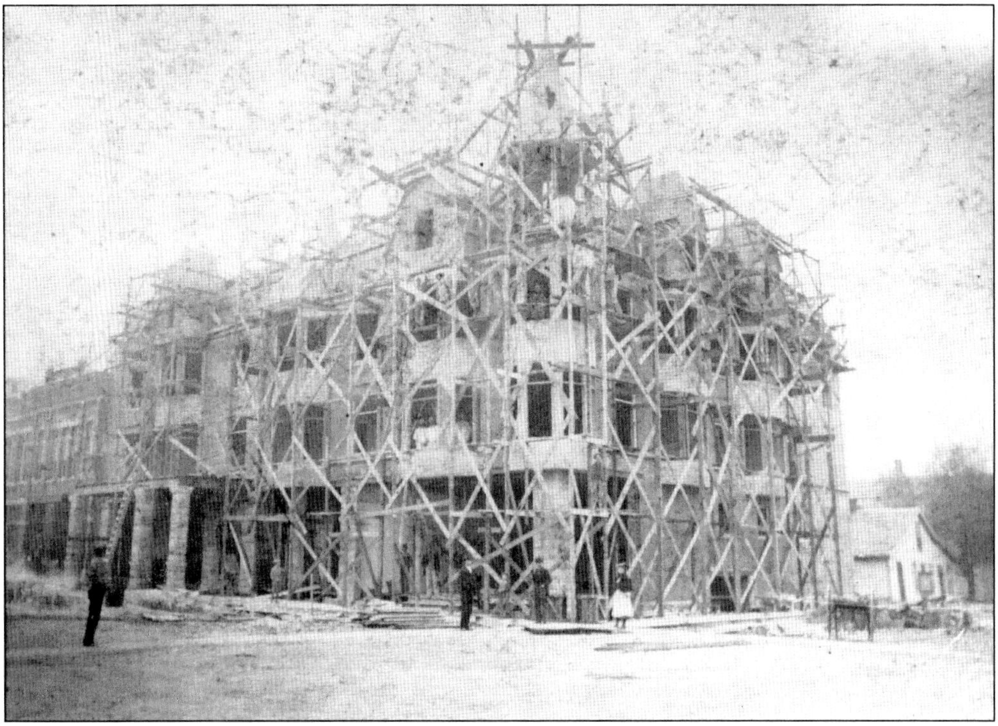

After the Alba House changed hands multiple times and was eventually destroyed in a fire, William Stolte Sr. and his son Edward G. Stolte decided to rebuild a hotel on the same site (above). The Stolte Hotel opened on January 1, 1897. It changed hands a few more times, and additions were made to the structure. The hotel eventually took on the facade recognized today (below). (Both, courtesy of Reedsburg Public Library.)

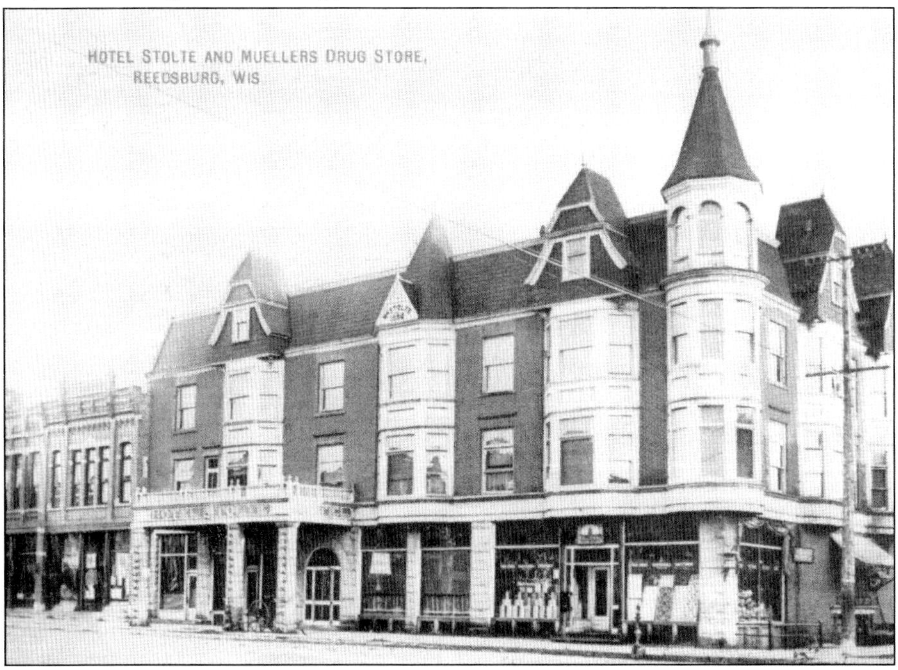

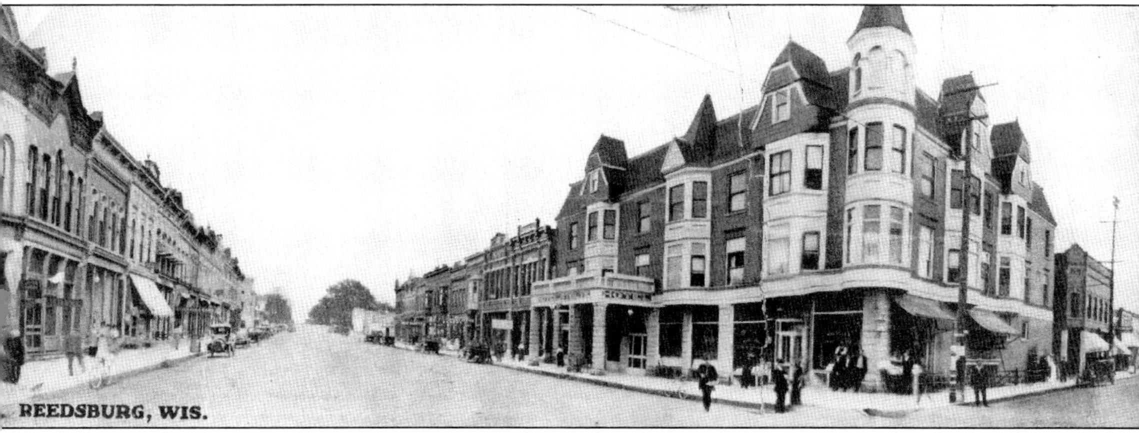

The Stolte Hotel, to the right in this photograph from the early 1900s, has been converted into street-level storefronts for local businesses and upper-floor apartments. Many of the elements of the old facade remain today. The old hotel is one of the most iconic buildings in Reedsburg. (Courtesy of Reedsburg Public Library.)

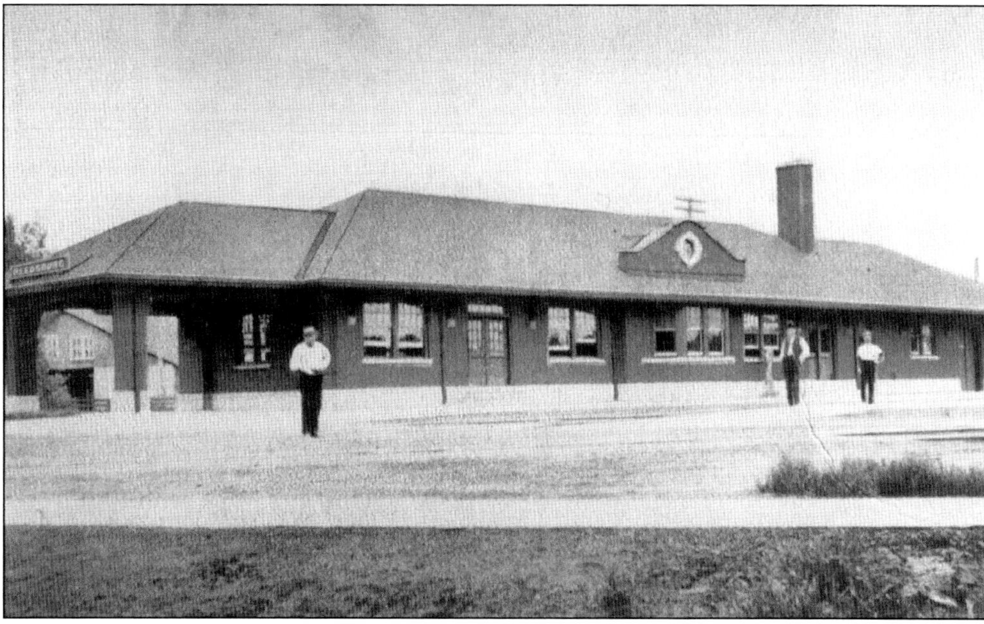

After the area was bypassed multiple times, a railroad stop in Reedsburg (above) was finally initiated in 1870. The line proved to be a success. Business had increased so much that a new depot was needed. The current building (below), which opened in January 1906, held a ticket office, waiting room, smoking room, restrooms, and baggage room. The number of trains passing through Reedsburg decreased drastically by the 1950s, and the final train passed through in 1963. Today, the depot houses the Reedsburg Chamber of Commerce. (Both, courtesy of Reedsburg Public Library.)

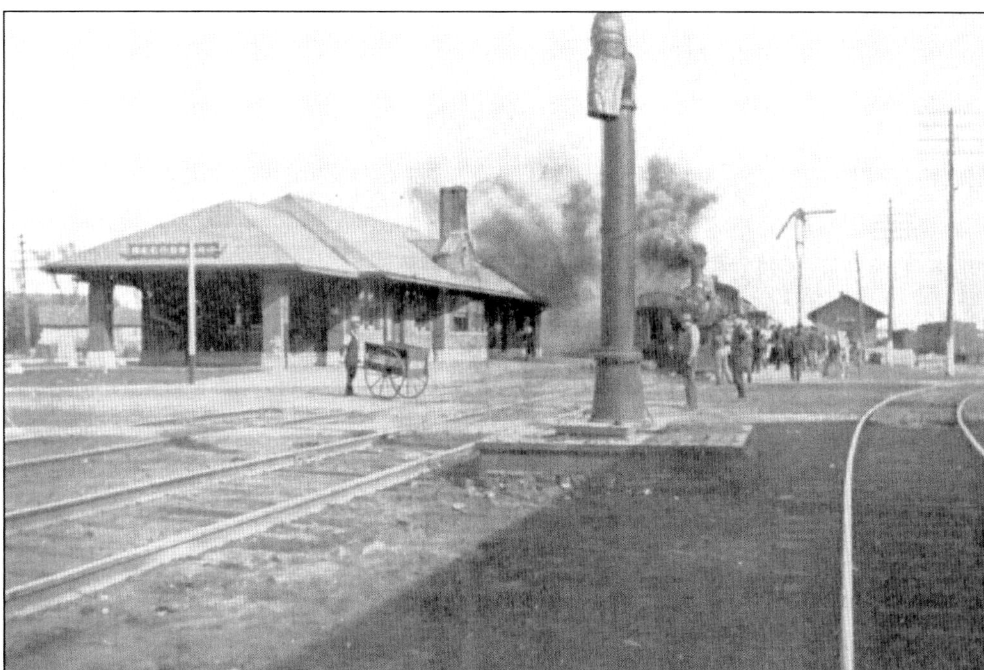

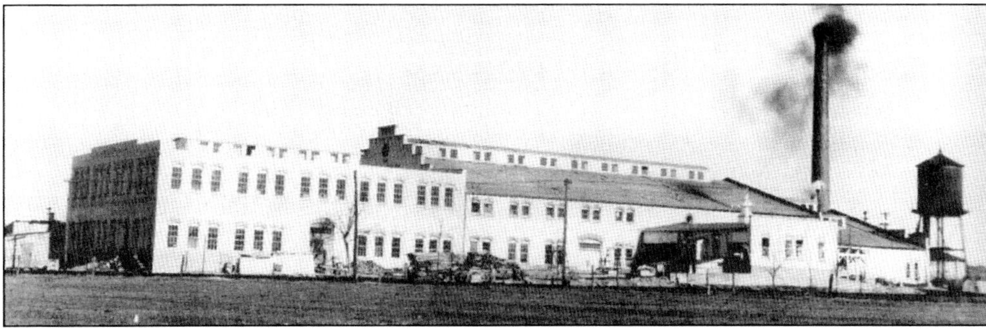

The Jay Wilde Milk Company built Foremost Farms in 1914. Two years later, Nestle purchased the plant and continued to operate it as a condensery. In 1946, Nestle sold the plant to Hillpoint Co-operative, which expanded production to include butter, nonfat dry milk, and cottage cheese. Hillpoint merged with Wisconsin Dairies Co-operative in 1967, and the plant began to focus solely on butter and powder production. Wisconsin Dairies merged with Golden Guernsey Dairy Co-operative on January 1, 1995, to become Foremost Farms USA Co-operative. Today, the Reedsburg plant is the company's only facility that produces butter. (Courtesy of Reedsburg Historical Society.)

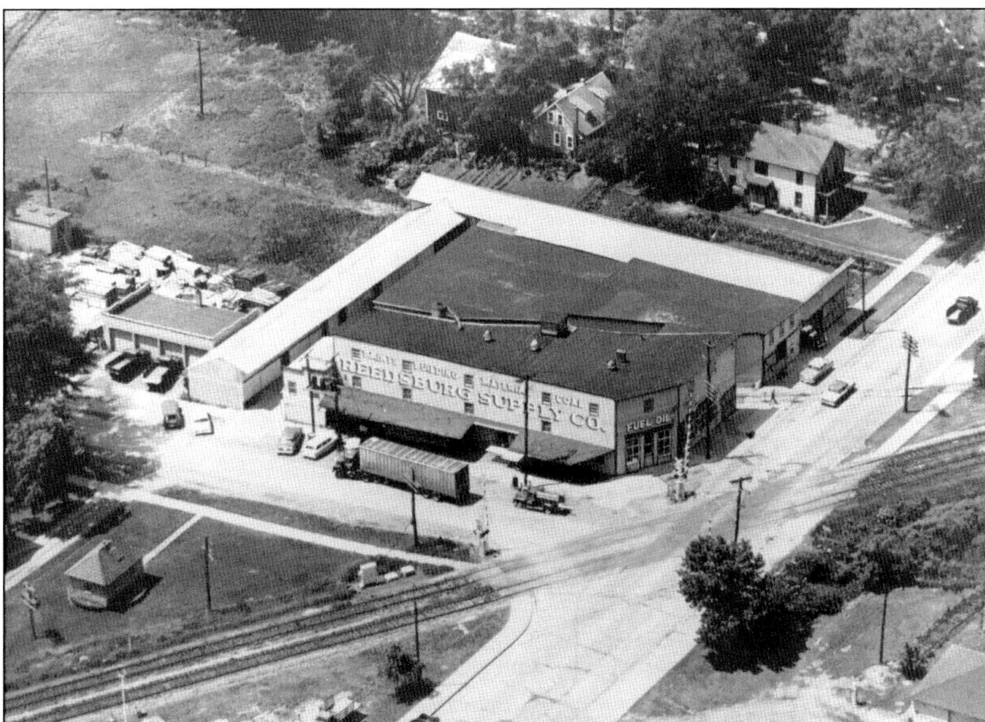

The Reedsburg Supply Company is pictured here in 1958. The company later became the Reedsburg Phillips Do-It-Center. The building is now Anytime Fitness. (Courtesy of Reedsburg Public Library.)

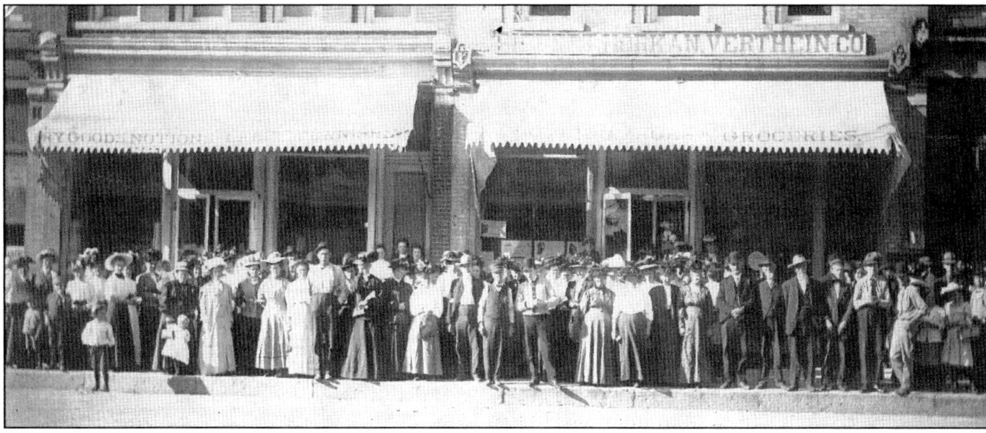

The Daylight Store was owned by E.A. Soefert, George Horkan Jr., and H.W. Verthein. The store carried a complete line of general merchandise, and did very well in the early 1900s. (Both, courtesy of Reedsburg Public Library.)

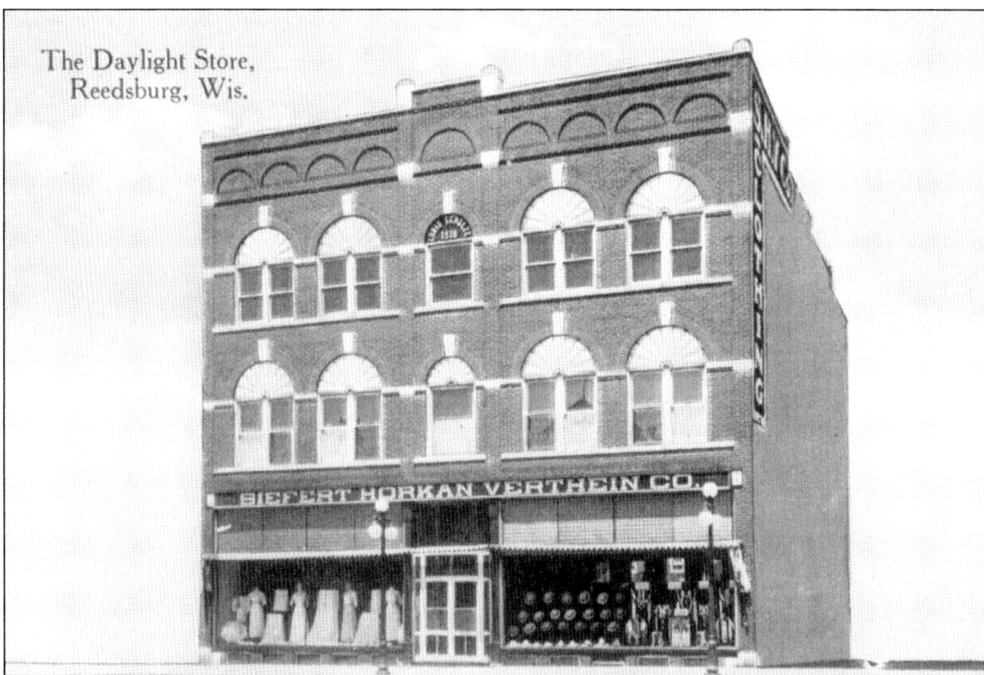

The *Reedsburg Free Press* started in 1860. In 1939, it merged with the *Reedsburg Times Press*. The *Reedsburg Times Press* and the *Reedsburg Independent* are the major newspapers in town. The building pictured here is where Gavin Brothers is located today. (Courtesy of Reedsburg Public Library.)

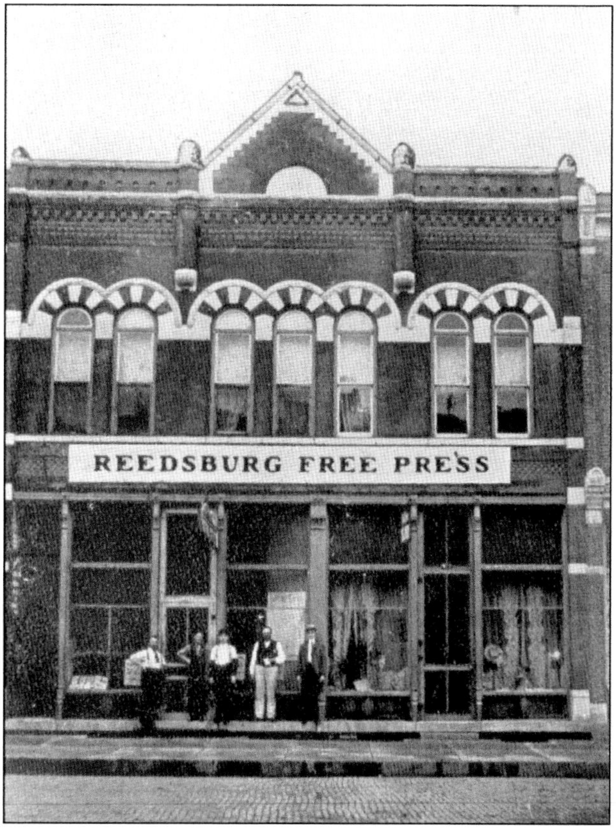

Collins Drugs was once the largest drugstore in Reedsburg. Its former location is now home to the Brides N' Belles store. (Courtesy of *Reedsburg Times Press*.)

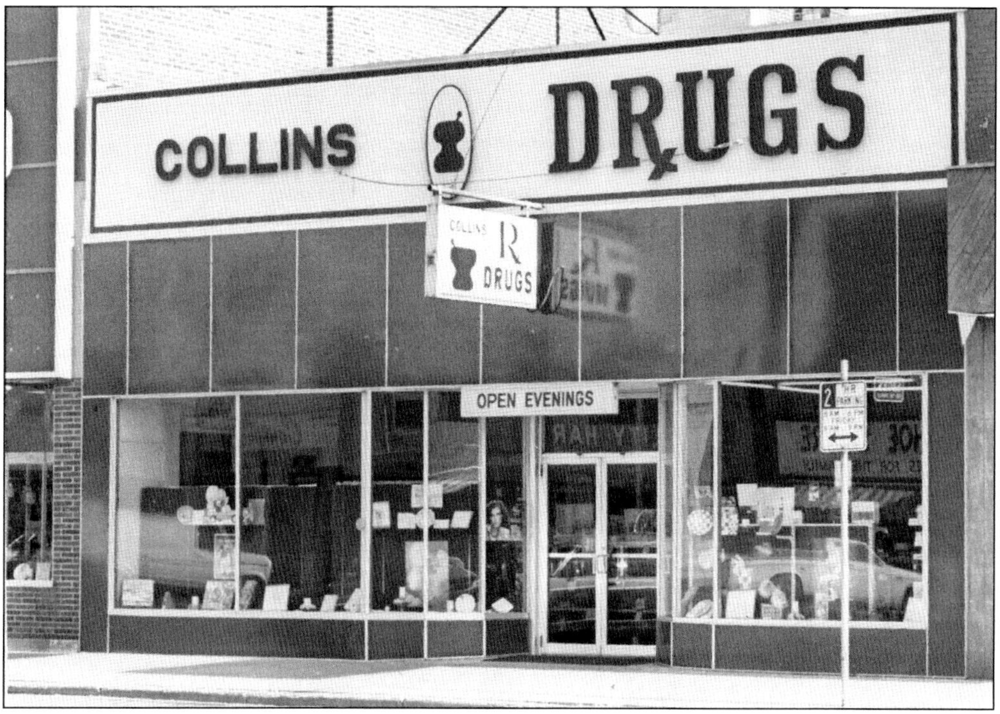

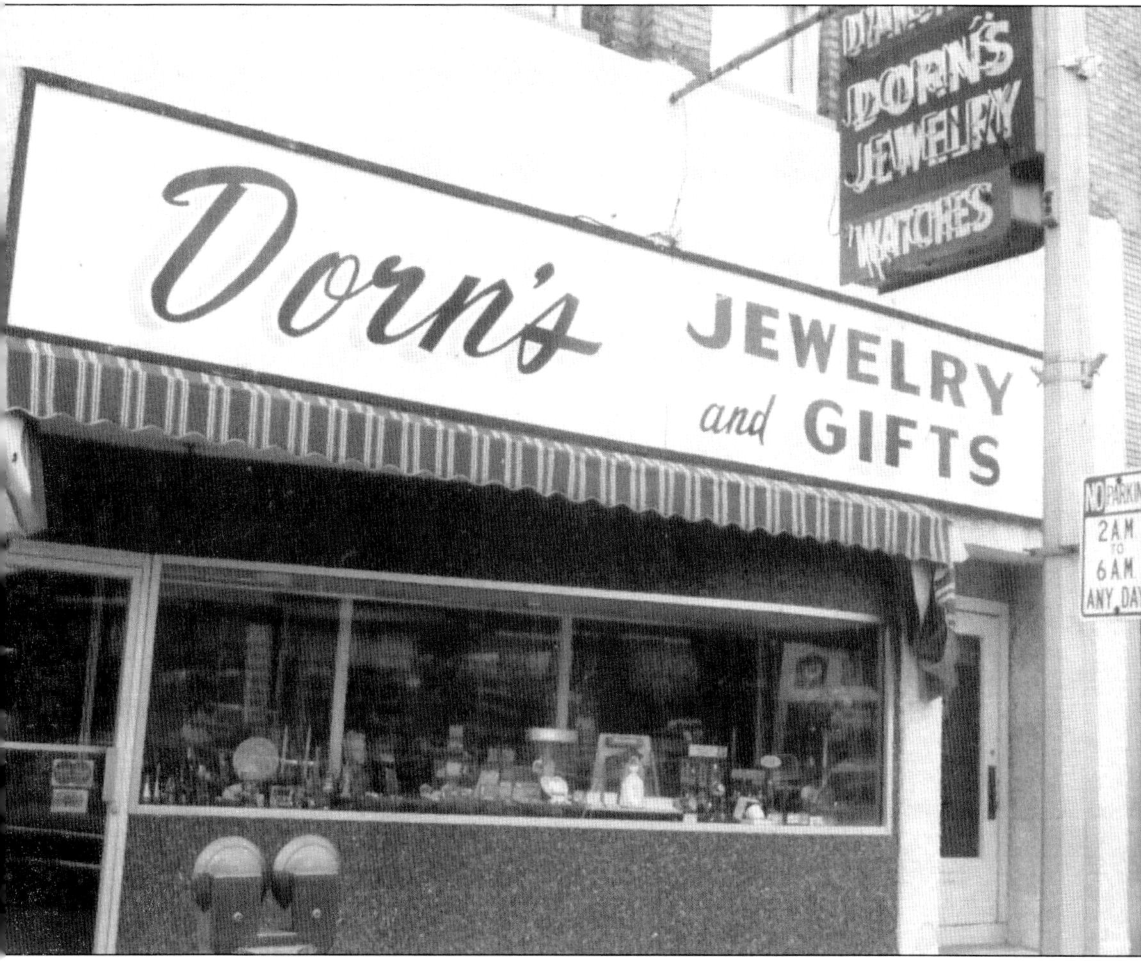

Dorn's Jewelry was started by John Dorn, who once worked at Brown's Drugs and Jewelry. The business started in 1972 on Main Street. Ron Dorn took over from 1987 to 1994. (Courtesy of *Reedsburg Times Press.*)

Four

Flood and Fires

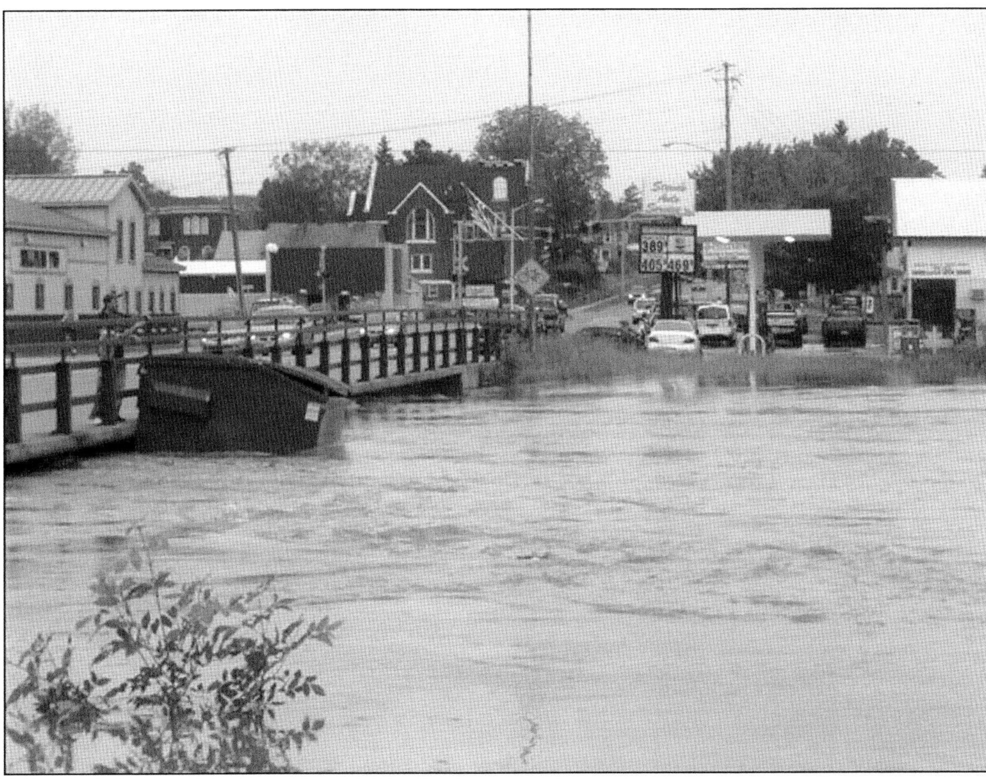

The Baraboo River runs through about 2.5 miles of downtown Reedsburg. In June 2008, due to heavy rains, the river flooded, which led to the destruction of many homes and a few businesses. The waters covered the Main Street Bridge (pictured), cutting off the entire west side of town. (Courtesy of Steve Braunschweig and Kelsey Jernander.)

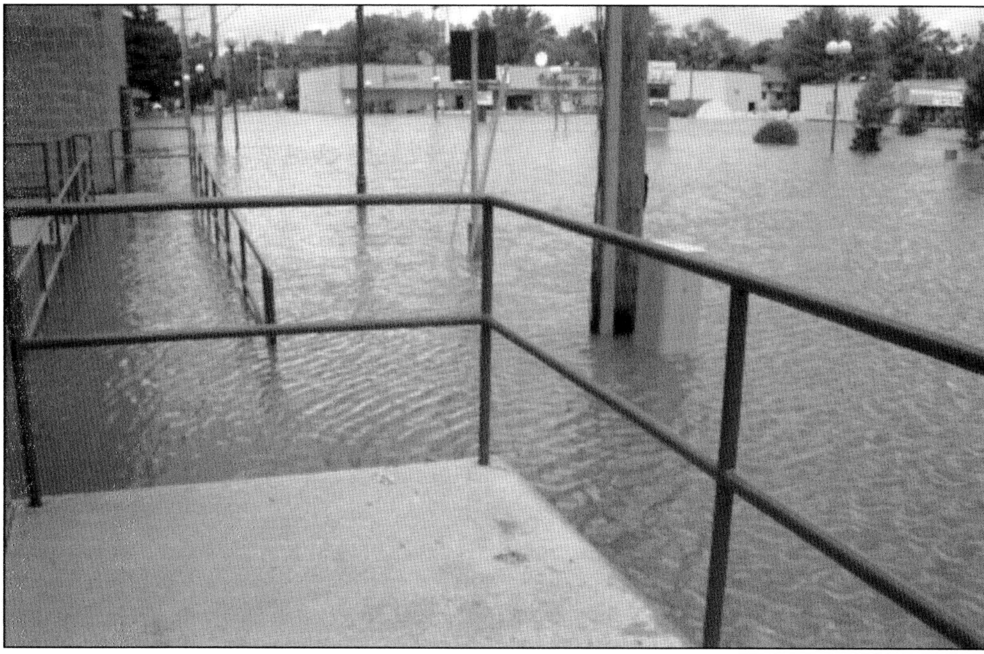

This photograph was taken by a brave employee who crawled to the front of the largest theater to see how deep the water actually was. Since the water reached the lobby at the peak level, the seats at the front of the theater were probably completely submerged at the time of this photograph. (Courtesy of Kelsey Jernander.)

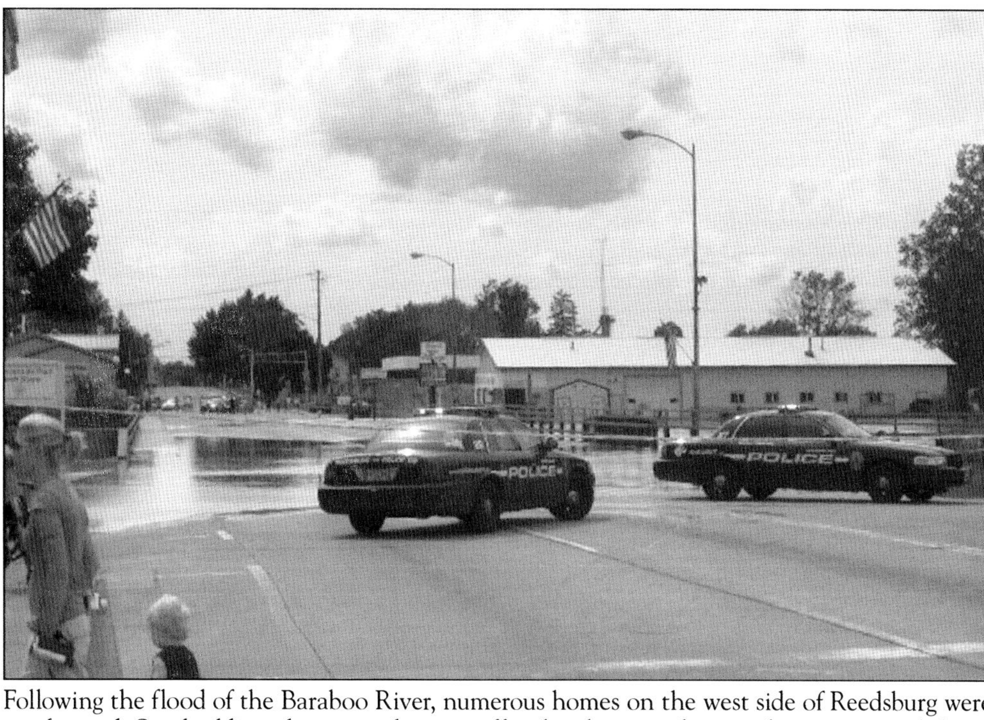

Following the flood of the Baraboo River, numerous homes on the west side of Reedsburg were condemned. One building, the movie theater, suffered such severe damage that it remained closed for nearly two and a half years. (Courtesy of Steve Braunschweig and Kelsey Jernander.)

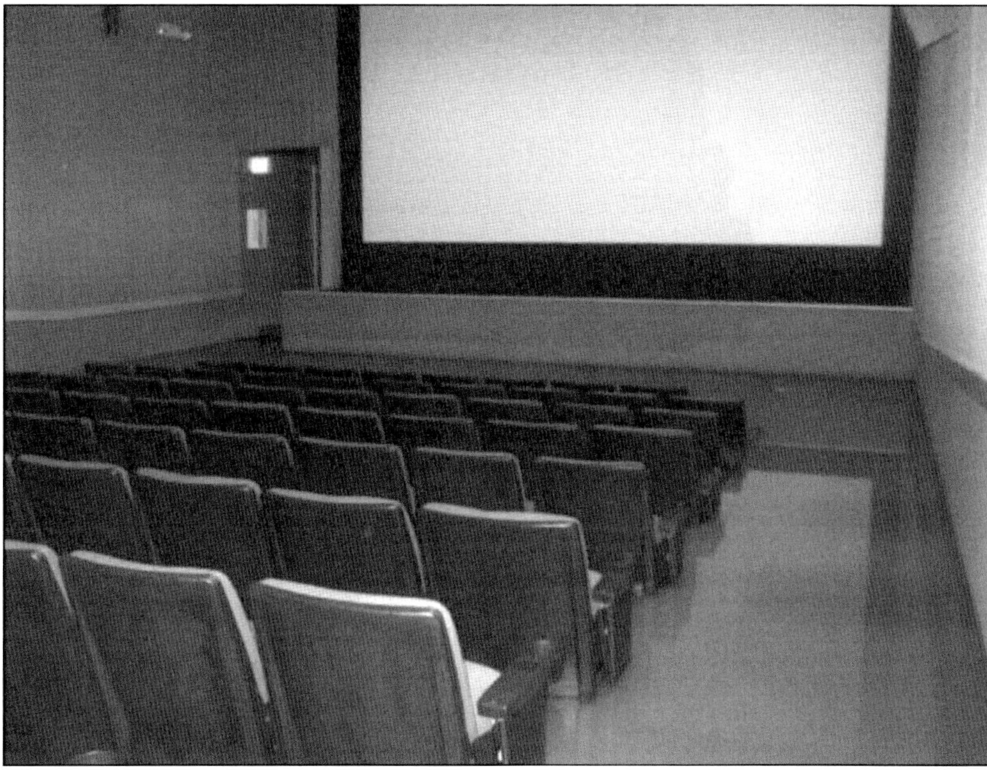

When the river began to recede, owners and employees of the movie theater were allowed inside to assess the damage. A view from the back of one of the screening rooms shows how far the water penetrated the building. The carpets in the lobby were so saturated that reflections were visible in the dark pattern. (Above, courtesy of Ashley Hentges; below, courtesy of Kelsey Jernander.)

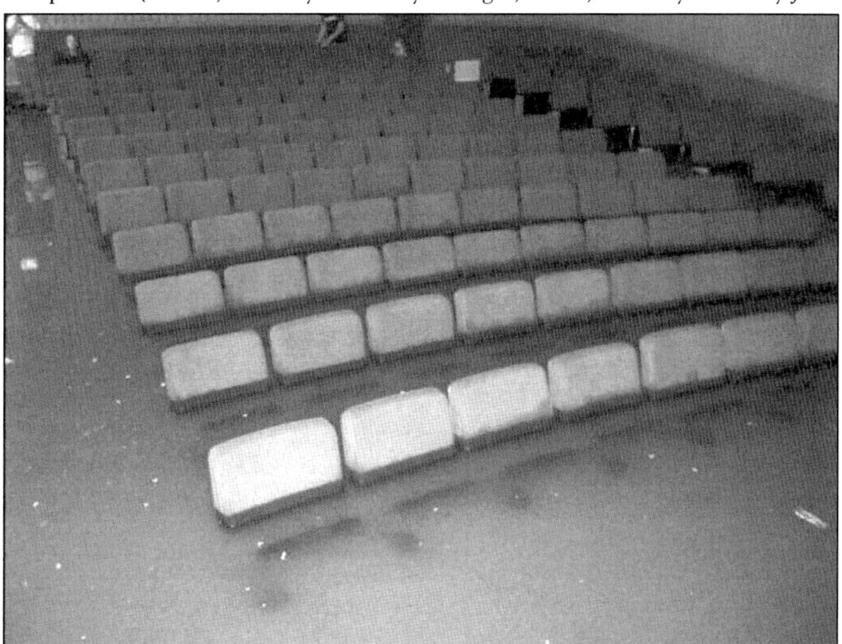

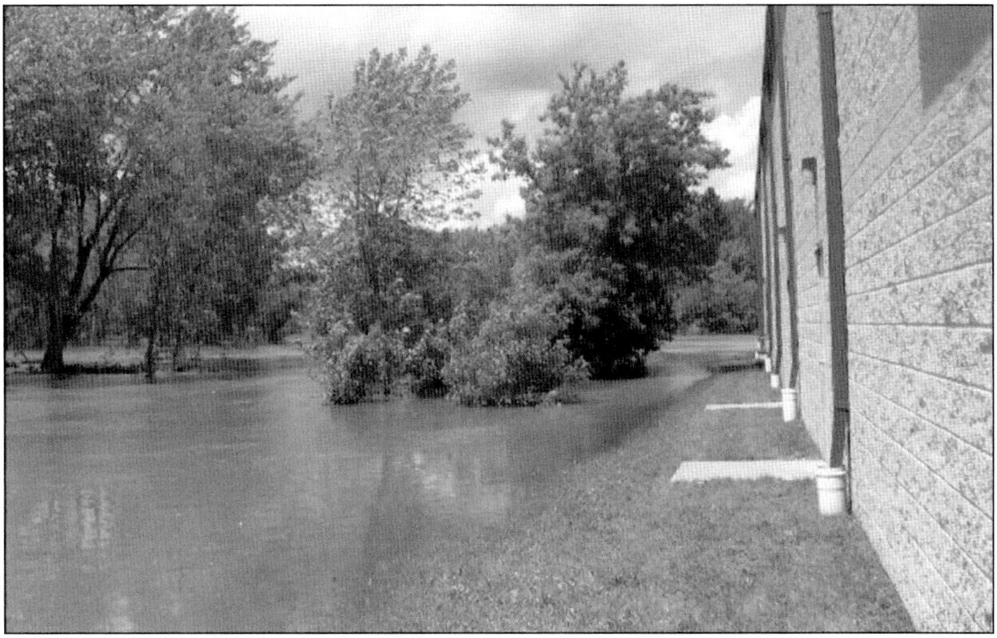

The Baraboo River runs behind Reedsburg's Star Cinema. Here, the waters have risen beyond their banks and taken over the parking lot and exit ramp. The water continued past the theater, across the street, and into the parking lots of nearby businesses. Sandbags were placed around most of the businesses in time to minimize damage from the waters, but the movie theater was completely flooded. Repairs did not start for two years, and the theater had to be completely gutted. (Both, courtesy of Kelsey Jernander.)

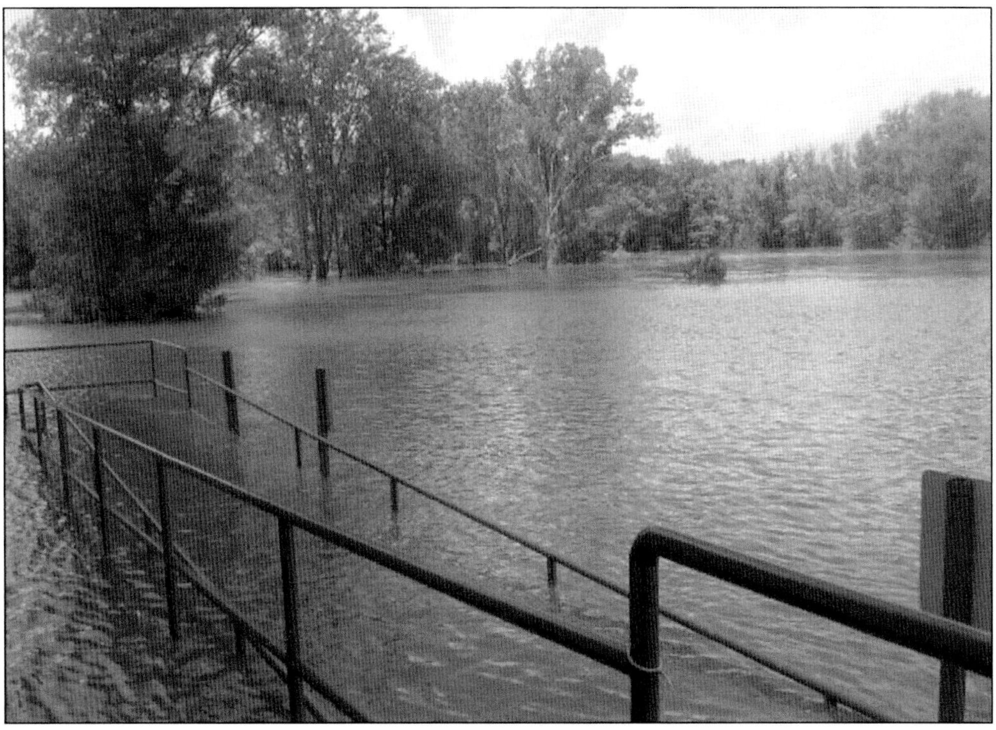

Since many streets were flooded, making car travel impossible, some residents resorted to boats. Parts of Webb Avenue, Main Street, and Granite Avenue, among others, were completely flooded. (Courtesy of Steve Braunschweig.)

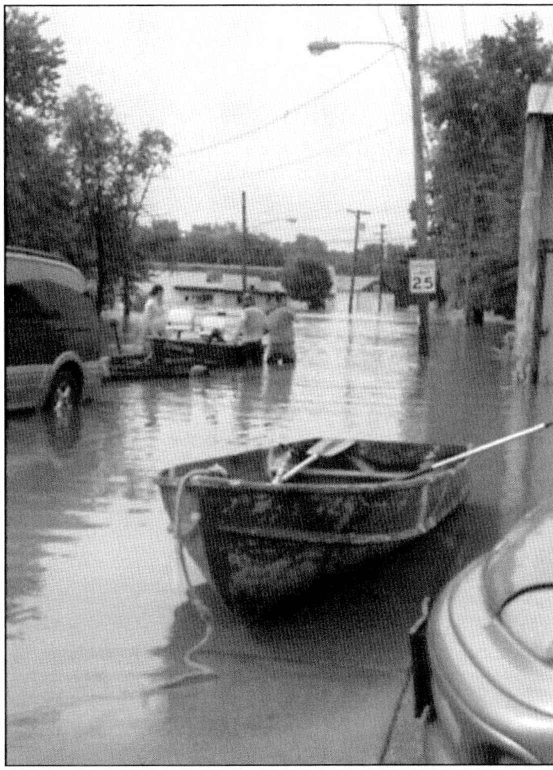

This photograph was taken on one of the first days after the water began to recede. Standing behind the movie theater, it was impossible to distinguish the natural banks of the river. The flagpole and bicentennial monument were also partly submerged, with the monument almost unrecognizable. (Courtesy of Kelsey Jernander.)

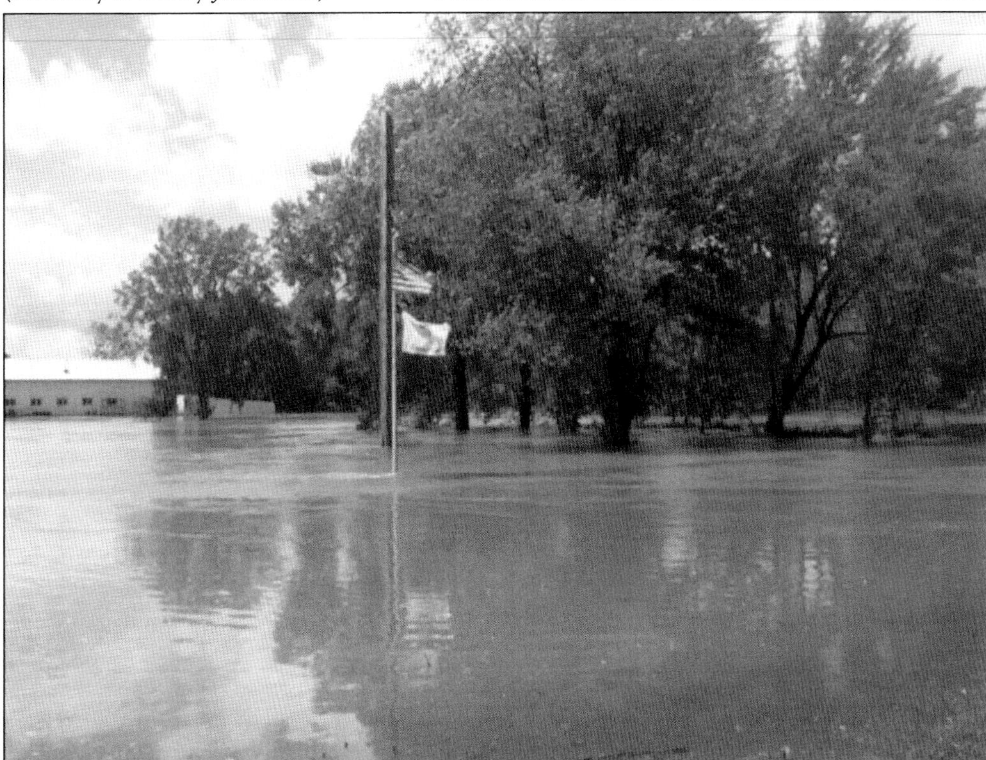

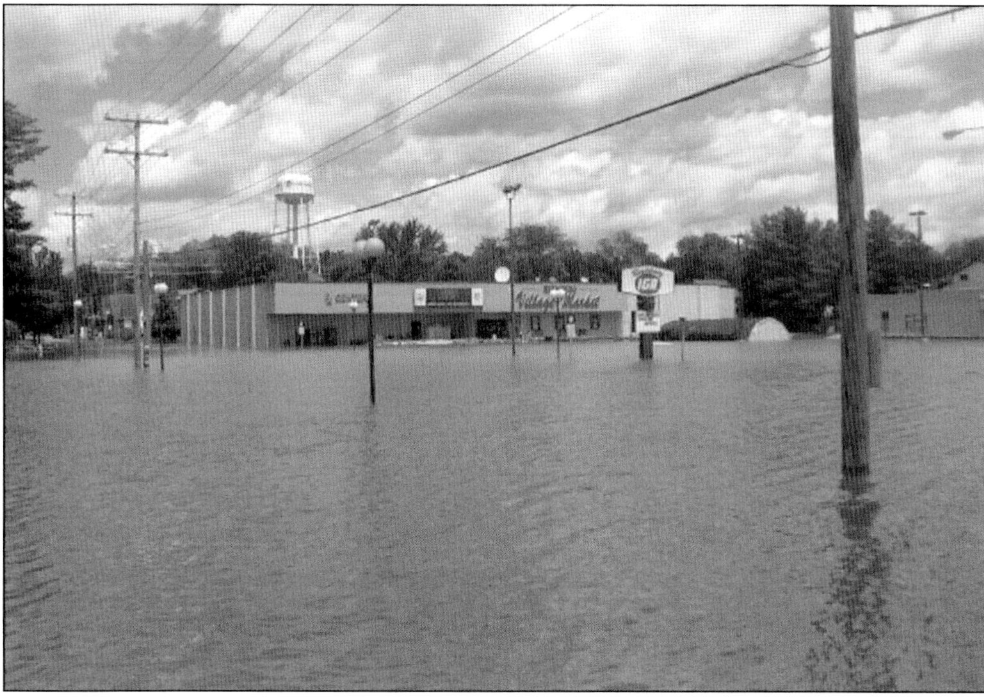

Many downtown businesses faced scenes such as these. Thanks to a great community effort, entrances were blocked with sandbags, which helped limit some of the water damage. As pictured in these two images, many city streets and parking lots were flooded and completely impassable. (Both, courtesy of Ashley Hentges.)

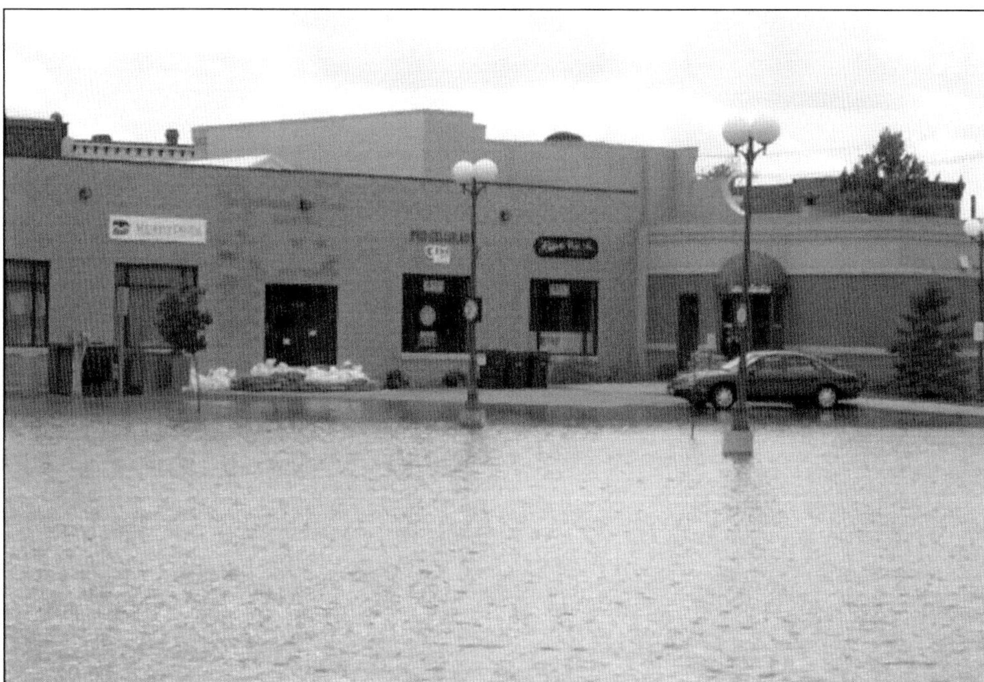

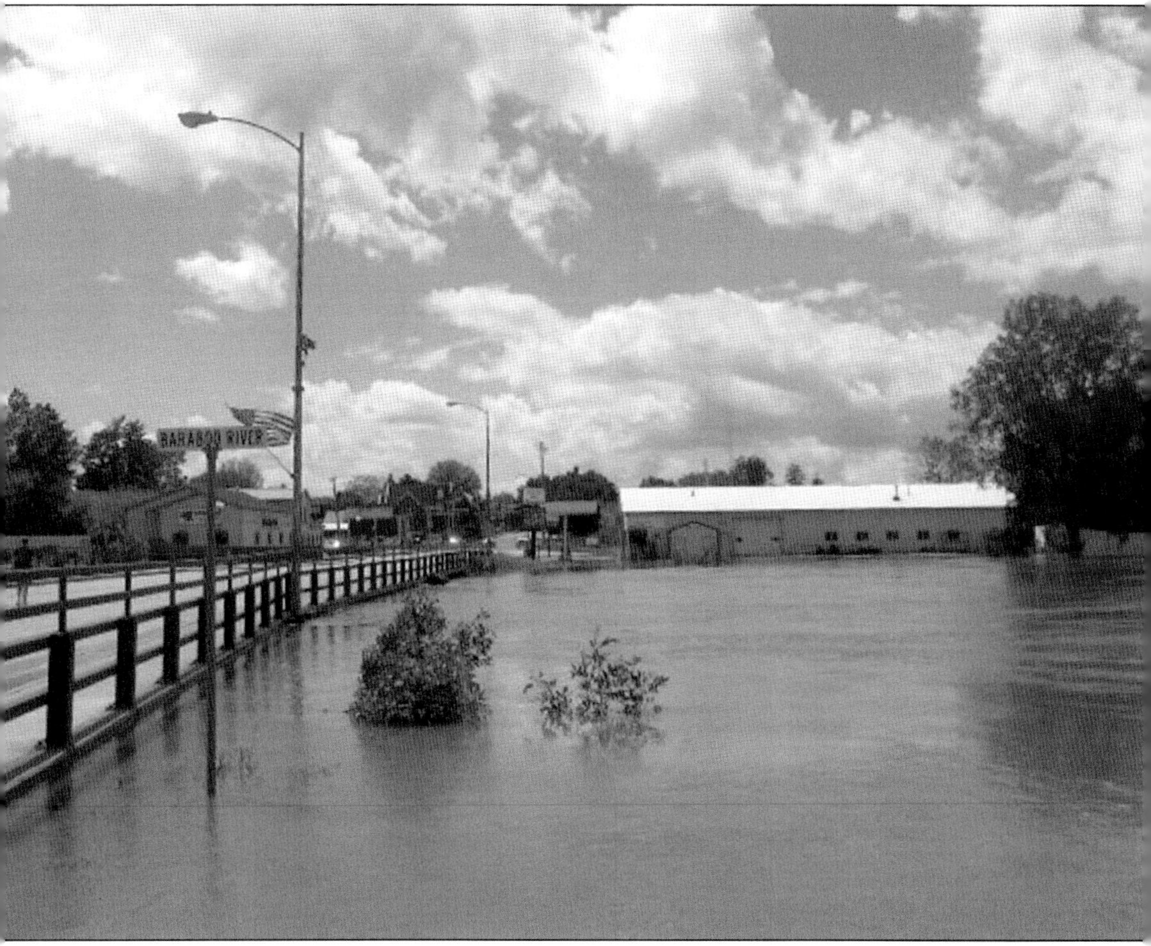

When Main Street Bridge reopened, those who lived on the west side could finally access the majority of businesses and supplies. In this photograph, the water is still level with the bridge and still inundates the gas station across the river. (Courtesy of Kelsey Jernander.)

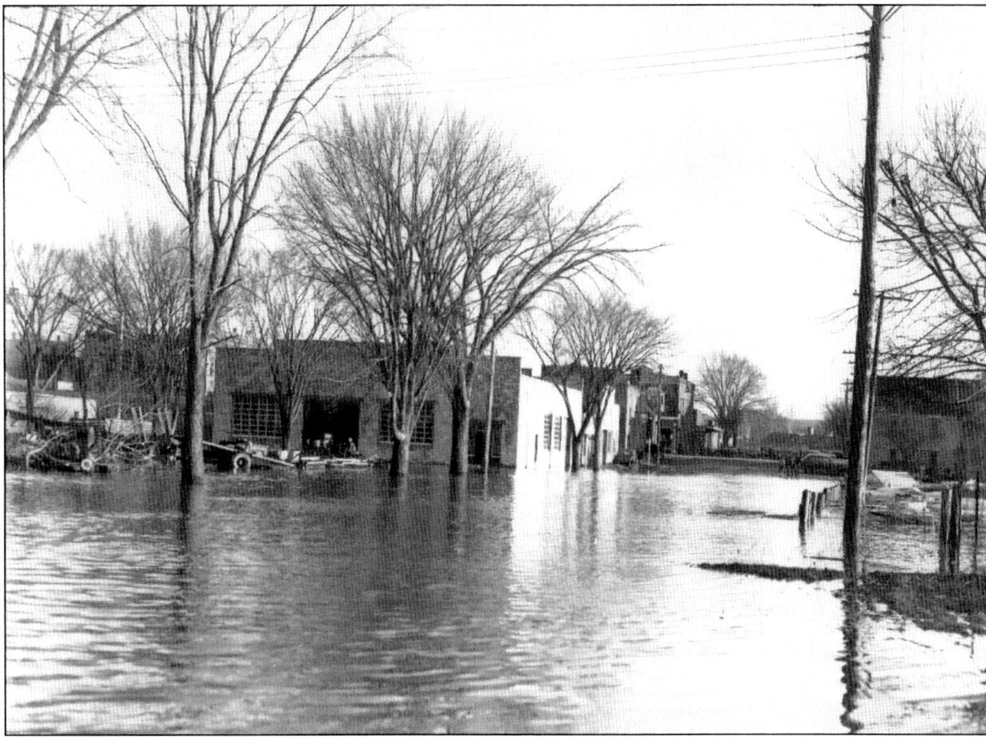

These two photographs show an earlier big flood that occurred on March 19, 1948. (Both, courtesy of Reedsburg Public Library.)

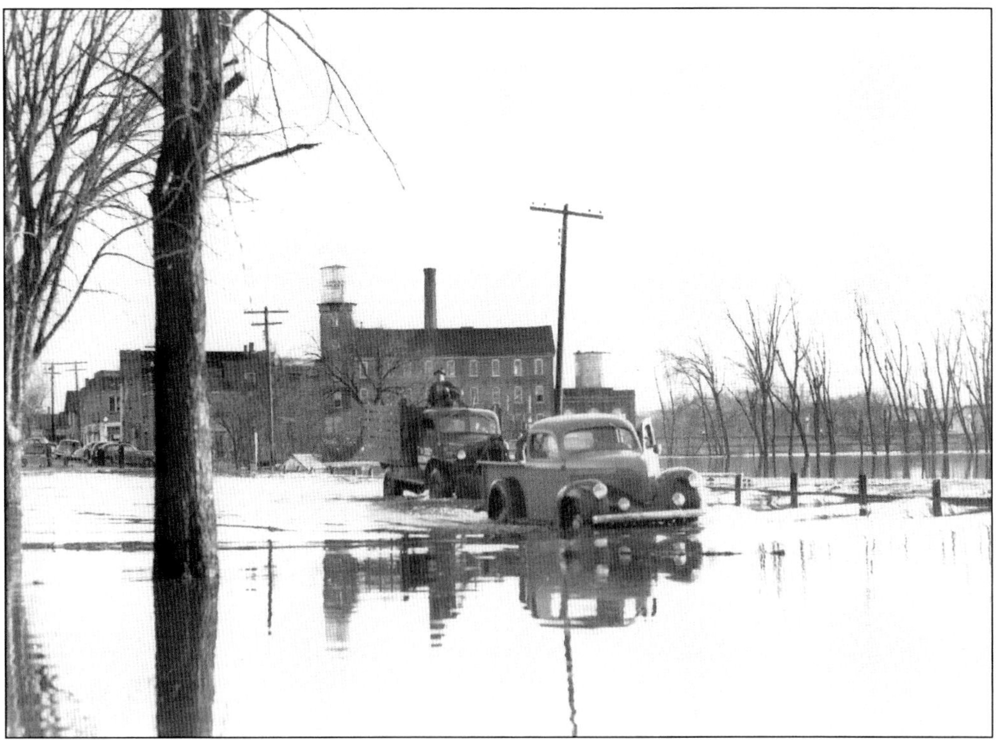

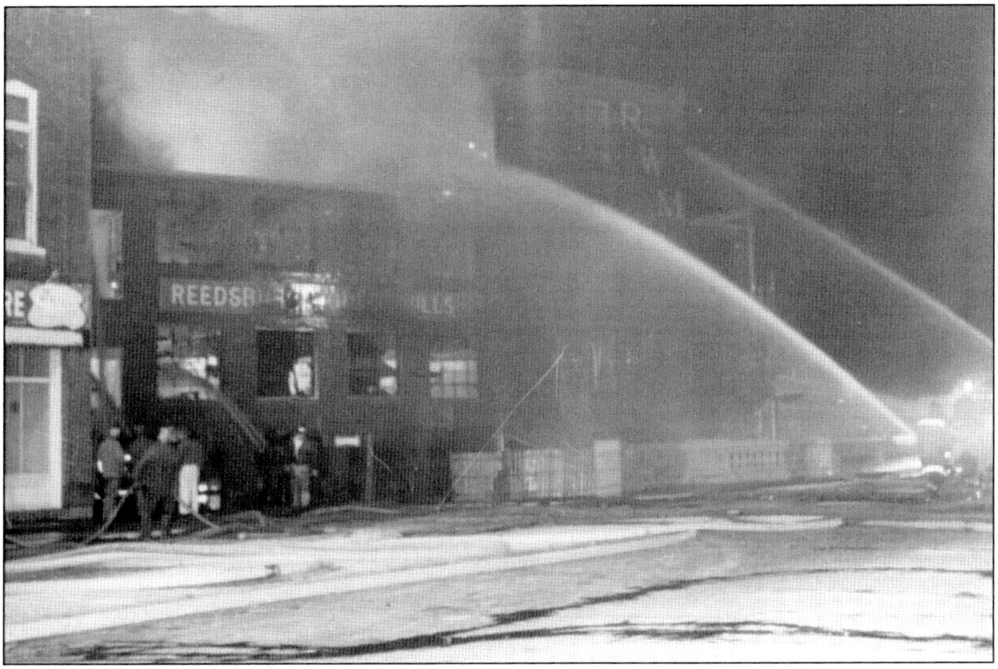

The Reedsburg Woolen Mills burned down on April 9, 1968. During the fire, the owners of surrounding businesses were worried about their own buildings catching fire, so they ran into their buildings to retrieve any important paperwork. The Woolen Mill's office building, still standing, is now home to Detiz Design. The dam once used to power the mill was torn down in 1973. (Both, courtesy of Reedsburg Public Library.)

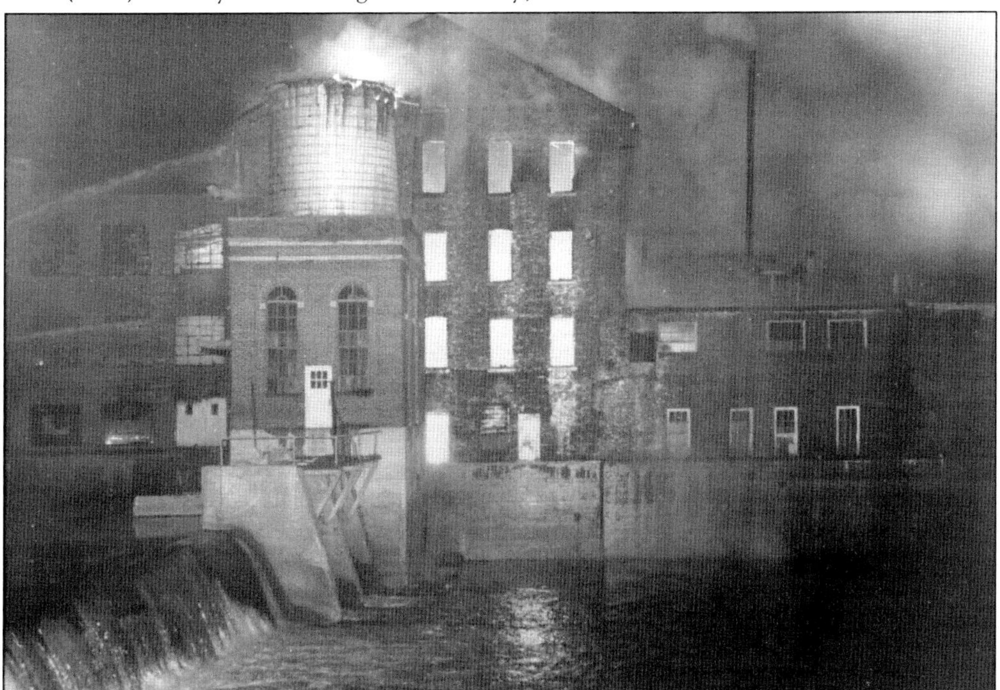

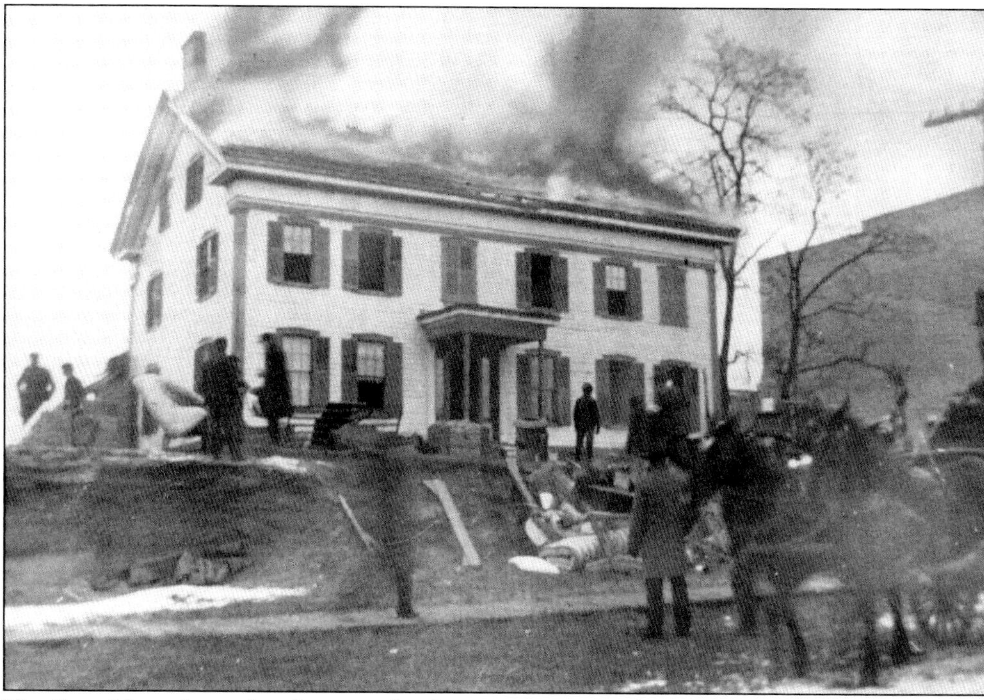

The Bates House burned to the ground in January 1900. In order to rebuild the hotel, rock had to be blasted from the site in order to build at street level. (Courtesy of Reedsburg Public Library.)

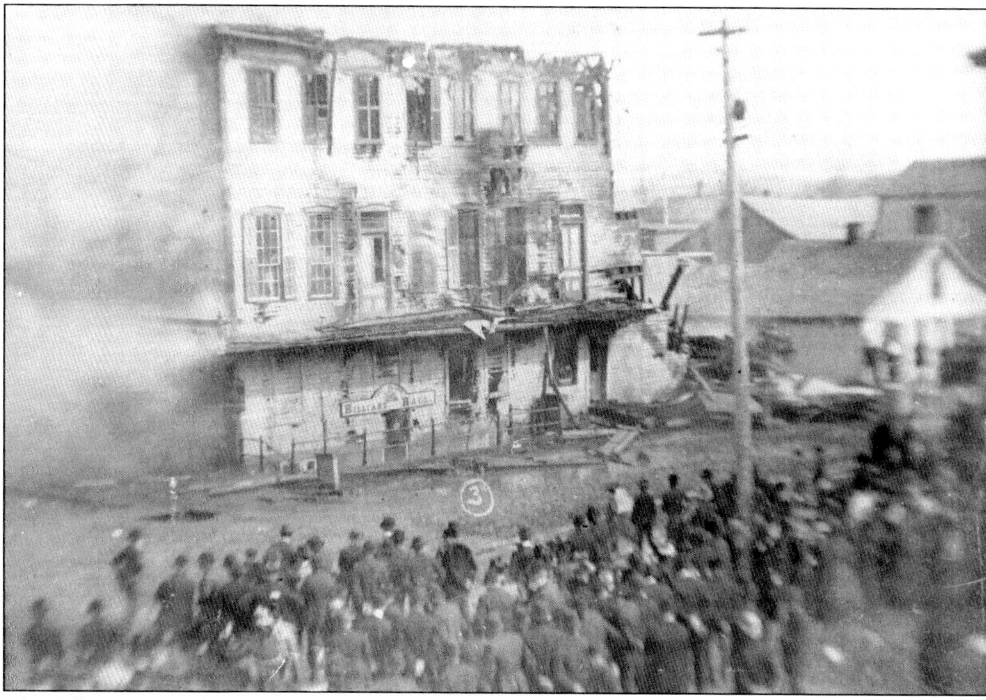

The Alba House, which came to be known as the Central House, burned down on April 12, 1896. William Stolte Sr., the proprietor, rebuilt the hotel on the same site, and it reopened on January 1, 1897. (Courtesy of Reedsburg Public Library.)

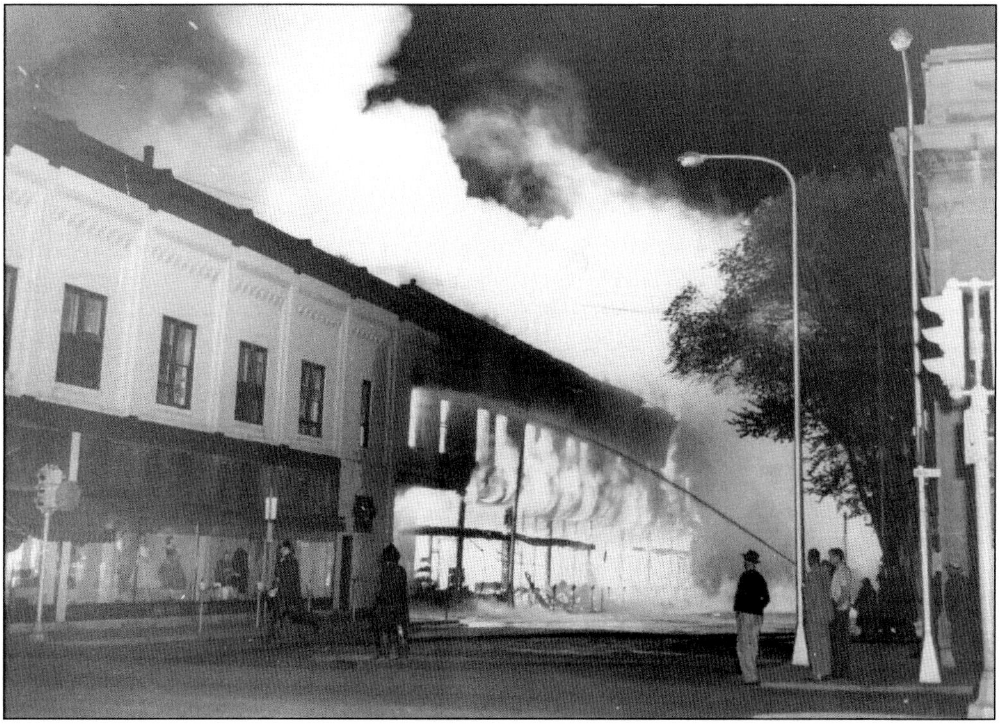

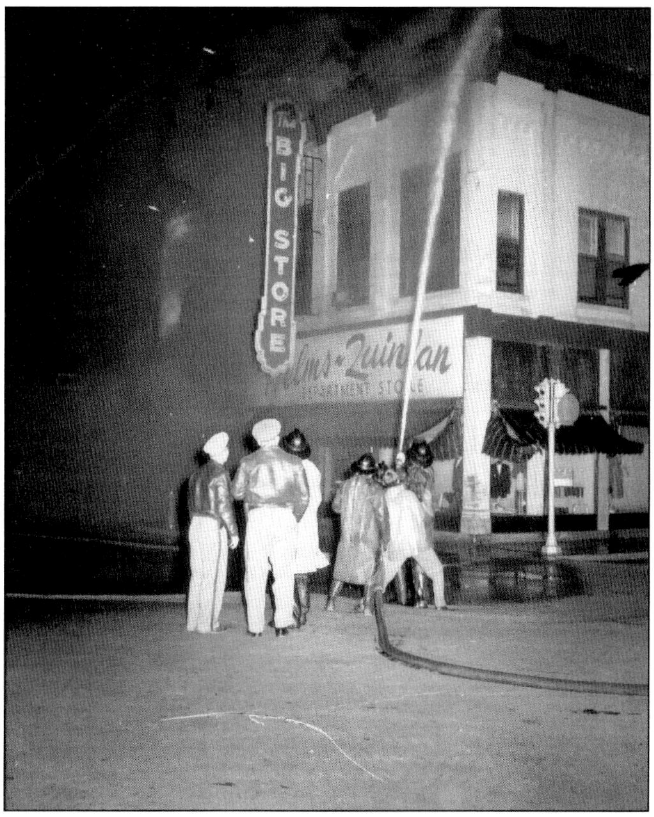

Paul Schrank, night watchman for the Big Store, discovered flames at 2:00 a.m. on Tuesday, August 27, 1957. The flames could not be controlled until 9:00 a.m. Firefighters from Baraboo, Portage, Lake Delton, Lavalle, Loganville, Rock Springs, North Freedom, and Badger Ordinance all aided in fighting the blaze. (Both, courtesy of Reedsburg Public Library.)

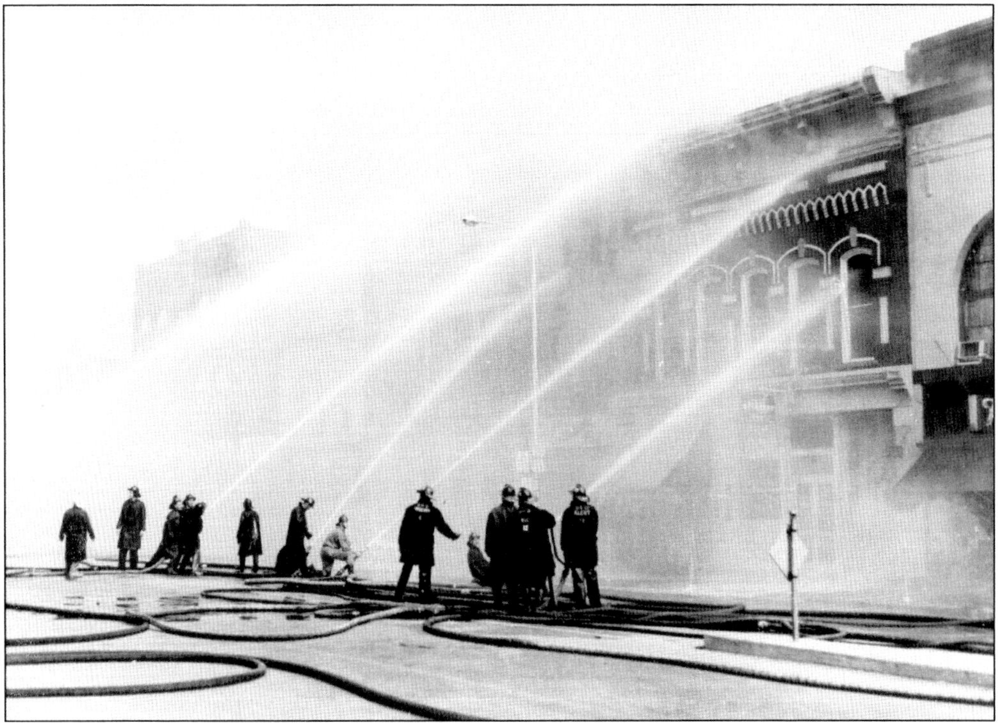

The heat from the Big Store fire was so intense that the apartments across the street had to be evacuated, and the front of the apartment building was charred. (Both, courtesy of Reedsburg Public Library.)

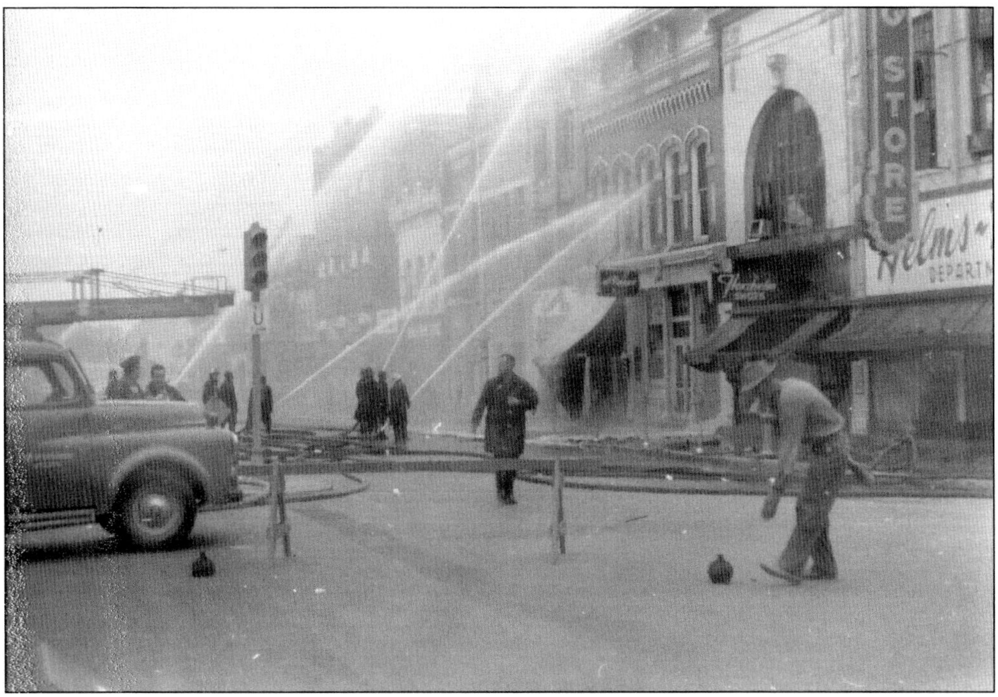

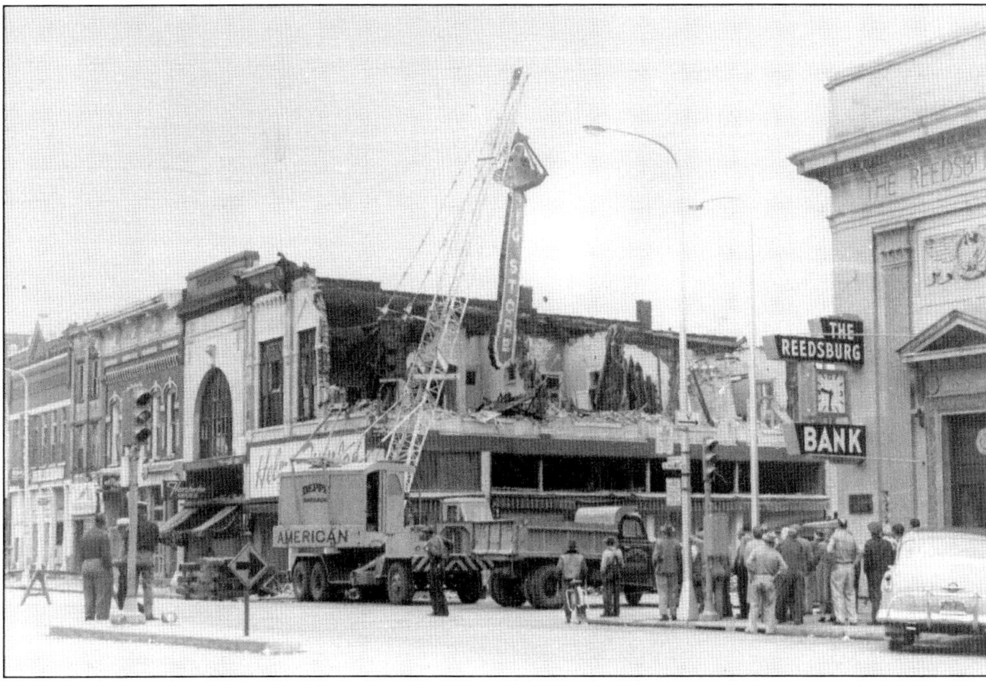

Schrank had seen flames in the meat cooler of the Big Store, but an official cause was never determined. The Big Store and some of the neighboring businesses that had been destroyed in the fire were rebuilt, but in a more modern style. (Both, courtesy of Reedsburg Public Library.)

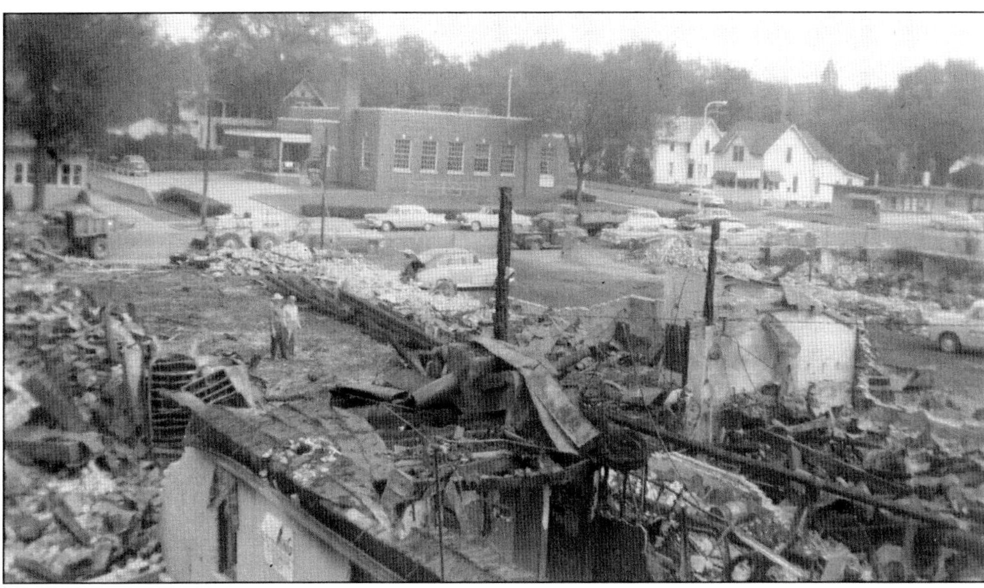

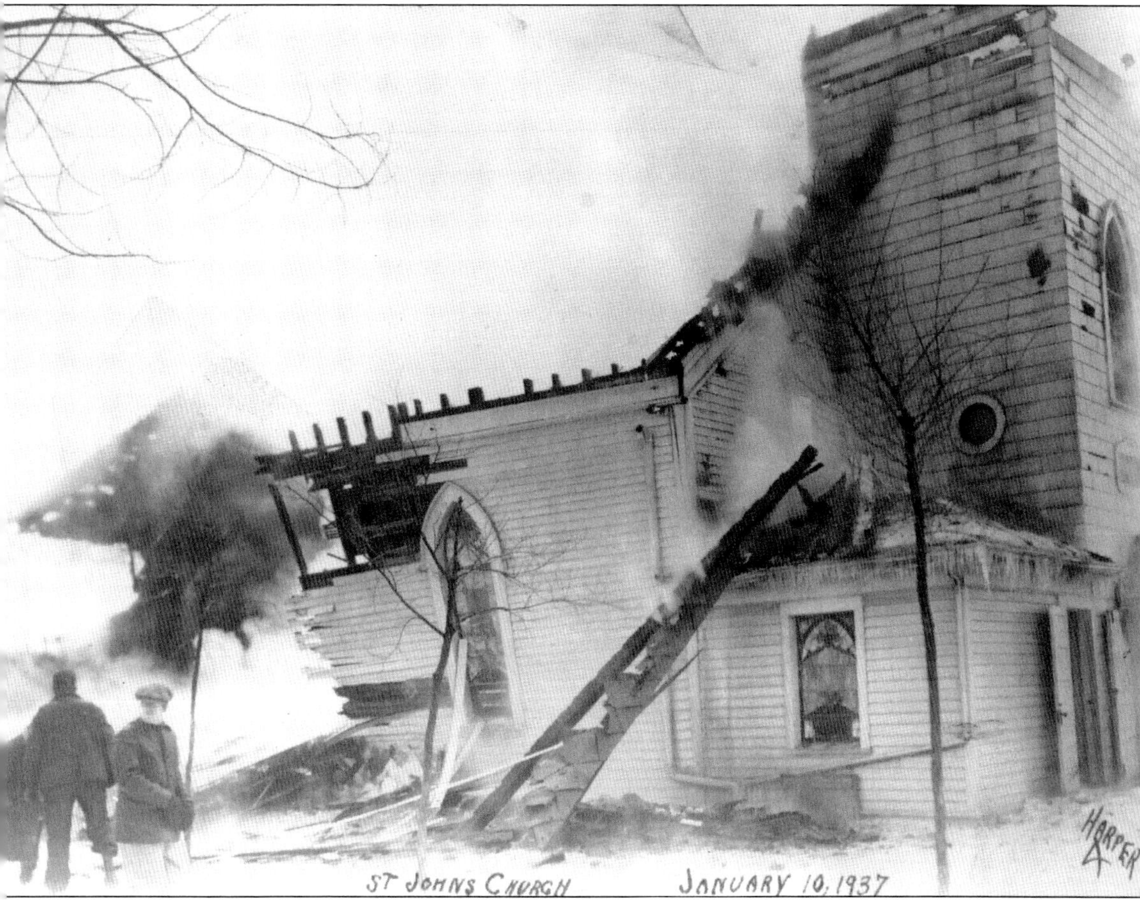

St. John's Lutheran Church was destroyed in a fire on January 10, 1937. The original nameplate, baptismal font, bell, and gold altar cross were the only items salvaged, and they were subsequently incorporated into the new church, which was dedicated on February 27, 1938. (Courtesy of *Reedsburg Times Press.*)

Five

Reedsburg Area Historical Society

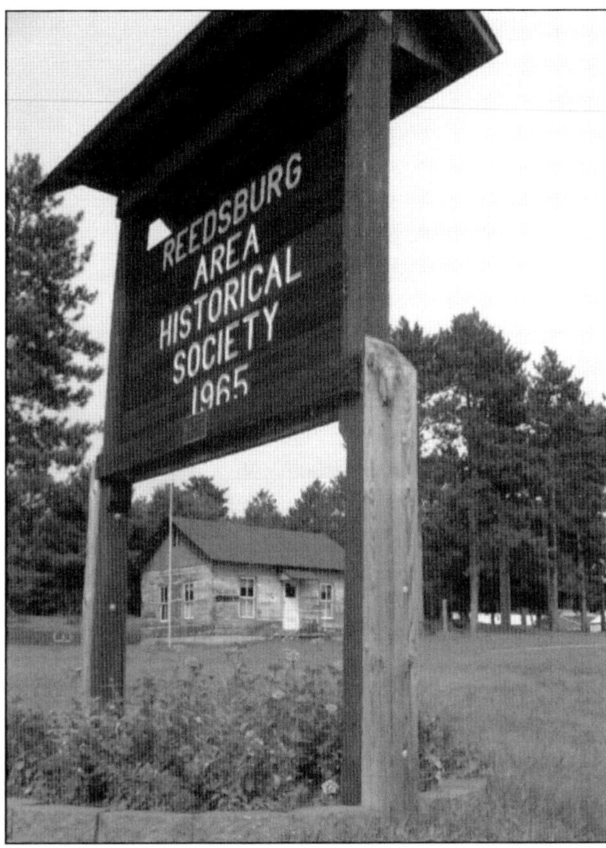

In 1966, the Reedsburg Area Historical Society received a charter for Pioneer Log Village from the Wisconsin State Historical Society. The Reedsburg Historical Society was begun by a group of people who wanted to preserve area log structures. (Courtesy of Steve Braunschweig and Reedsburg Historical Society.)

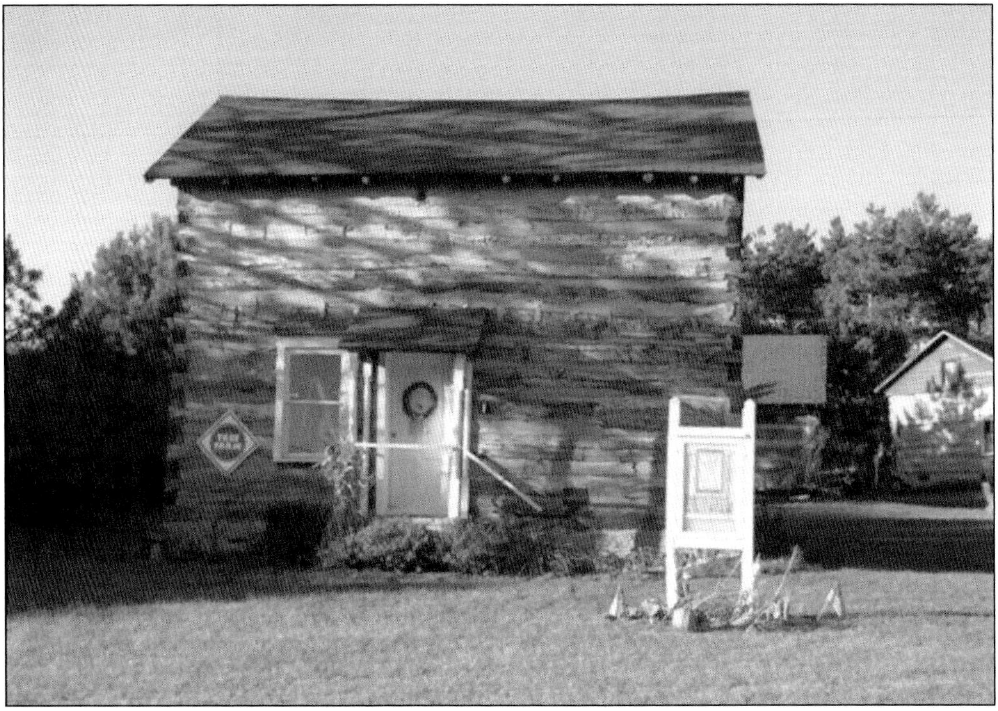

The log library (above) houses an extensive collection of antiquarian books and reference materials from the Reedsburg area. There are financial records from the old stores and businesses, journals, logbooks, census records, phone books, and Sauk County history books from the 1880s and before. Family scrapbooks and photographs are stored there as well. Plat books, maps, and magazines complete the large collection. The side room of the library contains memorabilia and relics from the Knights of Pythias, a fraternal society founded in 1864 by Justus Henry Rathbone in Washington, DC, and chartered by President Lincoln. The society, which carries on charitable works and places great emphasis on high moral standards, was organized in Reedsburg in 1898. Included in this collection are ceremonial robes and relics, a throne, and various furniture pieces used in ceremonies. Logs, records, and banners round out the collection. (Both, courtesy of Steve Braunschweig.)

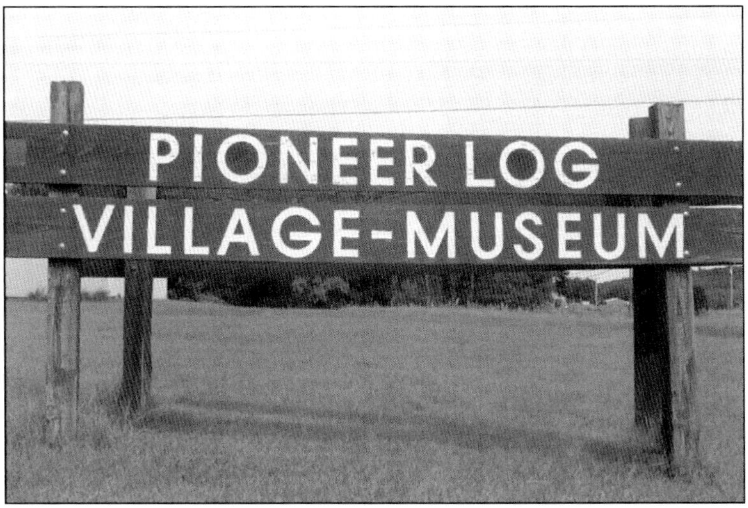

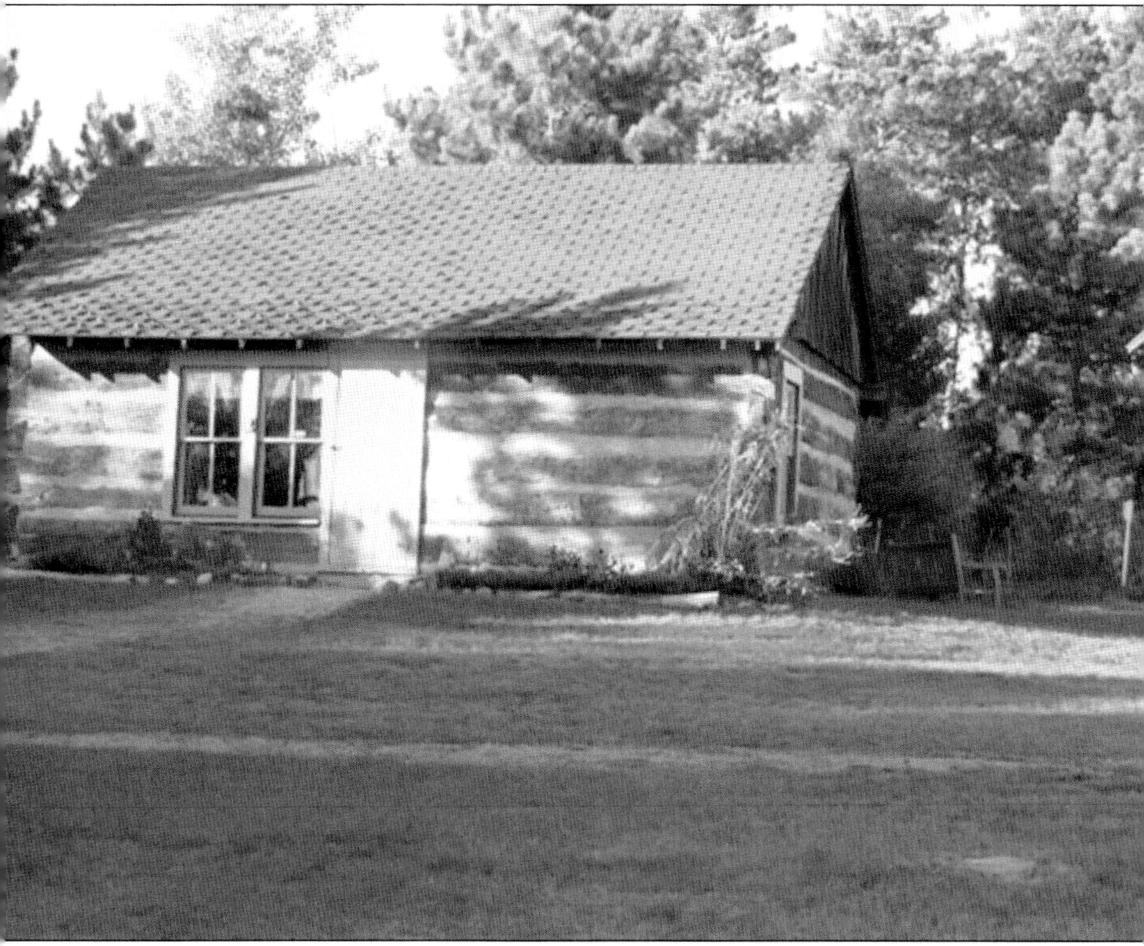

The Ligman-Cummings Cabin houses glass cases containing seasonal displays. The large bootjack collection is permanent, as are the cobbler's tools. The handmade shoes on display were found between the walls of an old house being remodeled on Myrtle Street in Reedsburg. (Courtesy of Steve Braunschweig.)

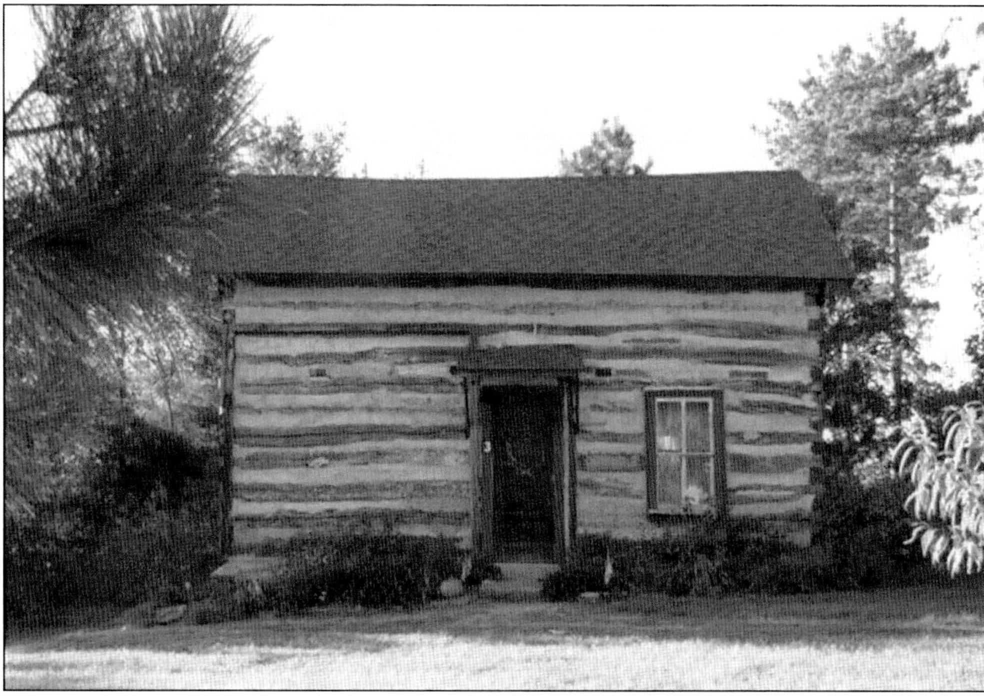

The Redstone Cabin formerly housed a family with 13 children. It has a loft and wide-board floors, along with a kitchen cabinet incorporating a built-in flour storage and sifter. The family did not have to carry in water because there is a pump from the cistern. (Above, courtesy of Steve Braunschweig; below, courtesy of Reedsburg Area Historical Society.)

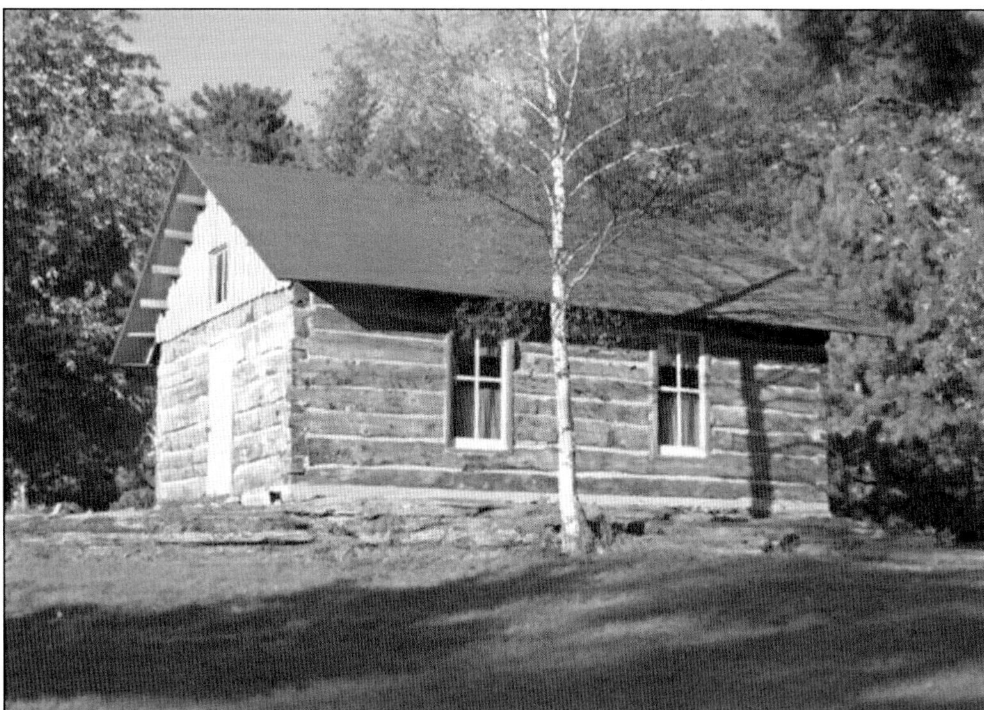

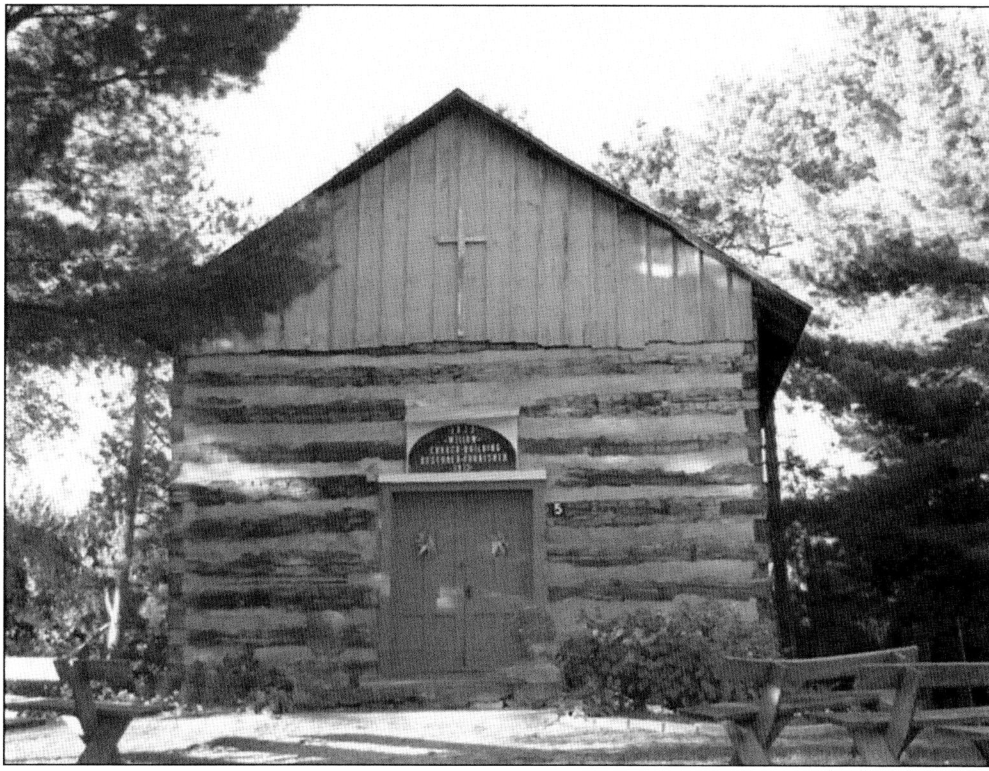

Willow Creek Church still houses its original altar, white marble baptismal font, and small reed pipe organ. Other artifacts found within the church are Bibles, pews, and the pump organ, all having been donated from other local churches. Originally a German Lutheran church, it now is nondenominational and represents aspects of all faiths. The church is available for weddings and other services. (Both, courtesy of Reedsburg Area Historical Society.)

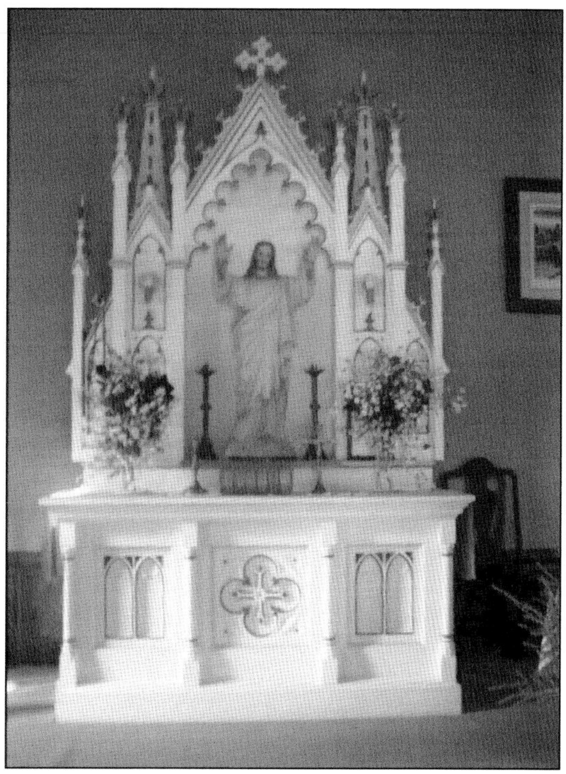

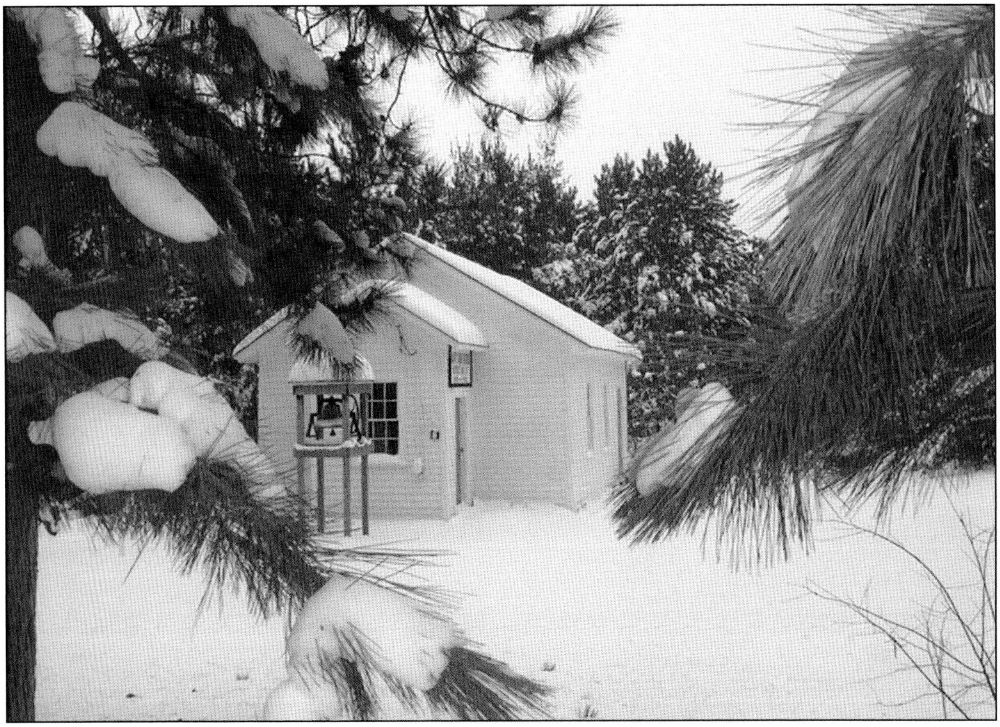

The County Farm School was built in 1865. The frame building houses various-sized desks, lessons written on the blackboard, books, benches, and much more. The one-room schoolhouse, which was a functioning school until 1962, was donated to the village by the Henry Vogel family. (Both, courtesy of Reedsburg Area Historical Society.)

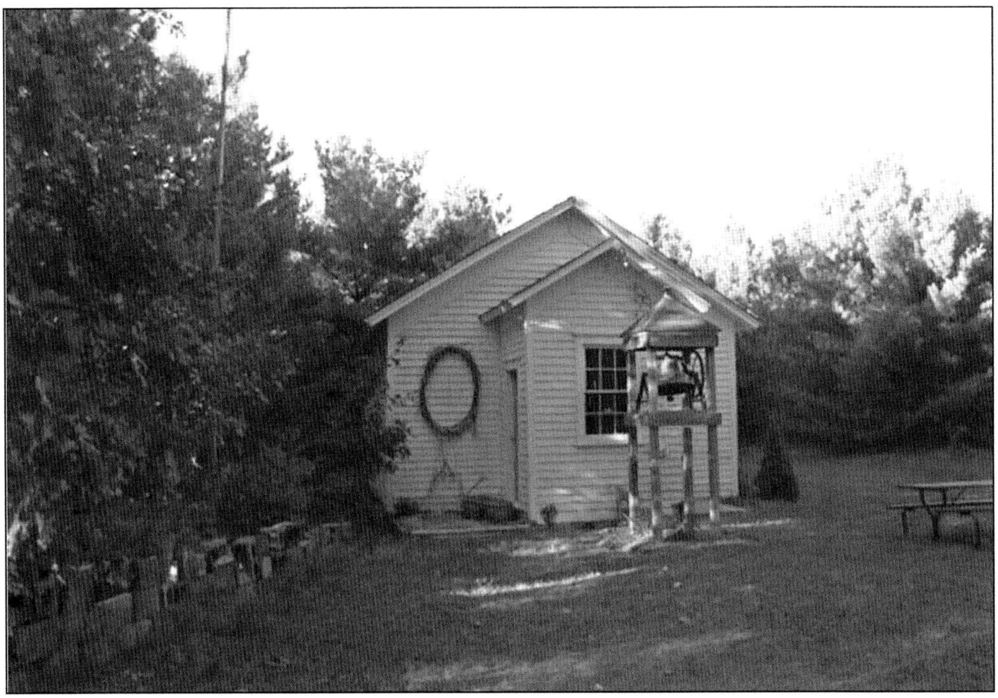

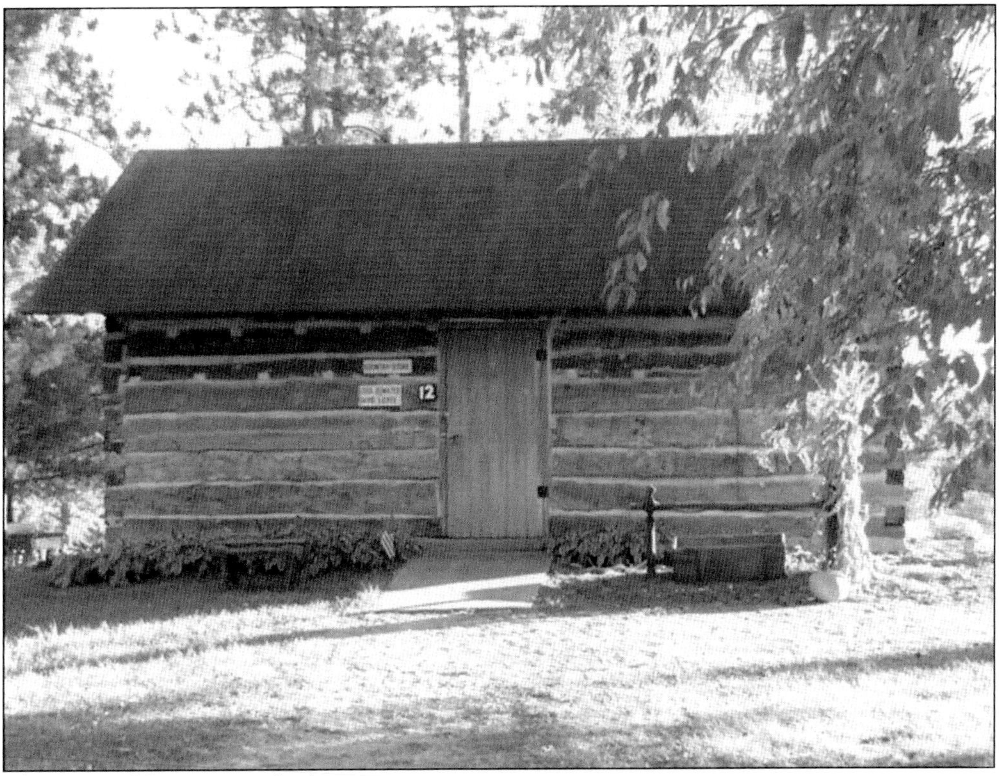

The General Store, once the home of the Lichte family, was discovered when their farm home was being remodeled. Hard work was undertaken by the "shopkeepers," Dale and Marcie Thompson (right), to make the store look like an authentic area general store. The display includes many items typically found in a general store, such as food, tools, houseware, shoes, and clothing. A reproduction of the Hillpoint post office is also in the building. (Above, courtesy of Steve Braunschweig; right, courtesy of Reedsburg Area Historical Society.)

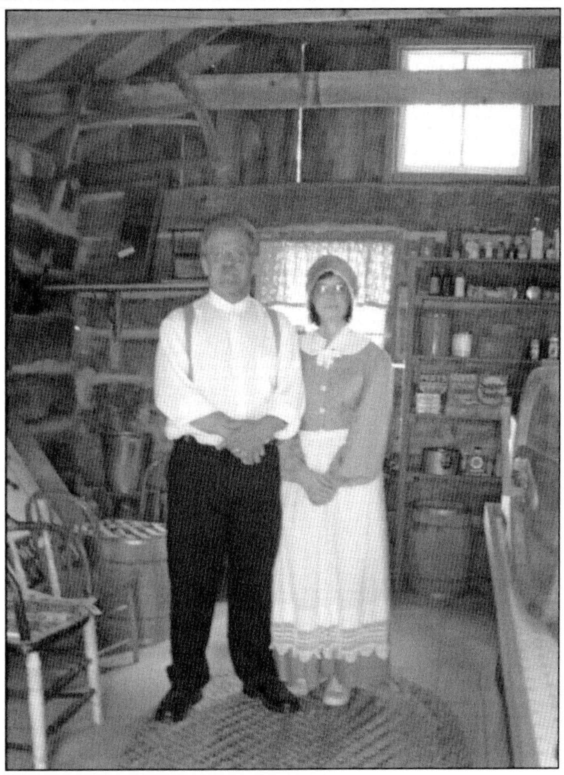

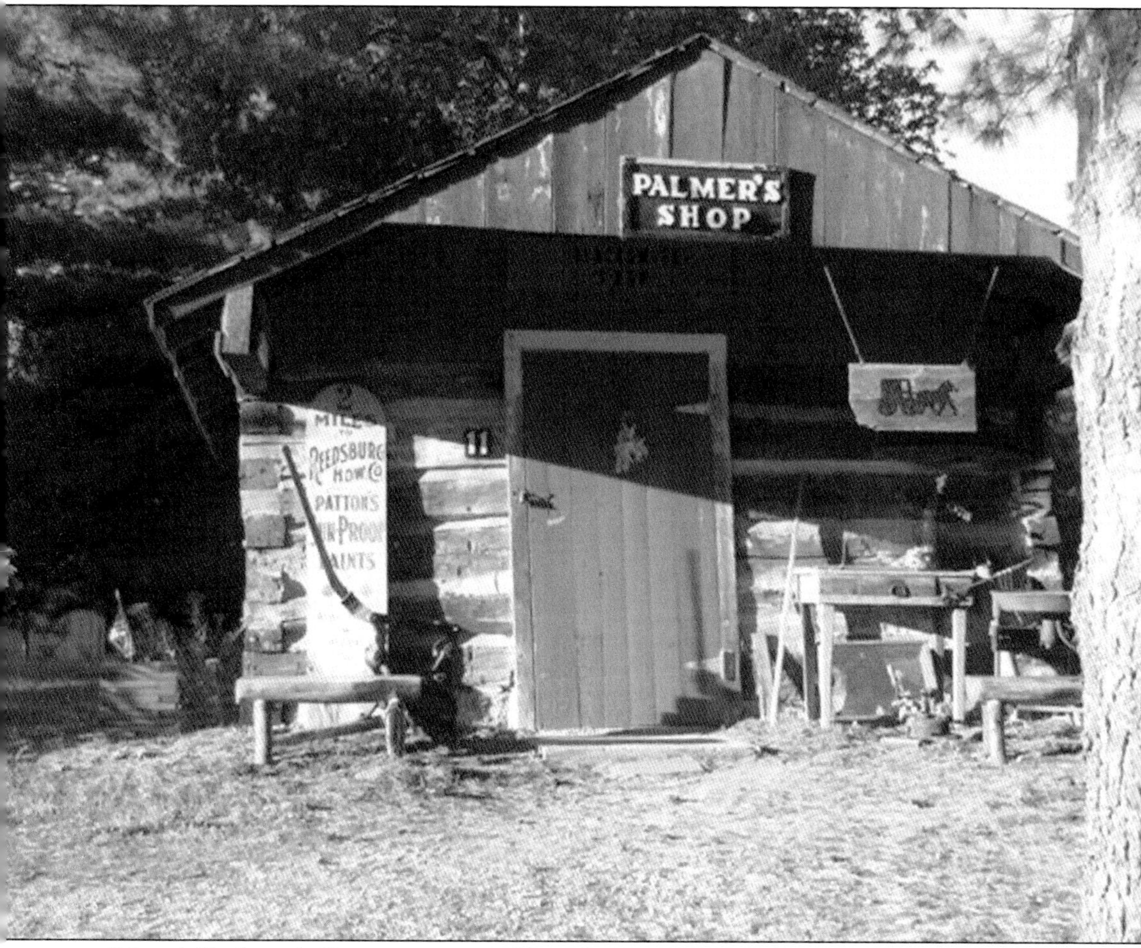

Palmer's Blacksmith Shop was re-created by volunteers using logs left over from other cabins. Ray Palmer was a retired blacksmith who donated the tools that are now on display. Handling and shaping tools for shoeing horses and oxen hang on the walls, and the forge, bellows, and anvil are located in the center of the shop. (Courtesy of Steve Braunschweig.)

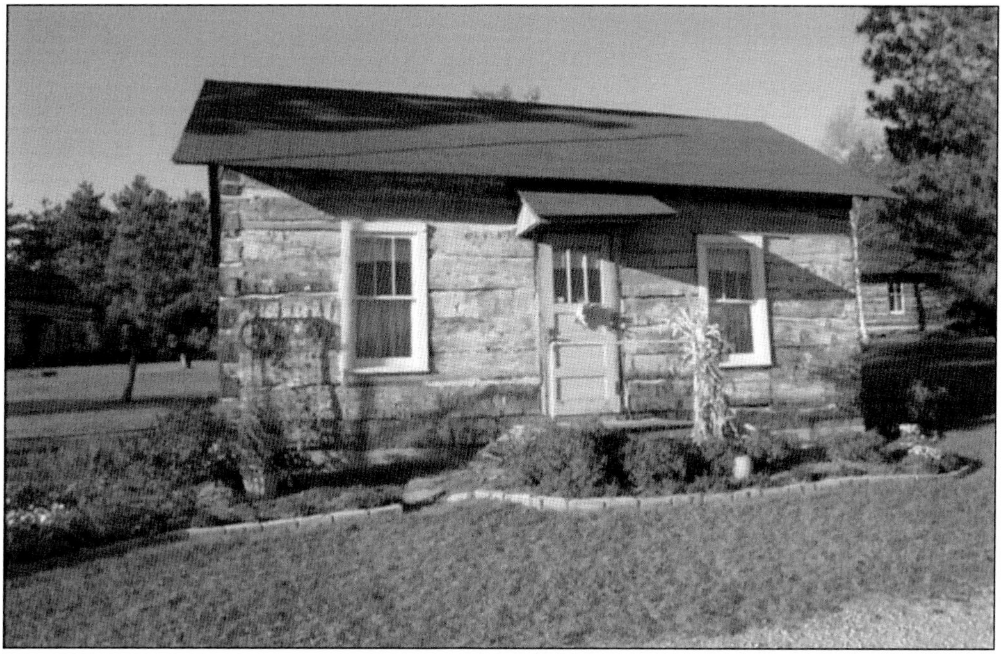

The Gluth-Kruse Cabin has a puncheon floor, which was made using four-inch-long stakes sharpened and driven into the dirt floor. The area between the stakes was then filled in with crushed limestone. The cabin houses a mountain goat coat brought from Switzerland by an early settler. There is also a tin lantern alleged to date to the time of the French Revolution, though its authenticity has not been verified. (Both, courtesy of Steve Braunschweig.)

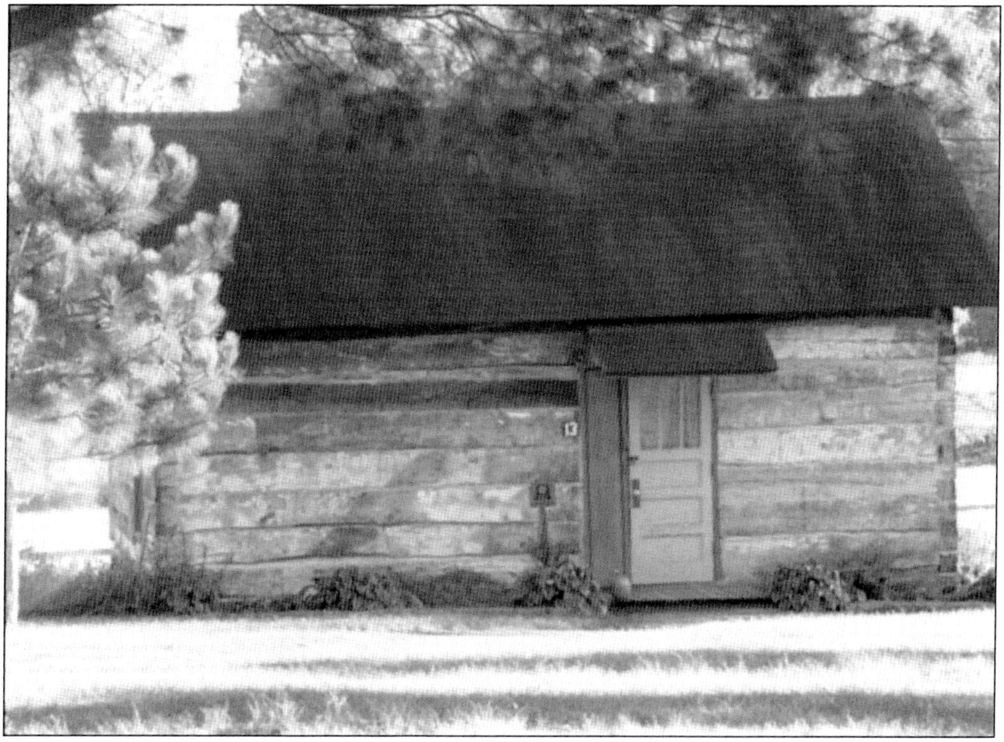

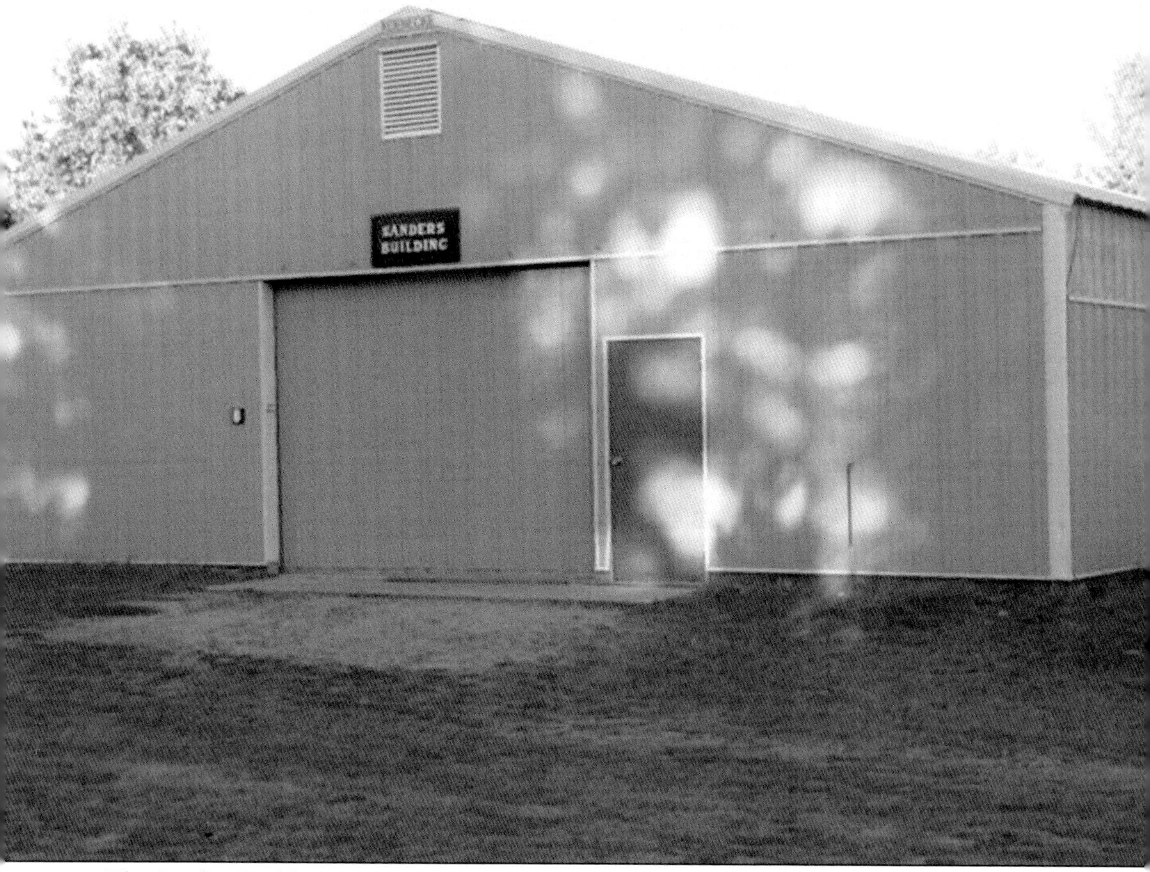

The Sanders Building serves a double purpose. During large gatherings, it can be used as a dining room. The large building is also home to a variety of farm implements and relics, including animal treadmills, mowers, plows, dairy equipment, a covered wagon that was used in parades, a horse-drawn fire wagon, and a buggy. (Courtesy of Steve Braunschweig.)

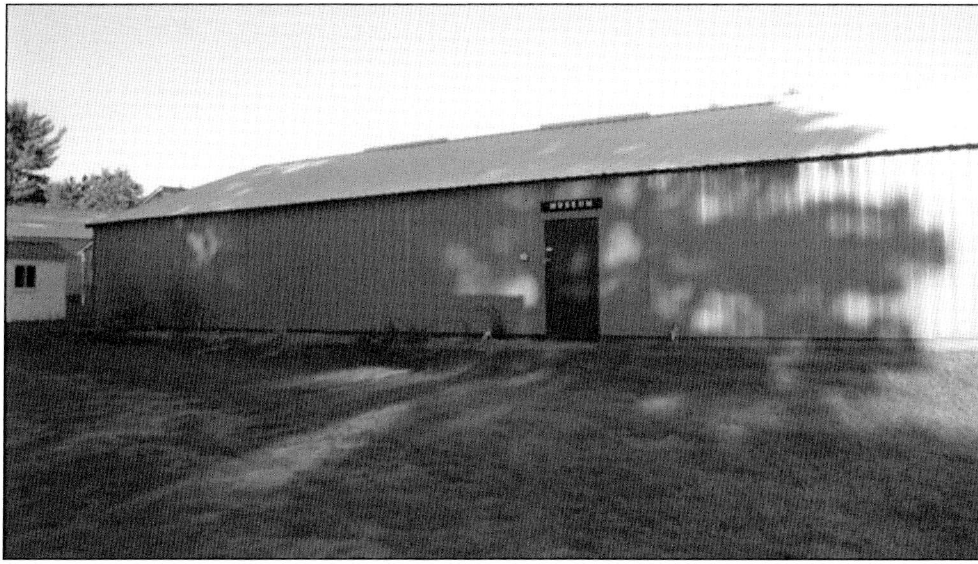

The museum building houses items of all sizes and styles. Clothing, musical instruments, woodworking tools, farm implements, tools for homemakers, and artifacts from the Winnebago Indians all help to provide an idea of early life in Reedsburg. The museum also houses displays from Native Americans and clothing worn by former Reedsburg resident, actress Agnes Moorhead. The museum also displays the evolution of clothes washing, from washboard to first electric machine; military artifacts from all American wars; and original works drawn by area cartoonist Clare Briggs, who spent his boyhood years in Reedsburg. (Both, courtesy of Steve Braunschweig.)

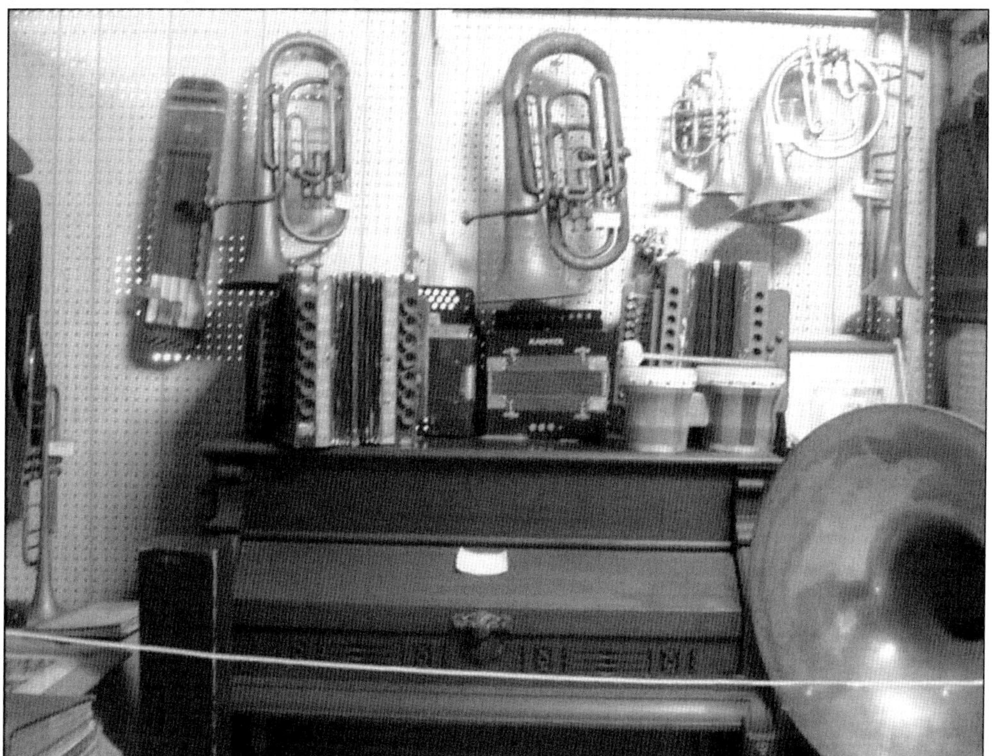

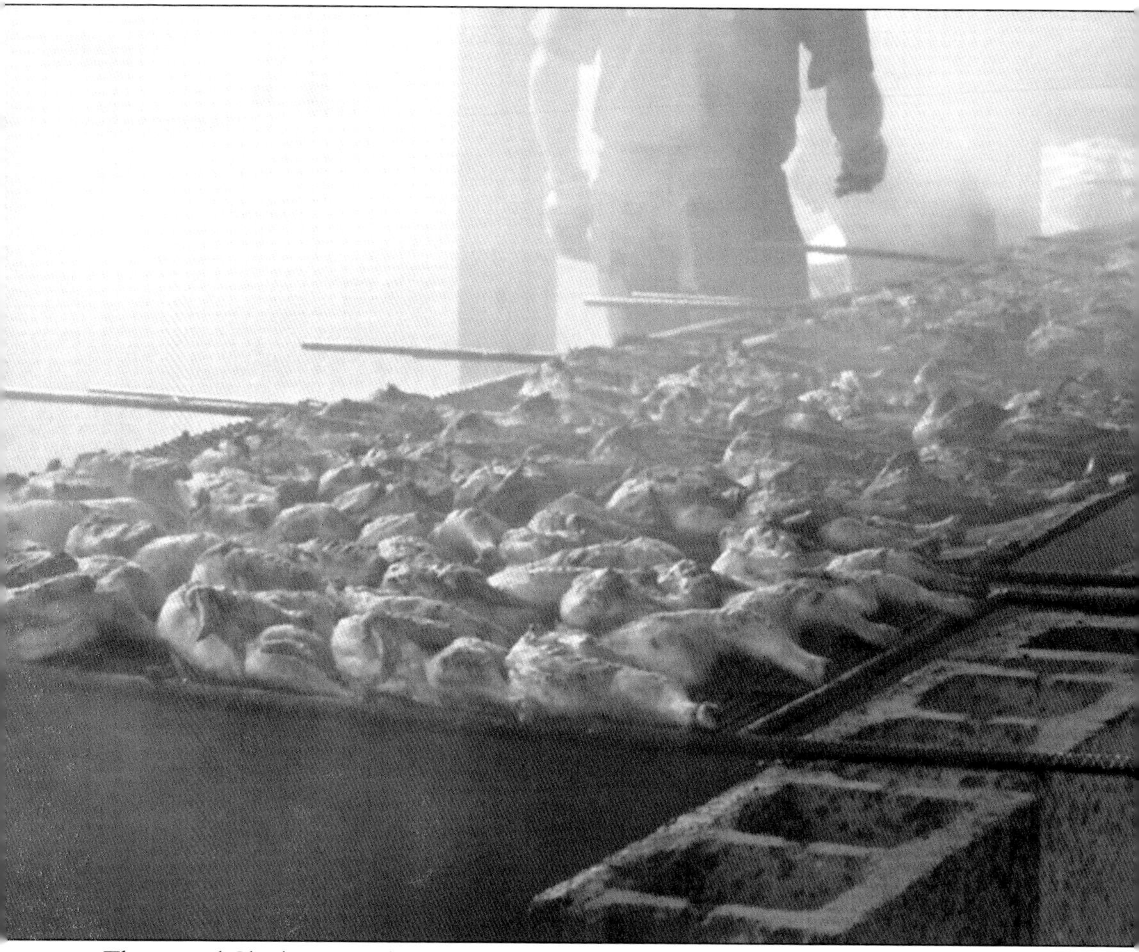

The annual Chicken BBQ, held in May, is one of the biggest fundraisers for the Reedsburg Area Historical Society. Members of the local Knights of Columbus grill their famous barbecue chicken. (Courtesy of Reedsburg Area Historical Society.)

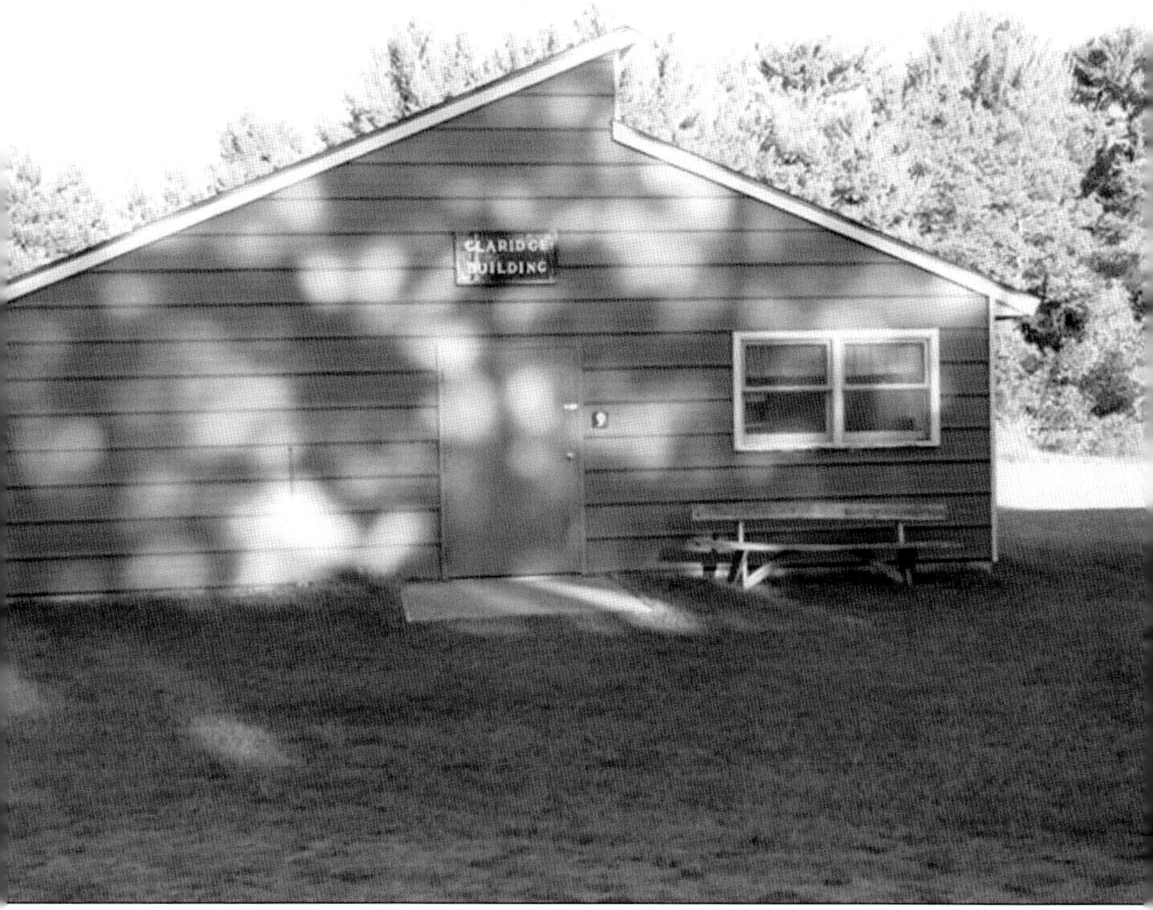

The Claridge Building is divided into sections, each providing a particular setting. Three sections include household items brought from England by the Claridge families. Another exhibit is the re-created 1970s living room of Elmer Krueger, a local author and former owner of the Badger Theater. (Courtesy of Steve Braunschweig.)

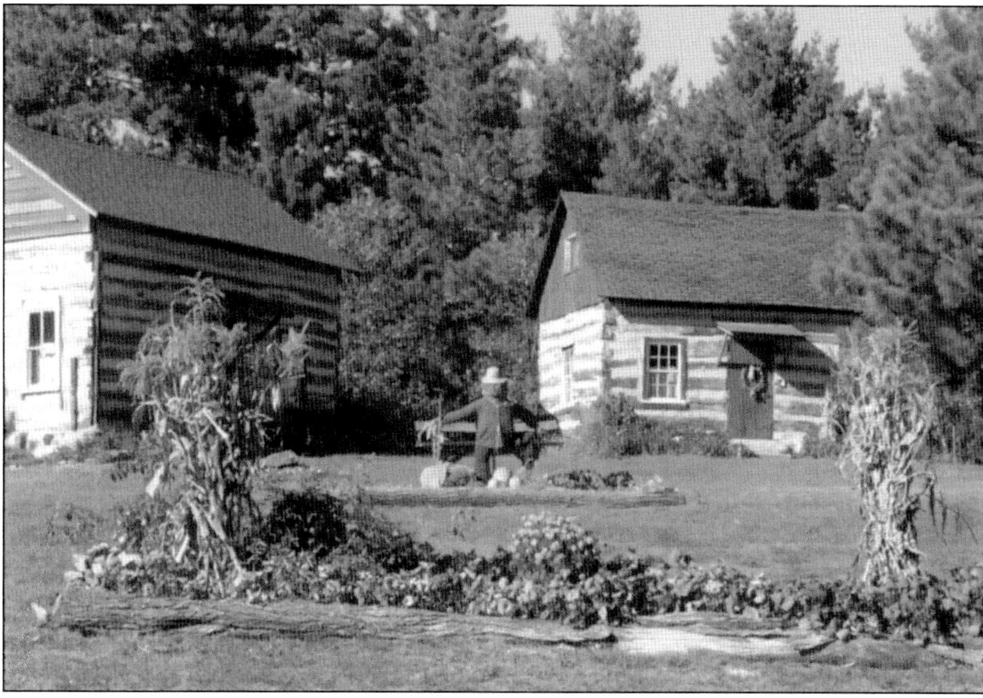

Gardens were created and are maintained by volunteers from the Sauk County Master Gardeners Association. A Huber Facility inmate crew assists with the gardening and the care of the village. The gardens consist of heirloom flowers and plants as well as vegetables and berries. A medicinal garden is in the planning stages. (Both, courtesy of Reedsburg Area Historical Society.)

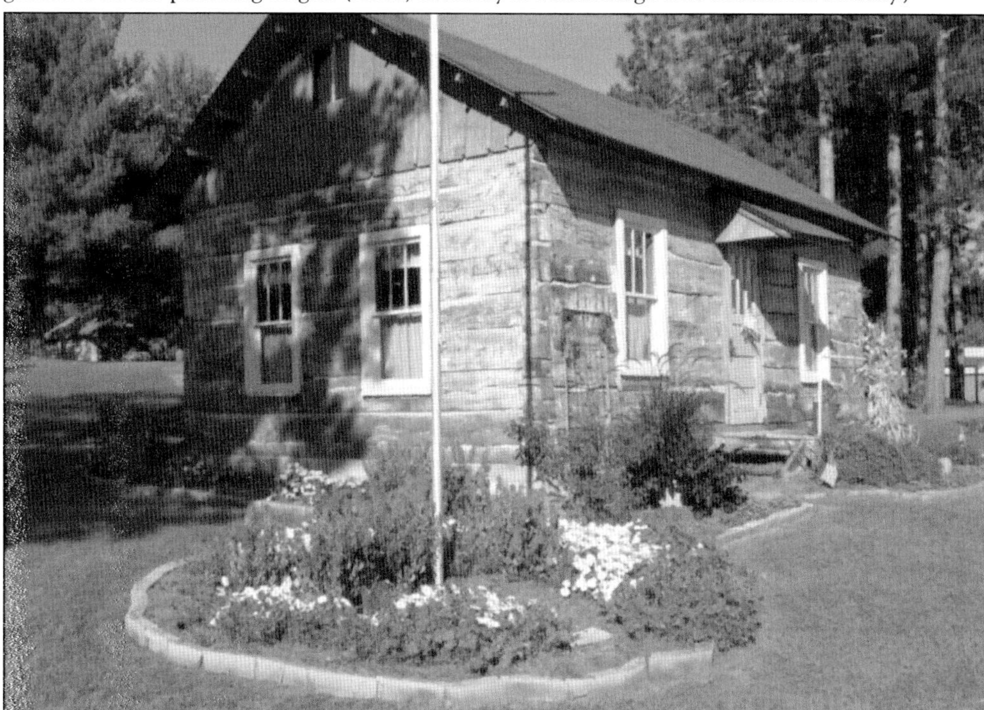

Six

Churches in Reedsburg

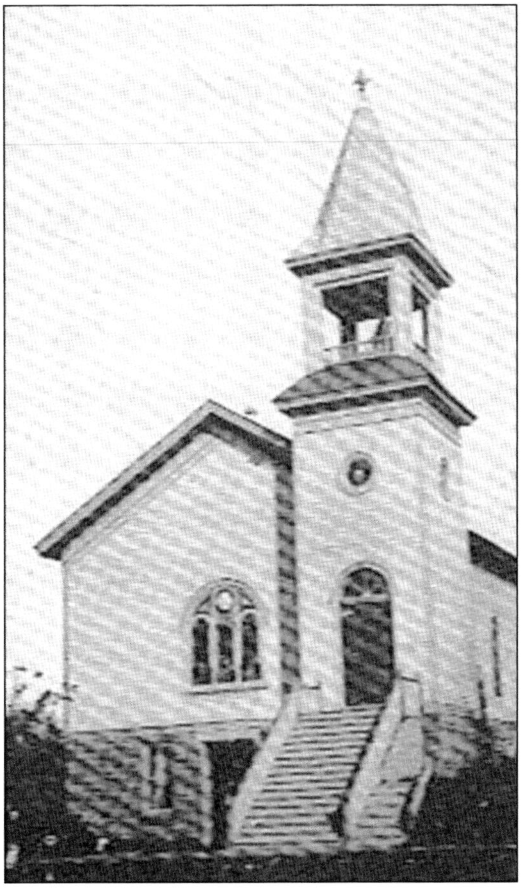

In November 1850, the Methodist Episcopal Church was formed at the home of John Clark. The original congregation of 12 grew to 63 by 1863, and the parish erected a tabernacle in 1865. (Courtesy of United Methodist Church.)

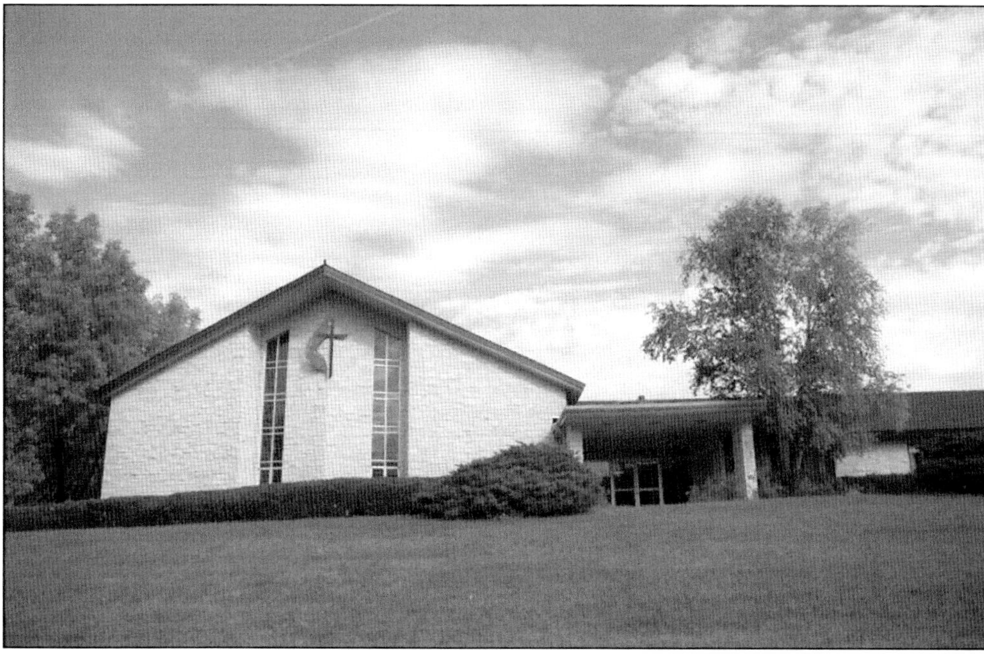

The parish built The White Church in 1872, which increased the congregation's seating capacity to 225. The brick church was built in 1908 and served the parish until 1968, when the congregation voted to move to their current structure (above), which was completed in 1969. (Both, courtesy of United Methodist Church.)

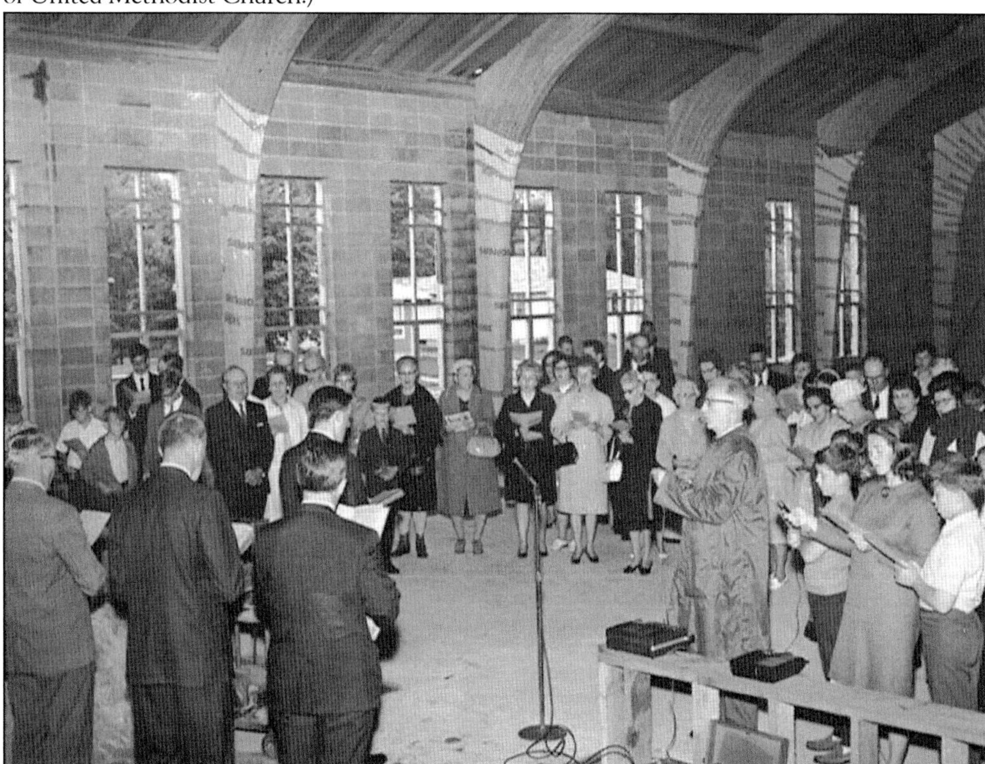

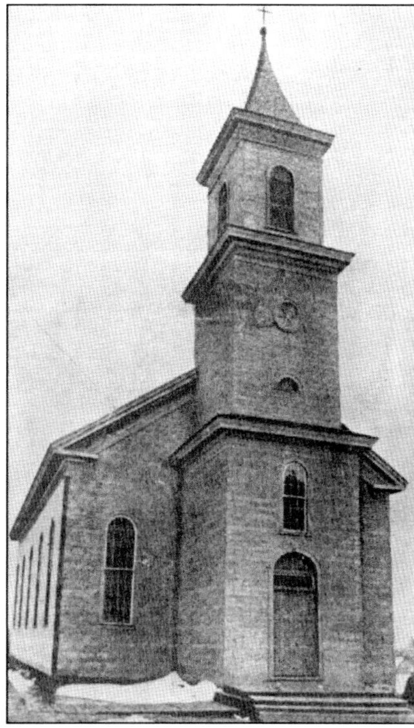

On November 16, 1867, the heads of 53 local families met to organize a Lutheran congregation. The attendants elected officers and chose a name: St. Peter's. Originally, the congregation met in a rented hall, but they quickly outgrew the space. Three years later, the church bought Block 8 of the village of Reedsburg. It built a small church (right) on the site in the 1870s, but outgrew that as well. In the fall of 1907, the congregation began building what is the current church (below), which was finished in 1909. The old building was sold and torn down that same year. (Both, courtesy of St. Peter's Church.)

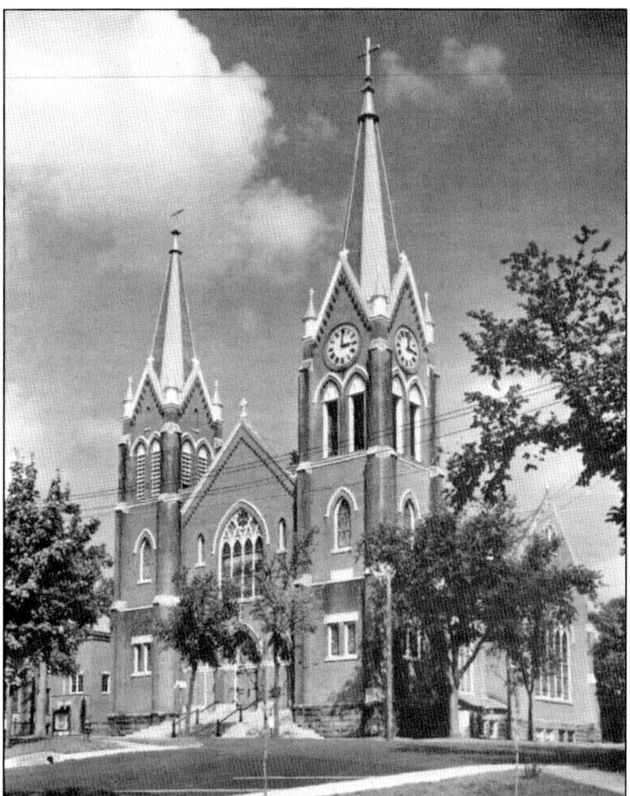

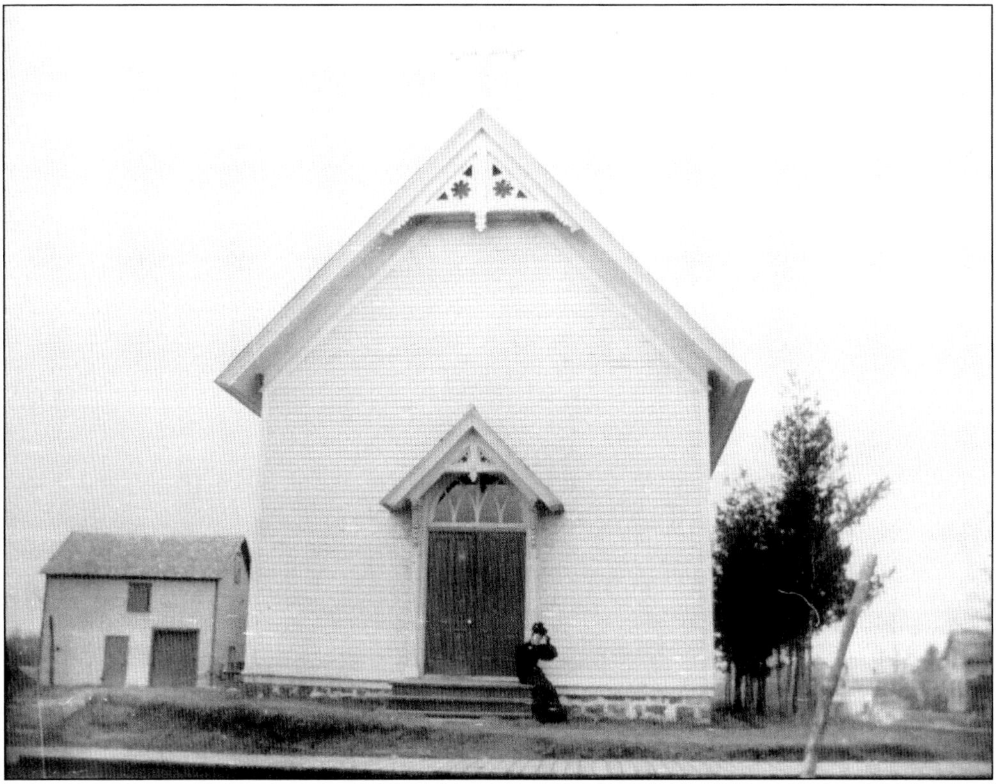

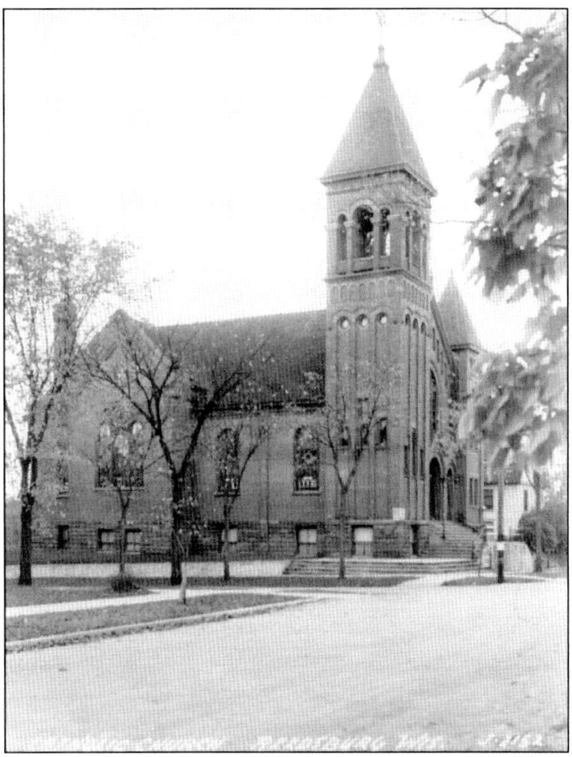

The Sacred Heart parish was organized in July 1878, and a church was built on the corner of Fourth and Locust Streets (above). This church burned down in 1902 and was replaced by a new one, made of brick, in 1903. A school was built in 1955 on Oak Street, and a third church (left) was opened in 1969 across the street from the school. (Both, courtesy of Sacred Heart Church.)

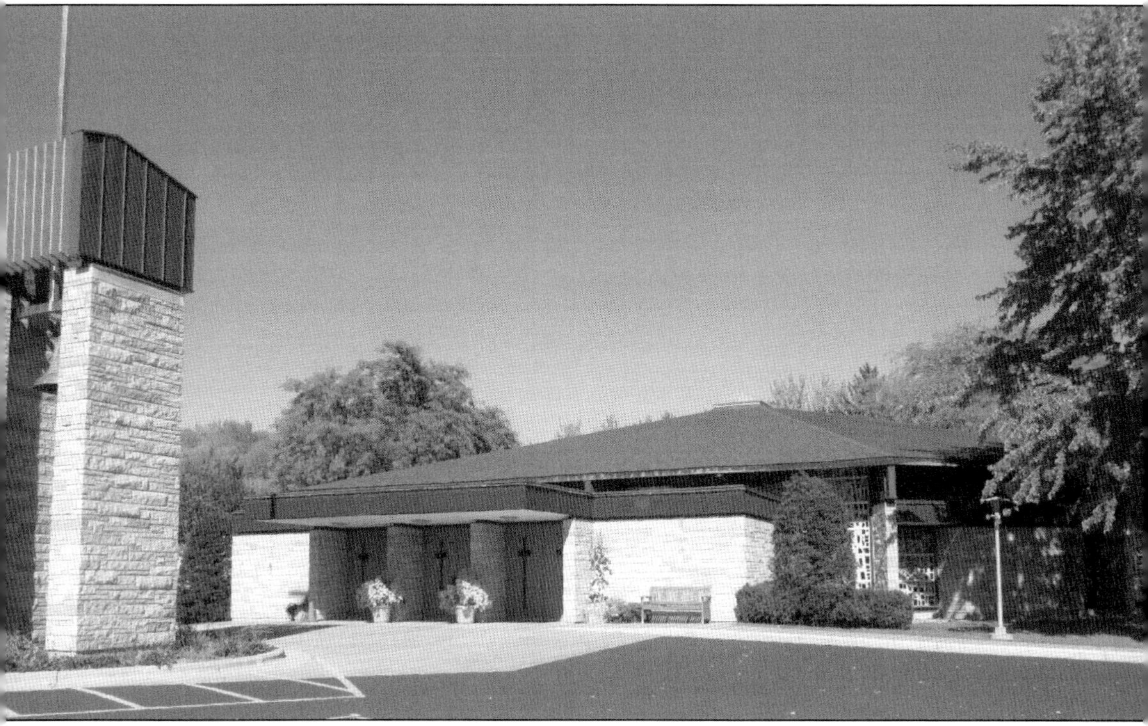

The church has grown to incorporate an office building, the Mazzuchelli Center (formerly a convent), and a house for the presiding pastor. In 2002, the street dividing the school from the rest of the buildings was eliminated and incorporated into a larger parking lot, making a more cohesive block. (Courtesy of Sacred Heart Church.)

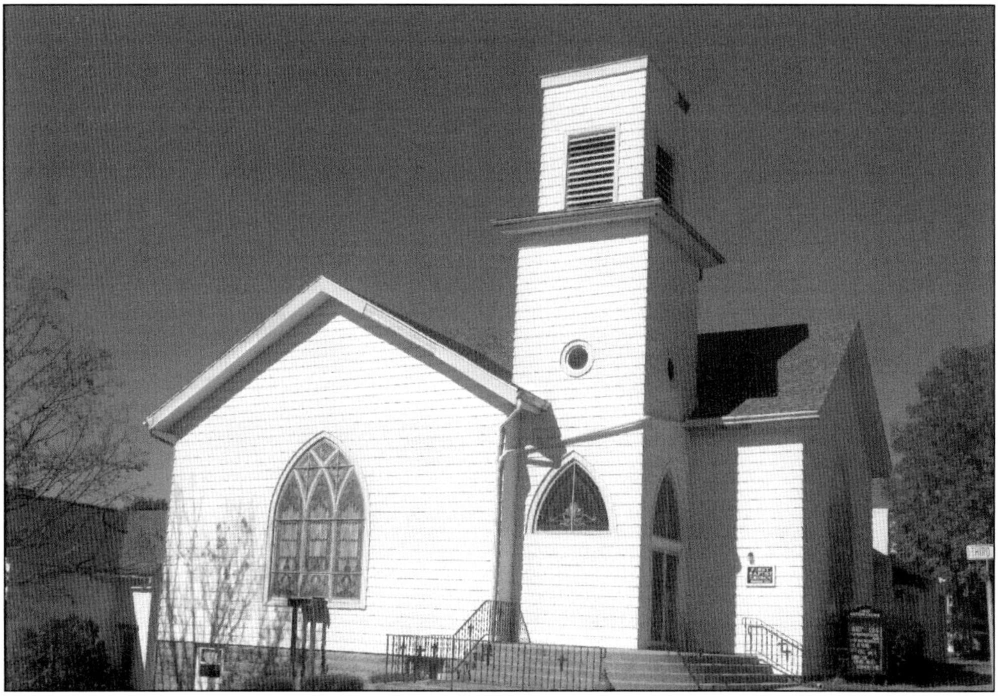

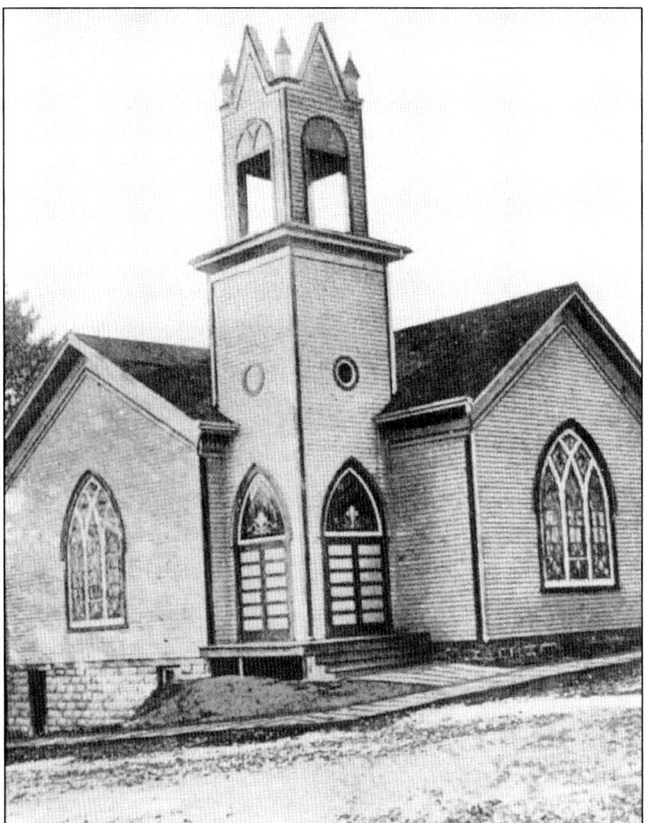

Prior to the fall of 1851, Baptists living in Reedsburg had to travel six to eight miles to attend services. Elder Peter Conrad began to give services in Reedsburg, and was asked to spend a quarter of his time preaching in the village. The congregation met to organize a church on January 24, 1852. A committee was formed in 1864 to build a church, and work began in 1872. The dedication for Corner Stone Baptist Church, pictured here, was held on October 12, 1873. (Both, courtesy of Bill Hentges.)

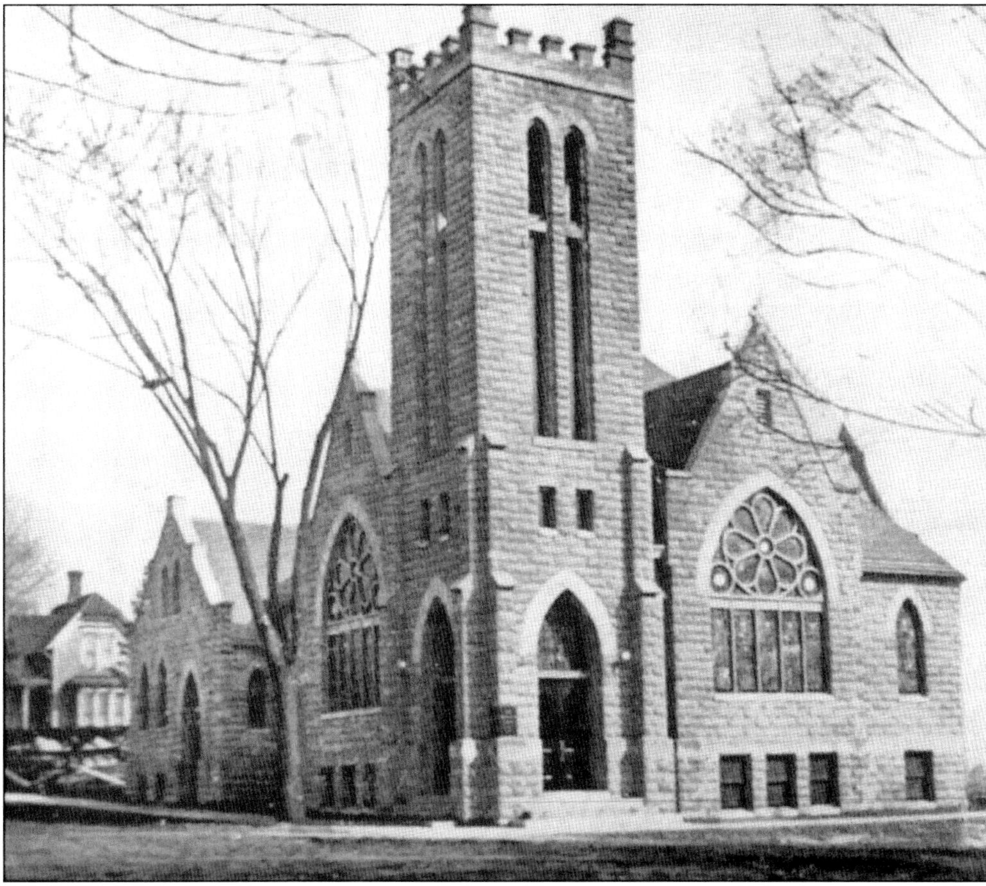

The first Presbyterian Church was formed in the fall of 1857 after a petition to organize a church in Reedsburg was sent to the Missionary Committee of the Columbus Presbytery and eventually approved. The current stone church was built in 1906 and dedicated in January 1907 (above). The church was completely redecorated following World War II, and the pastor's study was enlarged. (Above, courtesy of Reedsburg Area Historical Society; below, courtesy of Bill Hentges.)

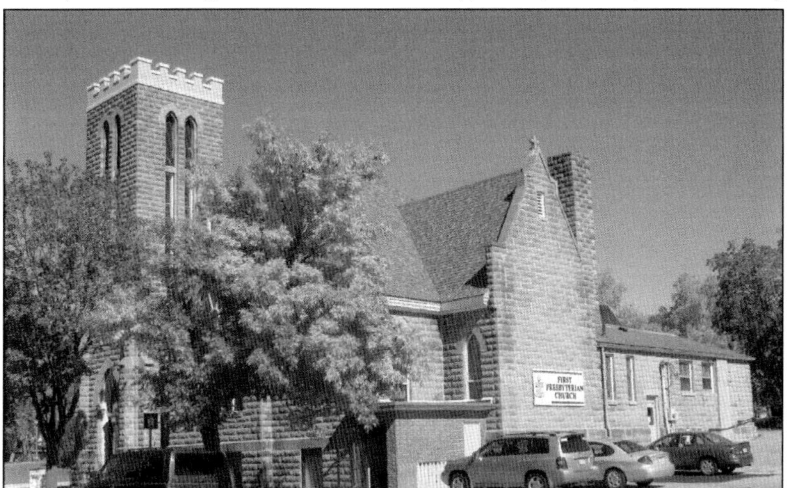

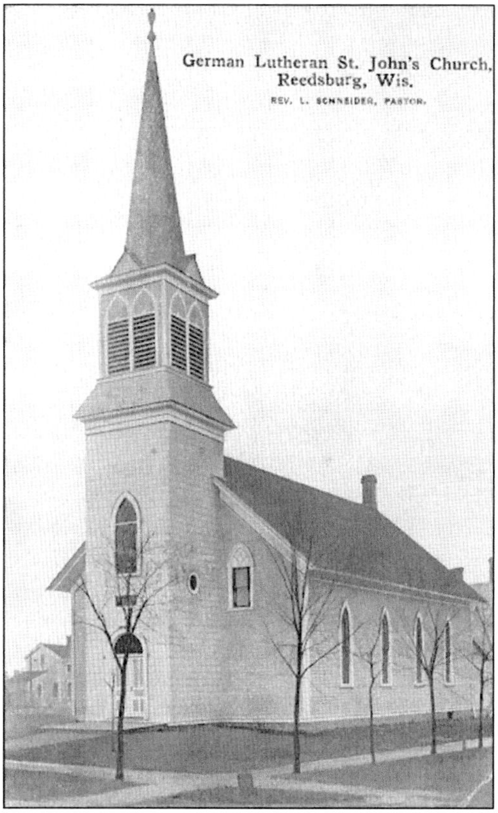

St. John's Lutheran Church was organized in August 1878 at a meeting in the home of William Raetzmann. The first church (left) was built shortly after organization, with a tower and bell added in 1892 and a pipe organ in 1913. The current church building is pictured below in the 1980s. (Both, courtesy of St. John's Church.)

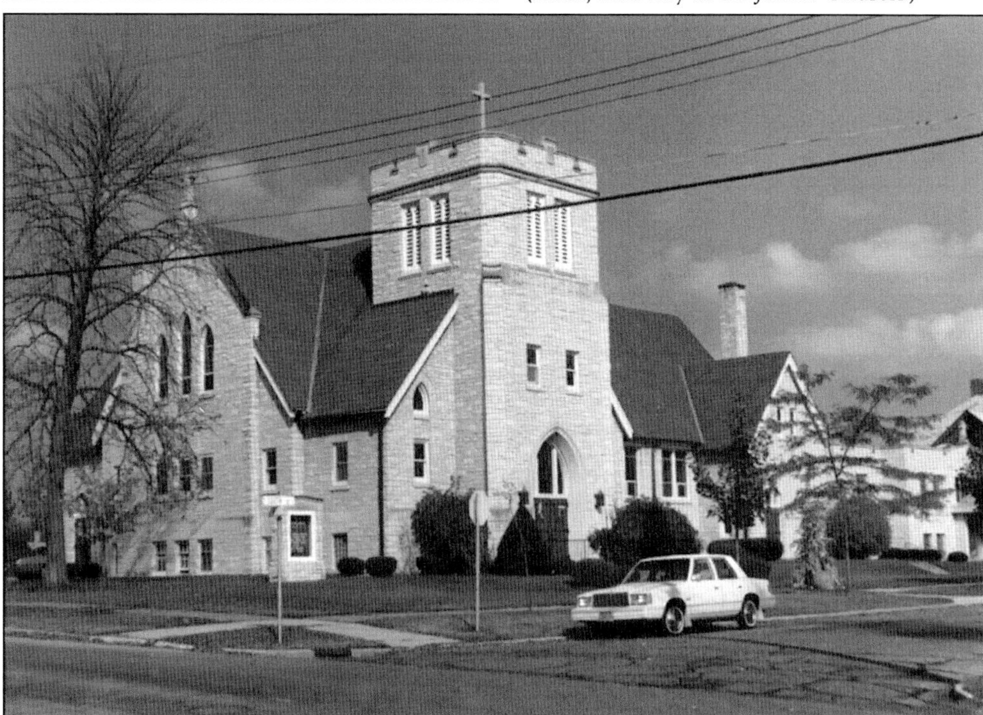

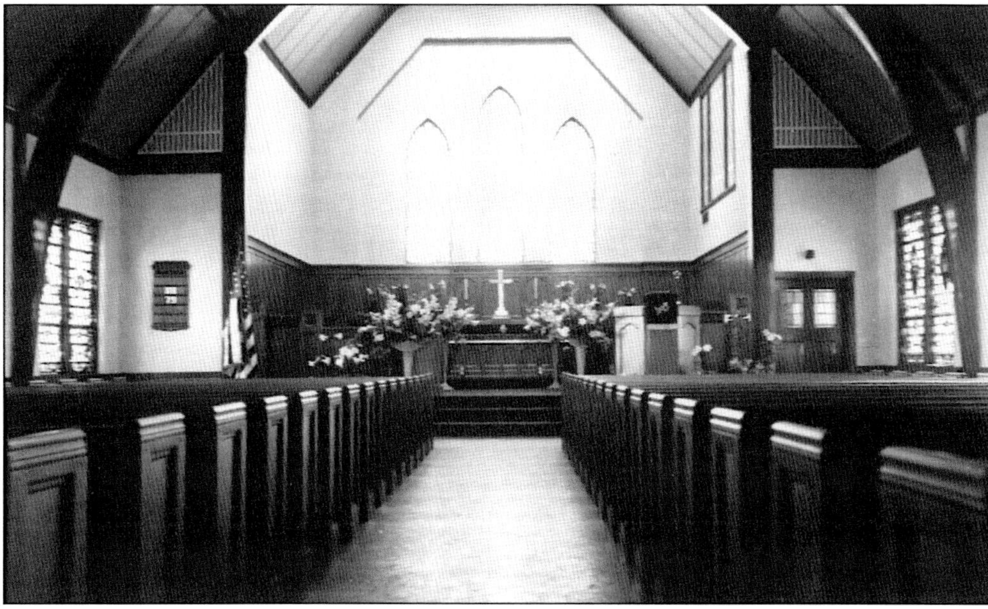

A fire destroyed St. John's on January 10, 1937. A new, larger church was dedicated on February 27, 1938, and this building is currently in use today. The church has since undergone renovations and an addition to accommodate the growing congregation. It later added an education wing to the church building and a reception room for people to meet and greet after services. (Both, courtesy of St. John's Church.)

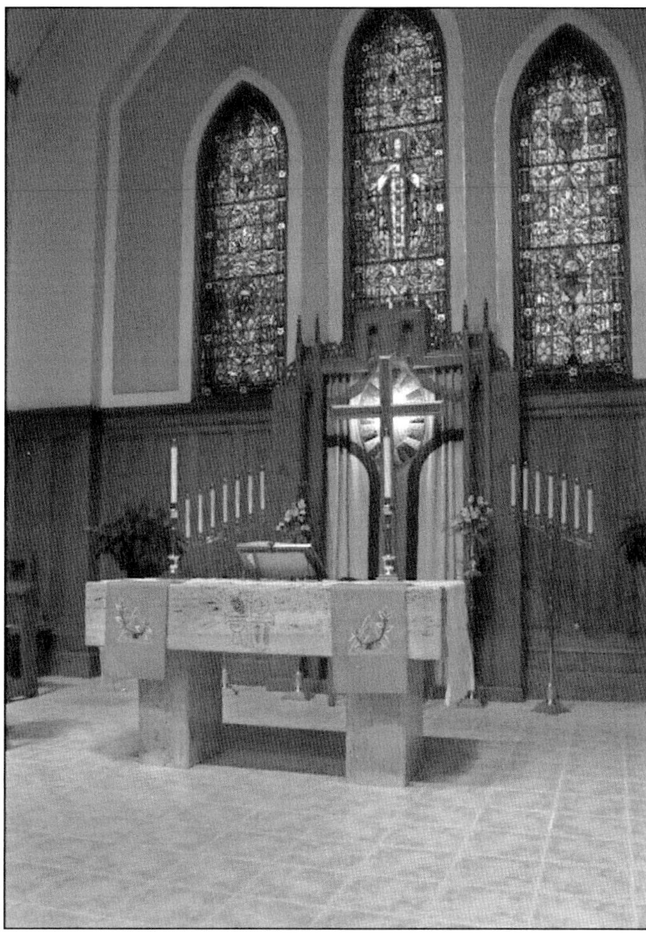

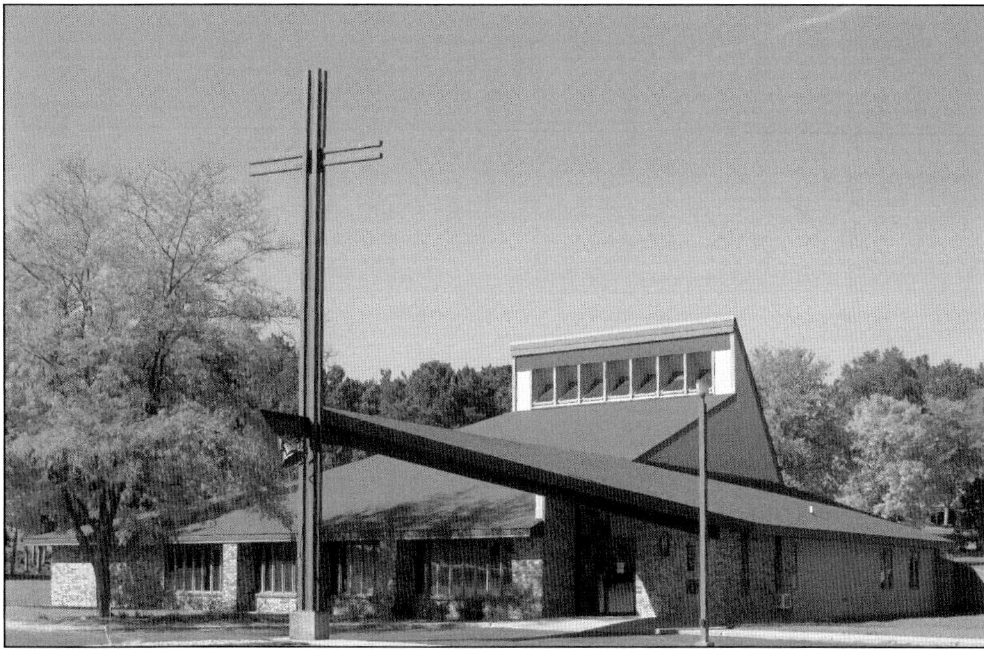

The Church of God was assembled on May 13, 1910. Services were originally held in various halls until the congregation decided to build in 1920. The lot for the current building was purchased in 1971, though construction did not begin until 1979. The first service in the new church was held on July 6, 1980. (Courtesy of Bill Hentges.)

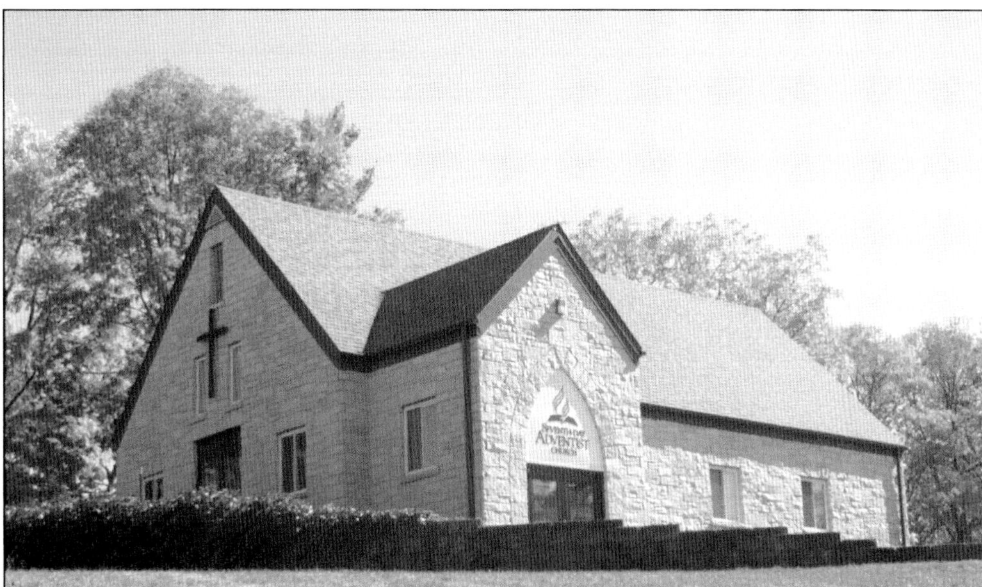

The Seventh-Day Adventist Church congregation began worshipping in 1936 in rented locations. Building began on the current structure in 1952, with the majority of labor and lumber donated by members. The church was dedicated in 1959. (Courtesy of Bill Hentges.)

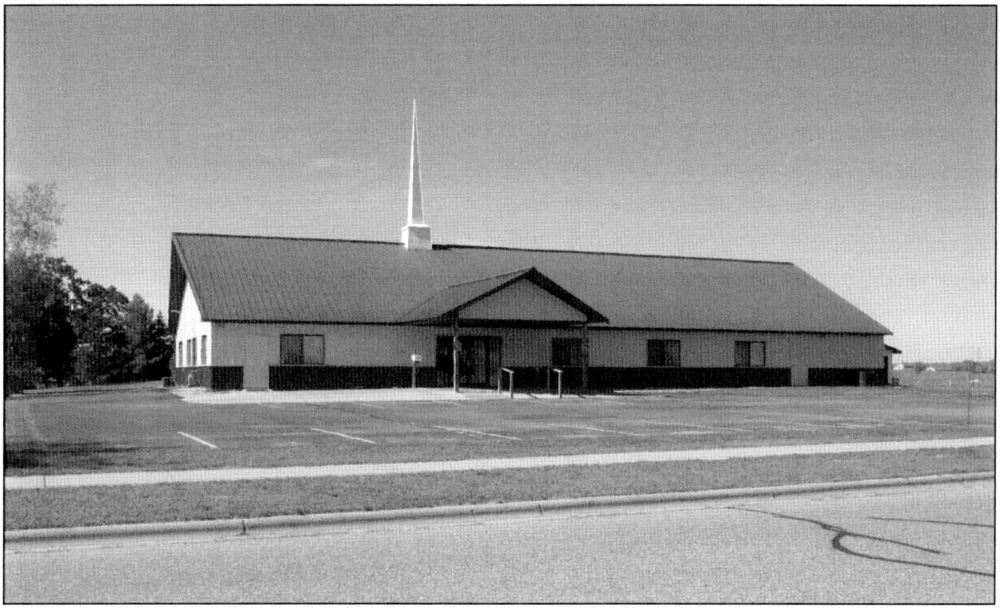

In 1951, the Bible Baptist Church was founded by 40 Reedsburg residents. The church on Main Street was dedicated in the fall of 1969, and the red brick church building was purchased in 1996 after merging with the First Methodist Church. The current building, shown here, is located just off of Reedsburg Road. (Courtesy of Bill Hentges.)

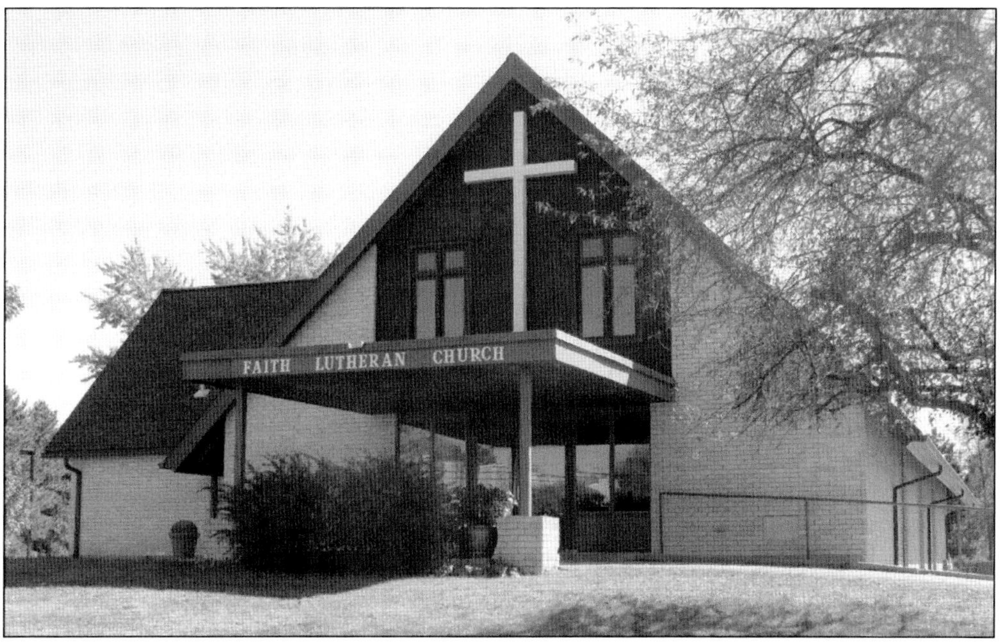

The first Faith Lutheran Church service was held on February 21, 1965, at the Seventh-Day Adventist church. The current building was erected in 1974, and a school was completed in 1981. (Courtesy of Bill Hentges.)

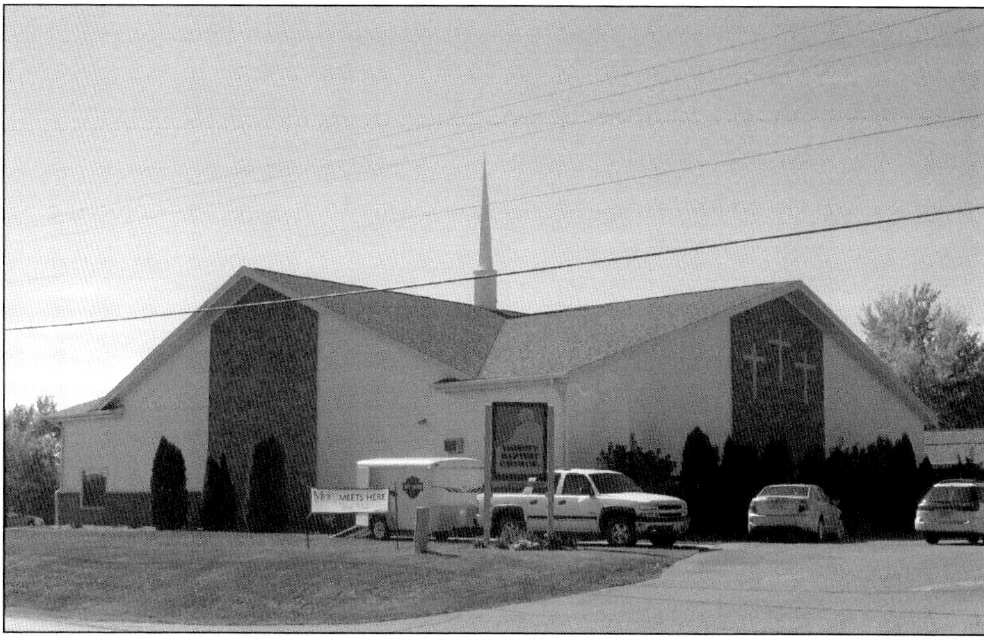

A number of families met in November 1976 to discuss establishing a new Baptist church. On January 23, 1977, ten adults committed to form the new church. The services were held at the Seventh-Day Adventist church and the middle school until the current building, shown here, was built in 1980. (Courtesy of Bill Hentges.)

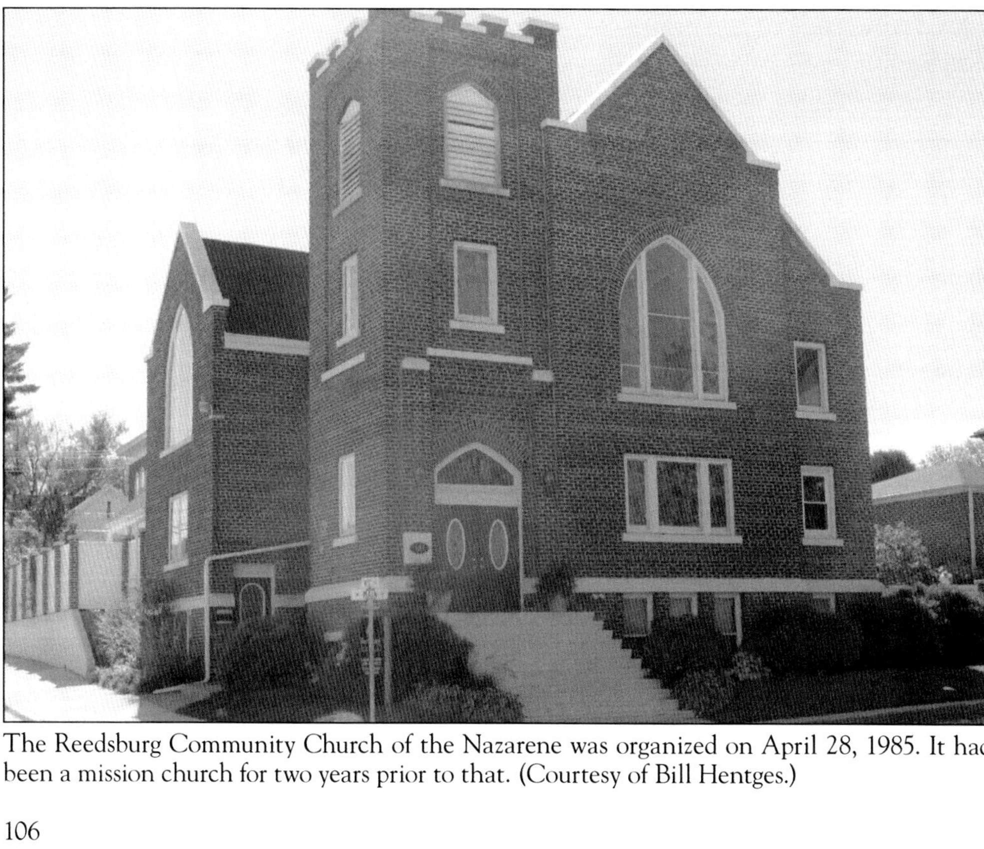

The Reedsburg Community Church of the Nazarene was organized on April 28, 1985. It had been a mission church for two years prior to that. (Courtesy of Bill Hentges.)

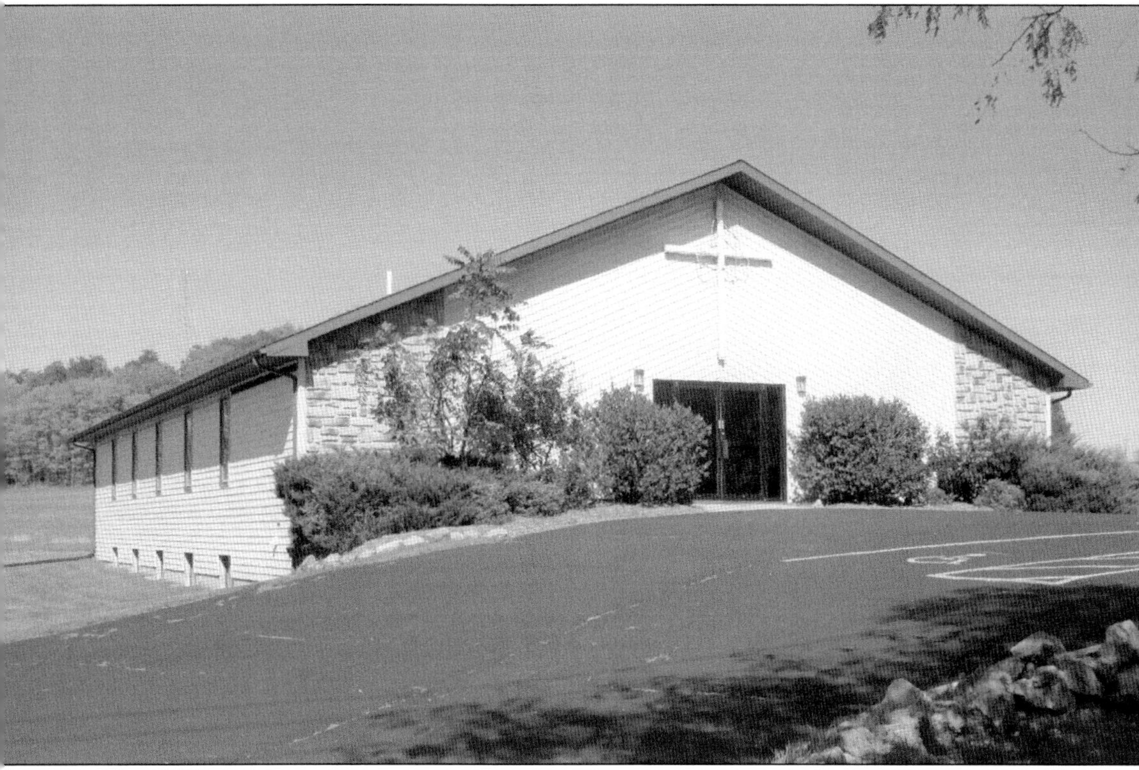

New Life Assembly of God began on November 5, 1983, as the Life Christian Fellowship. Meetings were originally held in Reedsburg's Town Hall. The church was accepted into fellowship with the Assemblies of God on June 7, 1985, and the church was built by 1988. (Courtesy of Bill Hentges.)

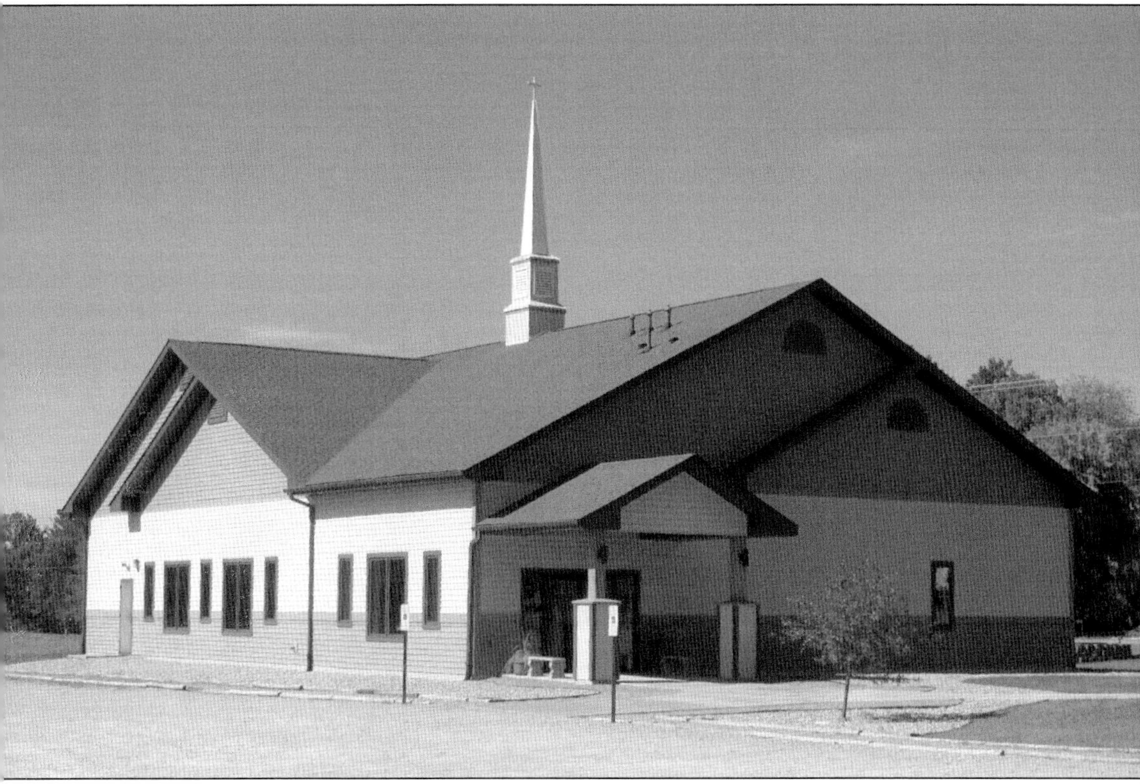

The First Missionary Baptist Church of Redlands, California, was formed in 1941. This became the sending church for the Reedsburg location in 2000. Cornerstone Missionary Baptist Church started small, but has grown to a steady presence in the Reedsburg community. (Courtesy of Bill Hentges.)

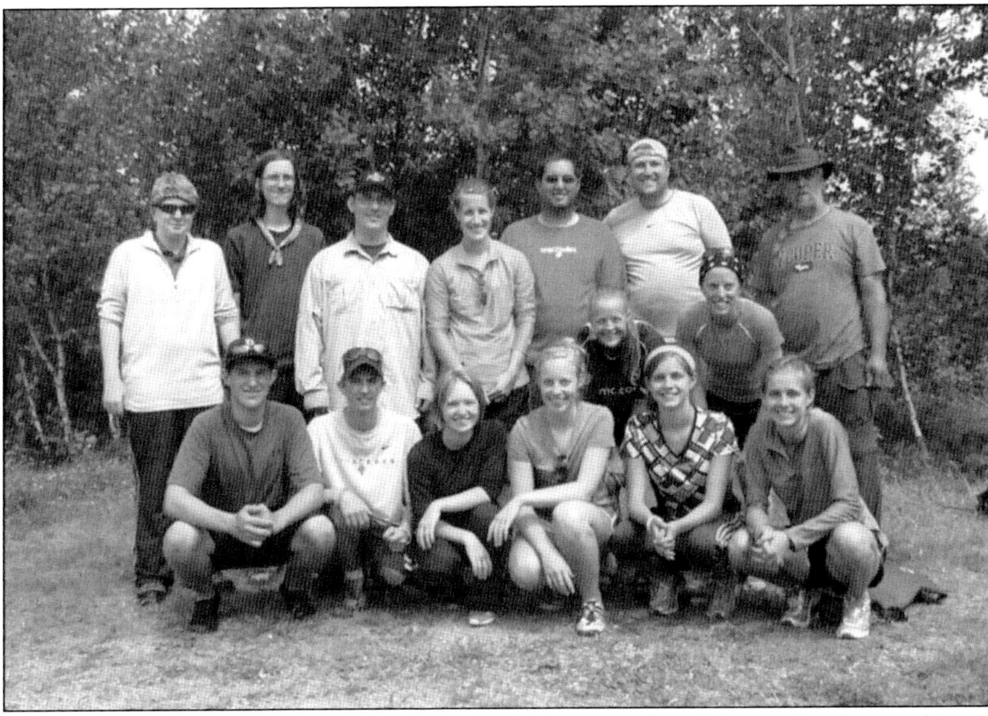

Pictured in the St. John's youth group photograph above are, from left to right, (first row) Jacob Hacker, Tanner Hahn, Chelsea Bernien, Katie Kitson, Becky Rataczyk, and Katie Rataczyk; (second row) guides Mary ? and K.P. ?; (third row) Jorden Bernien, Daniel Glesne, Travis Simon, Cassie Hacker, Craig Braunschweig, Ben Berg, and Todd ?. Pictured below is a youth group made up of several churches. (Both, courtesy of Ben Berg.)

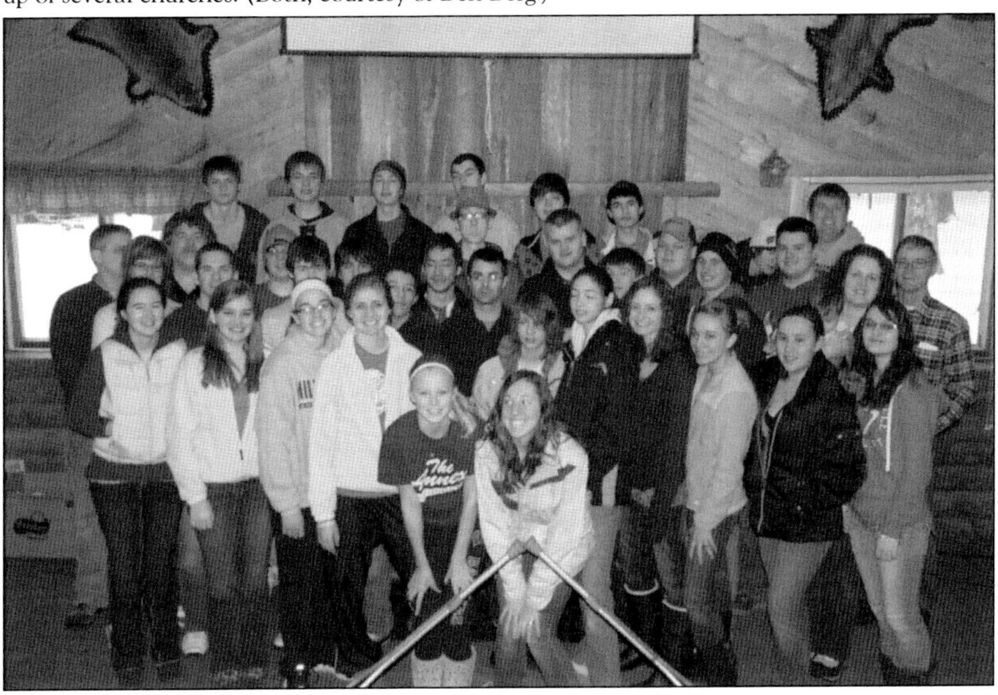

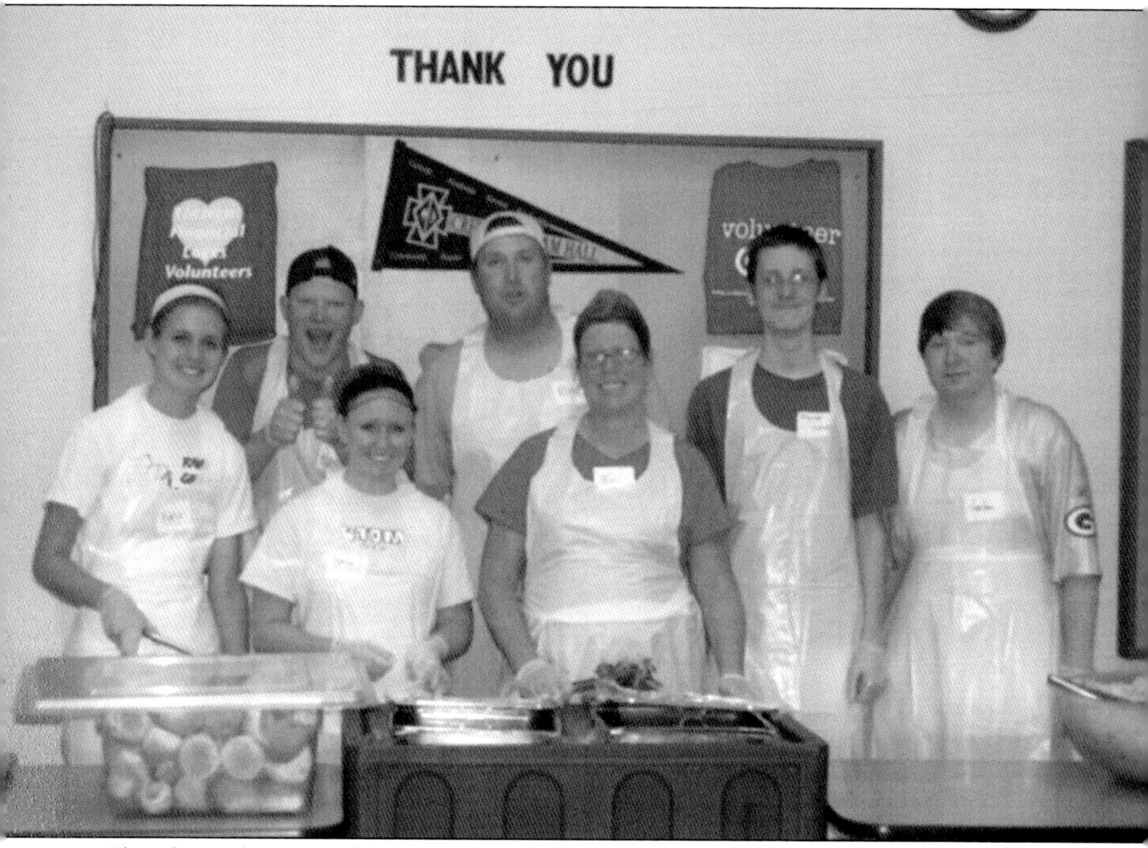

Church youth groups also go on trips to places around the United States on mission trips, conventions, hikes, or camping trips to further their faith, grow as a group, and help people in need. Pictured here from left to right are Katie Ratajczyk, Rydge Craker, Danica Polk, Ben Berg, Tori Maxfield, Daniel Glesne, and Jordan Bernien. (Courtesy of St. John's Church.)

Seven

Sports in Reedsburg

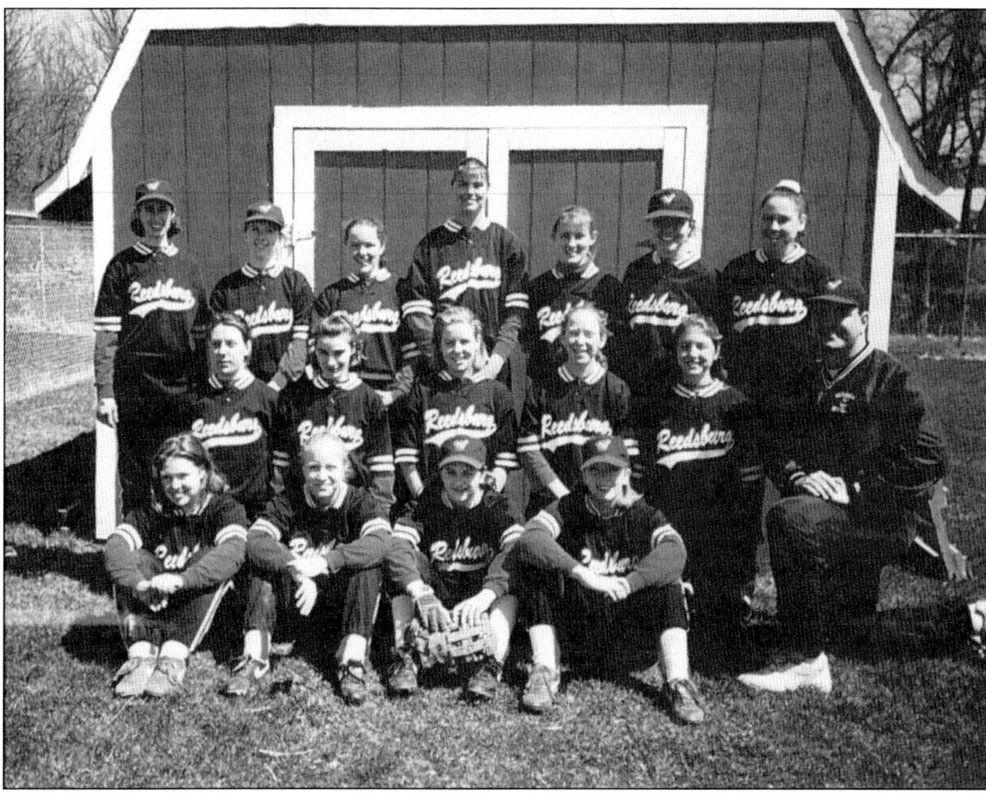

From the late 1980s through the early 1990s, no sports program at Webb High School was more consistently successful than Beavers softball. Beginning with coach Gary Lemieux and continuing into the tenure of coach Kevin Runde, the school's teams piled up South Central Conference titles. Pictured here is Coach Runde's 1995 conference title squad. (Courtesy of Reedsburg Area High School.)

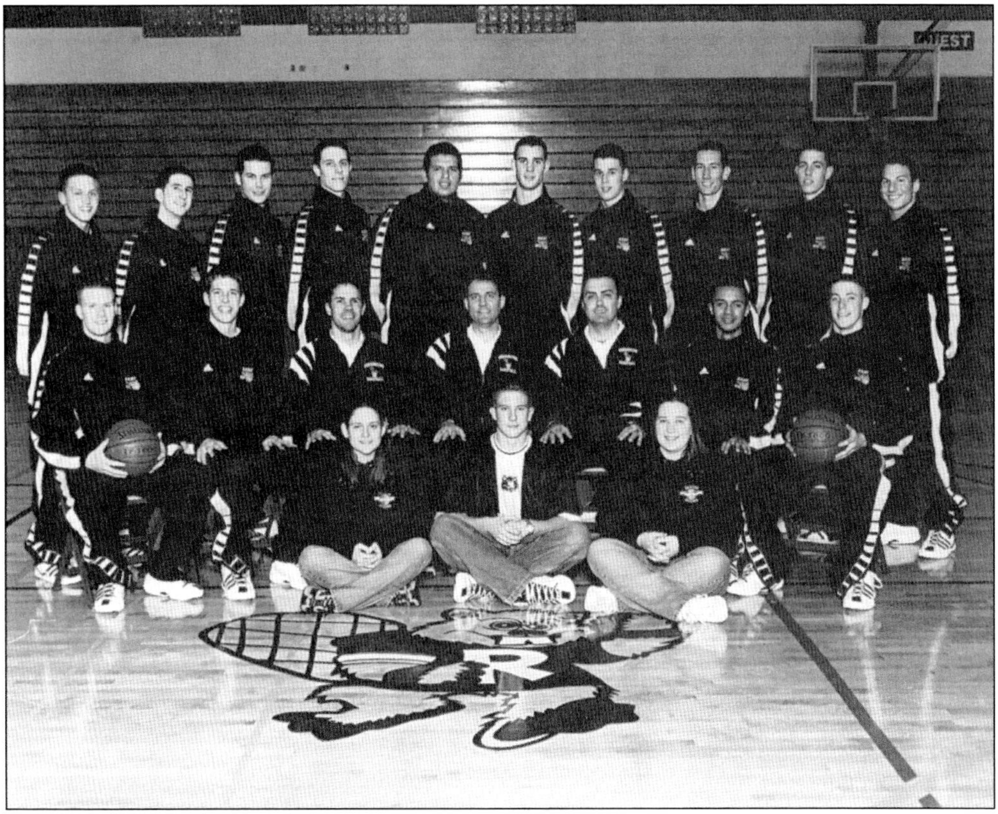

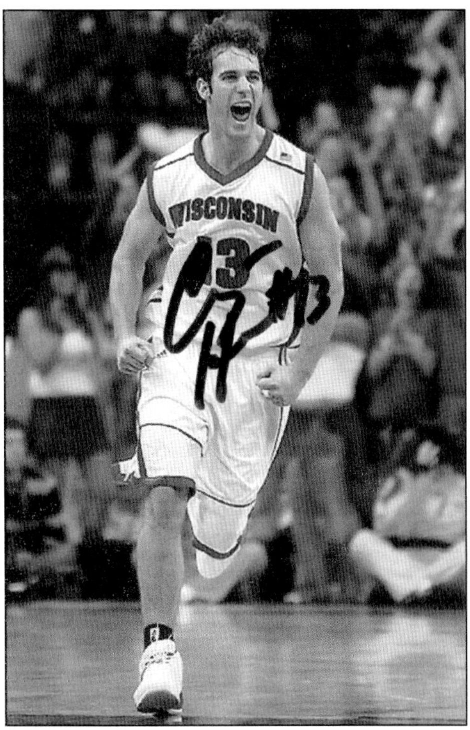

The 2000–2001 boys' basketball team is pictured above. Reedsburg's sports programs moved from the South Central Conference to the Badger North Conference after the 2000–2001 school year. Before exiting the SCC, however, the Beaver basketball team won the South Central title in 2001. Coach Andy Gesteland's squad featured future University of Wisconsin–Madison standout Clayton Hanson (left), who would go on to help Bo Ryan's Badgers reach the NCAA Sweet 16 in 2005. (Above, courtesy of Reedsburg Area High School; left, courtesy of Craig Braunschweig.)

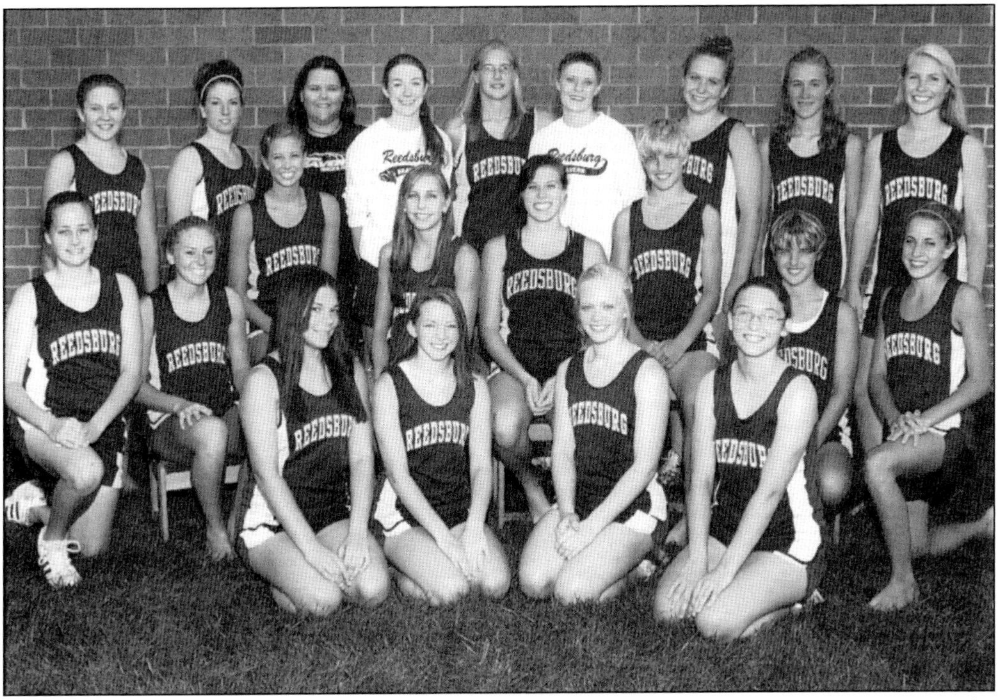

Pictured here is the 2007 cross-country team. The Reedsburg girls' cross-country program, under the direction of head coach Nicole Bruer and assistant coach Katie Matthews, had a very talented roster and went to state as a team. Several runners on the varsity team went on to compete in cross-country and track in college. On the varsity team were Brea Goodsman, Dakota Goodman (both ran track for LSU), Nichelle Roessler, Madeline Roznos, Rachel Hasler, Anna Walker, and Sophie Roznos. (Courtesy of Reedsburg Area High School.)

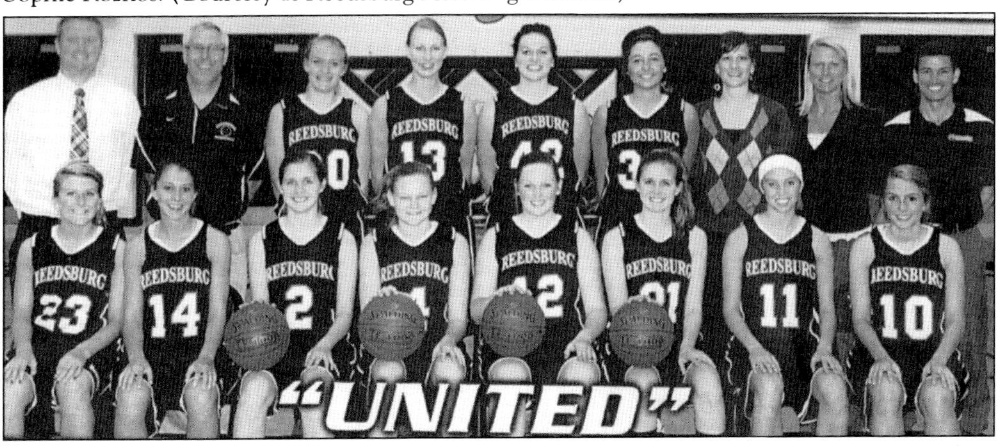

The 2011–2012 girls' basketball team went 23-4 and advanced to the state tournament. On their way to state, they faced their rivals, the Baraboo Thunderbirds. Reedsburg defeated Baraboo in the sectionals 56-53, in three overtimes. The team's players and staff are, from left to right, (first row) Meghan Douglas, Chelsey Schulenburg, Becky Ratajczyk, Emily Kellner, Kelsey Mazur, Katie Ratajczyk, Carly Yager, and Jennie Bindl; (second row) head coach Mark Simon, assistant coach John Brandt, Tiernee Schrank, Beth Maenpaa, Sophie Lichte, Elika Marten, assistant coach Kelly Cunningham, assistant coach Jamie Nebel, and assistant coach Todd Polk. (Courtesy of Reedsburg Area High School.)

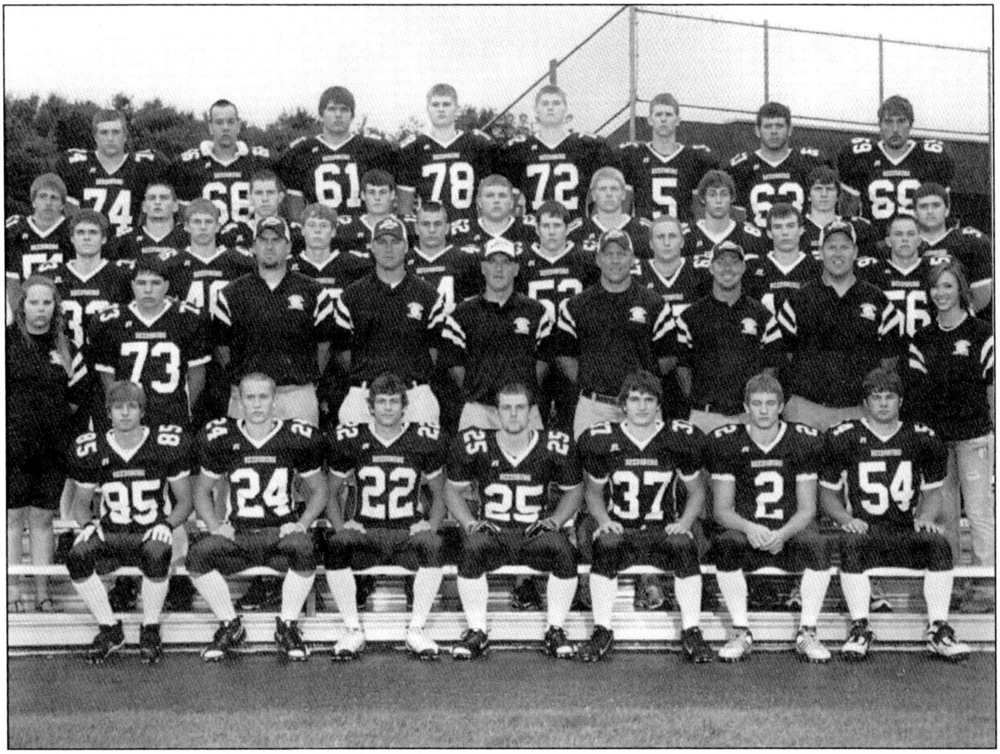

The 2009 Reedsburg football team (pictured) put it all together. The team went 11-3 and were Badger North champions. It also made its second trip in two years to the Division 3 championship, this time winning against West De Pere High School, 34-27. This was Reedsburg's first state football championship. The team, filled with players in their senior year and other upperclassmen, possessed experience from the 2008 state run. (Both, courtesy of Reedsburg Area High School.)

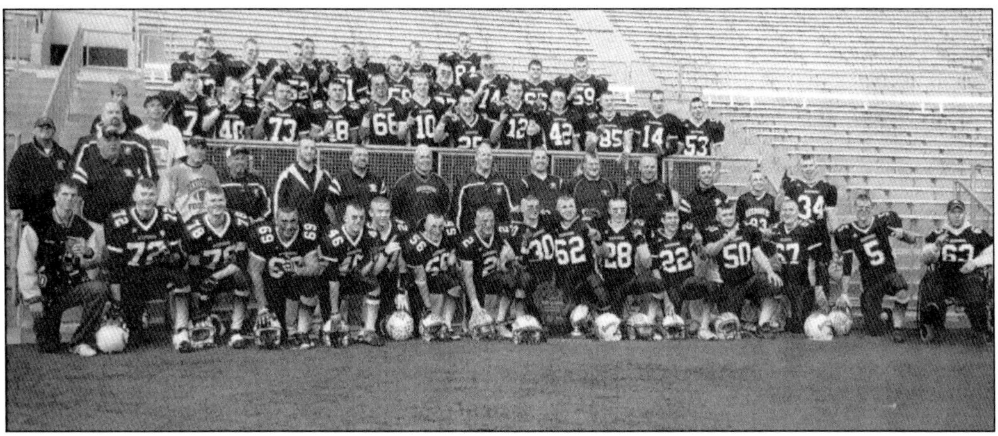

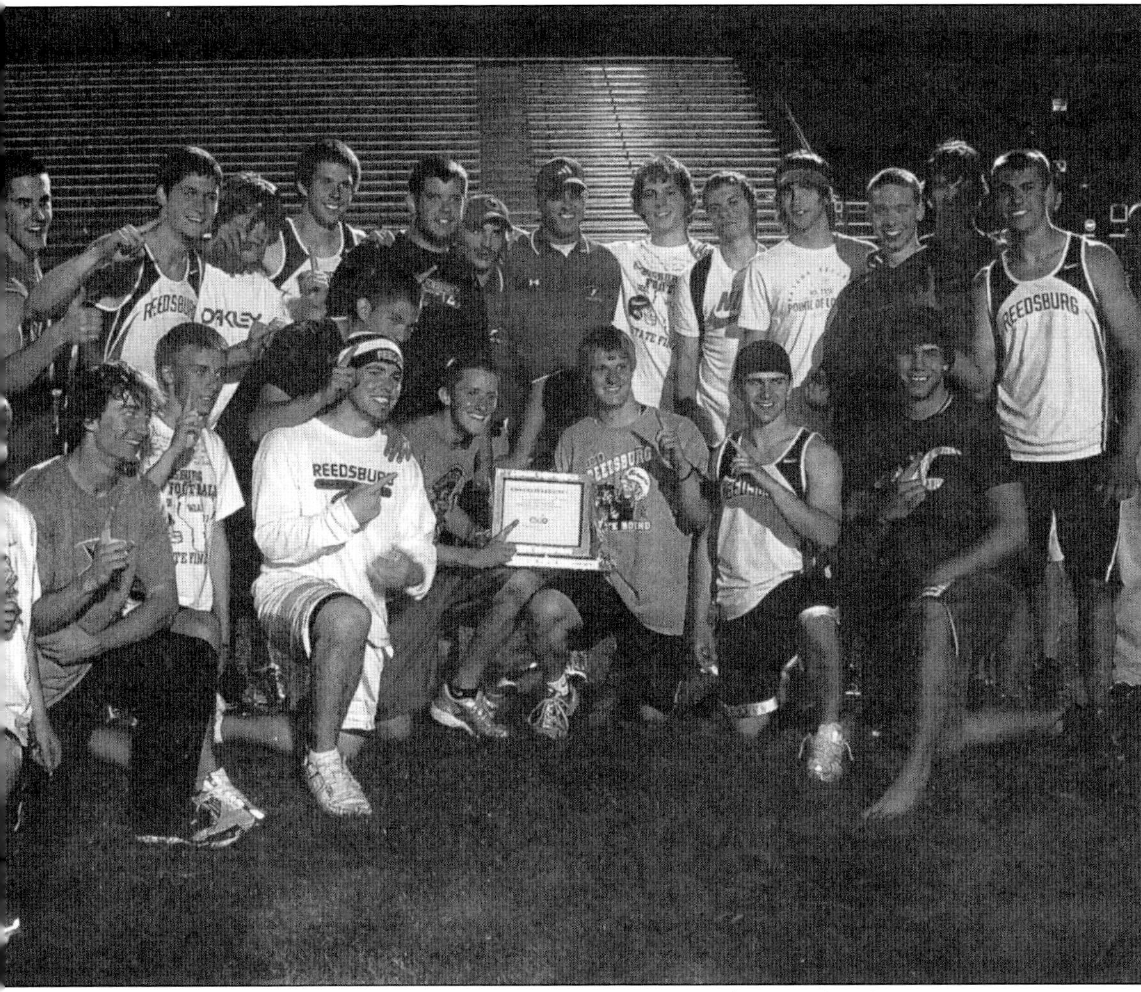

In 2009, boys' track head coach Phil Hasler led his team to a Badger North title. Having major talent on the team certainly facilitated winning the conference. Pictured are, from left to right, (first row) Taylor Roessler, Tyler Archambo, Ryan Dischler, Bob Kruger, Mike Turner, Zach Meyer, Derrick Kinsman, and Nick Kokenzie; (second row) Jacob Gonzalez, Matthew Rockweiler, Tyler Mazur, Ryan Mathews, Kyle Smith, Nate Brey, coach Michael McCarville, coach Phil Hasler, Matt Pingle, Matthew Hartje, Rob Taylor, Jared Wertz, Cassidy Denman, Jerry Weiss, and coach Matt Bauer. Everyone on the team worked hard to bring a Badger North title to Reedsburg, and many members went on to compete at the state level. (Courtesy of Reedsburg Area High School.)

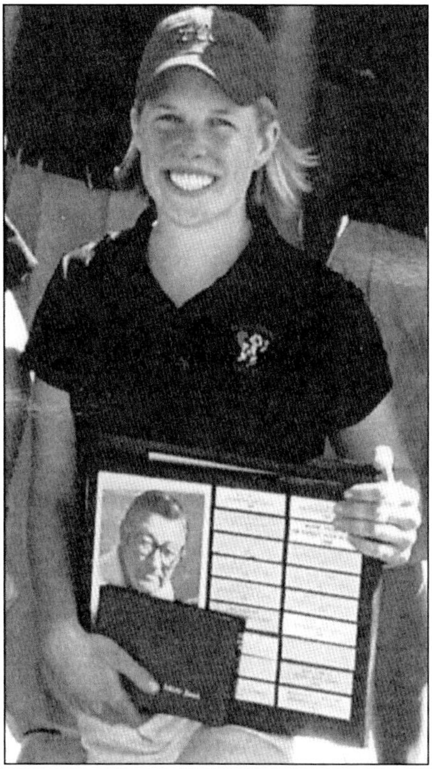

Because Reedsburg did not have a girls' golf team at the time, Elle Arkin had to play on the boys' team. In her senior year, she finished 14th in the WIAA Boy's High School Championship. The Reedsburg team as a whole finished fourth. Arkin went on to compete in golf at the University of Wisconsin–Madison, playing on the varsity team from 2008 to 2012 (not playing the 2009–2010 year). Arkin, also a great hockey player, was named Ms. Hockey Wisconsin in her senior year of high school. (Both, courtesy of Reedsburg Area High School.)

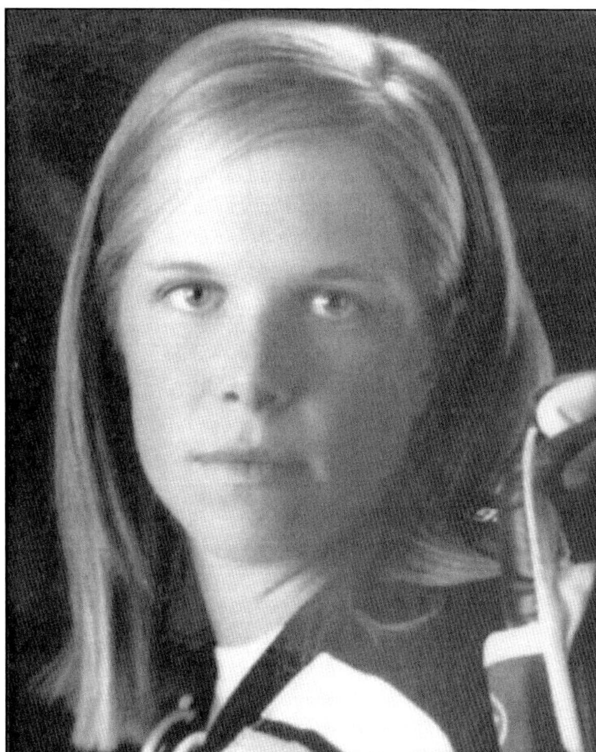

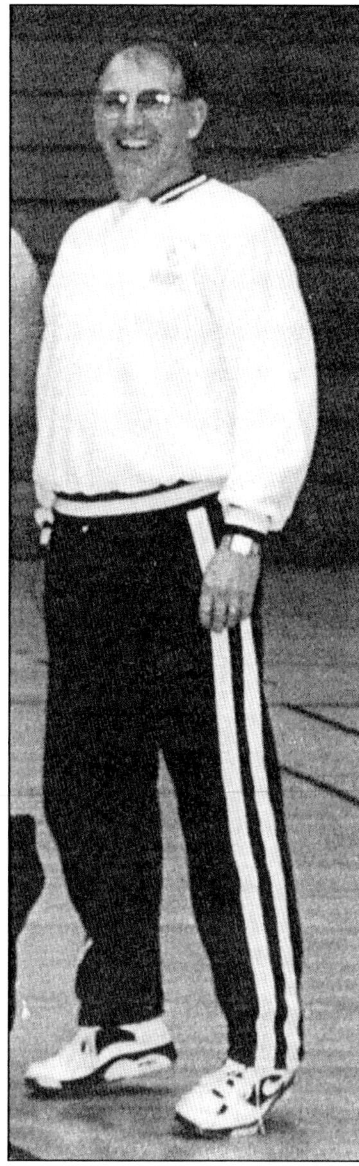

David "Doc" Koehler coached both basketball and baseball at Reedsburg's Webb High School through parts of four decades. Koehler completed his baseball coaching career in 1994, shortly after his induction into the Wisconsin Baseball Coaches Association Hall of Fame. He continued to coach basketball through the 1997–1998 season. (Both, courtesy of Reedsburg Area High School.)

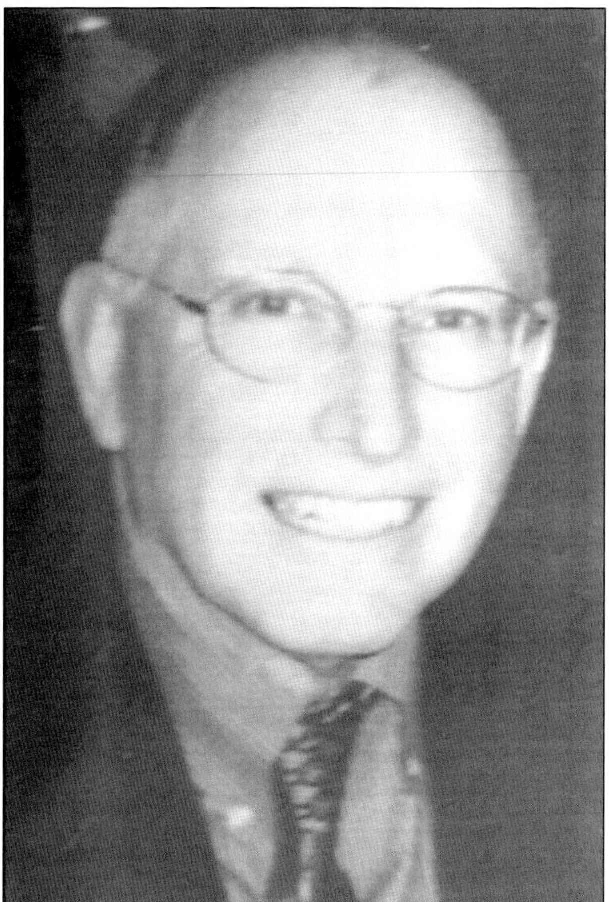

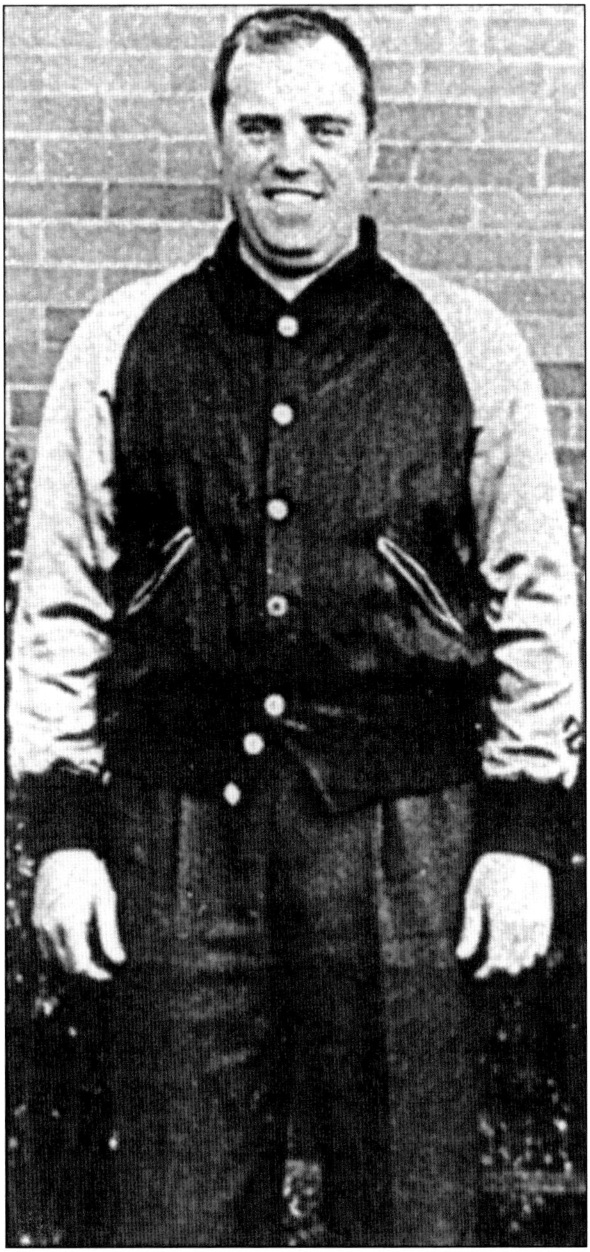

In 1952, Nick Homes started his career at Reedsburg as football and basketball coach, as well as serving as the athletic director. He was the football coach at Reedsburg for 13 years; his career record stood at 82-22. During his final 10 years, starting with the 1955 squad, Holmes's teams won a total of 72 games while losing only 8, and during that time, five of his teams were the undefeated South Central champions. The 1959–1960 team won 17 consecutive games, and the 1961–1964 squad won 23 straight. Holmes also served as the head basketball coach for nine seasons and organized Reedsburg's baseball program. As a basketball coach, his teams were 120-52, winning three South Central Conference championships. During the 1959–1960 season, his team was 18-0. In his four seasons as baseball coach, his record included three championships and a runner-up trophy at the state tournament. (Courtesy of Jeff Seering.)

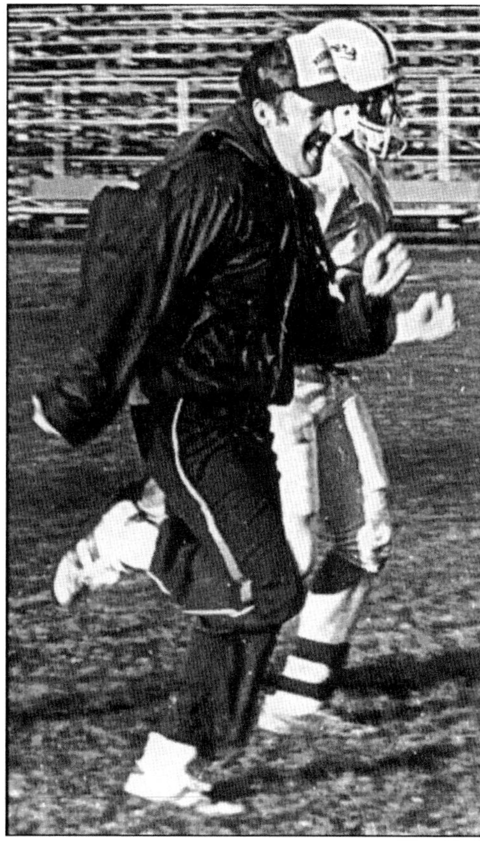

Jerry Griffin took the head football coaching position at Reedsburg High School in 1983. During his career at the school, he was part of five conference championships, and his teams appeared in the playoffs 10 times. Griffin was selected District Coach of the Year three times and was elected to serve as a district representative for the Wisconsin Football Coaches Association in three different conferences over 10 years. He taught physical education at Reedsburg until his retirement in 2007. (Both, courtesy of Jeff Seering.)

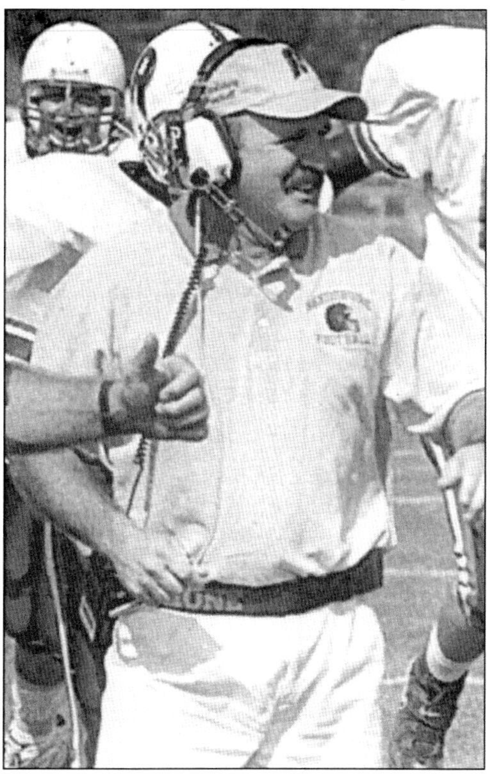

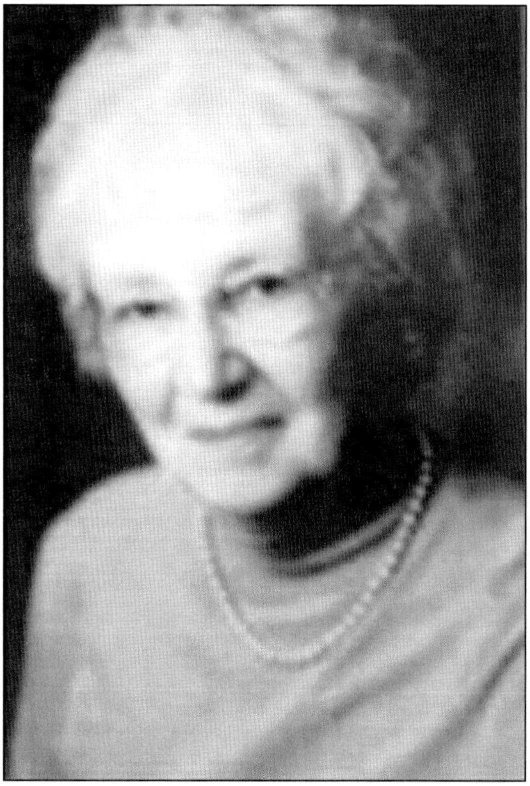

Betsy DeMerit attended the University of Wisconsin–La Crosse before coming to Reedsburg to teach physical education and coach the girl's track-and-field program, which she started in 1967. DeMerit coached Reedsburg girls' track for 18 years, compiling 58 dual meet victories, one conference championship, five conference championship runner-up finishes, one Wisconsin Interscholastic Athletic Association (WIAA) regional championship, two sectional championships, and many other achievements. DeMerit was elected into the WIAA Hall of Fame in 2007. Reedsburg's home track invitational is named after DeMerit. (Courtesy of Reedsburg Area High School.)

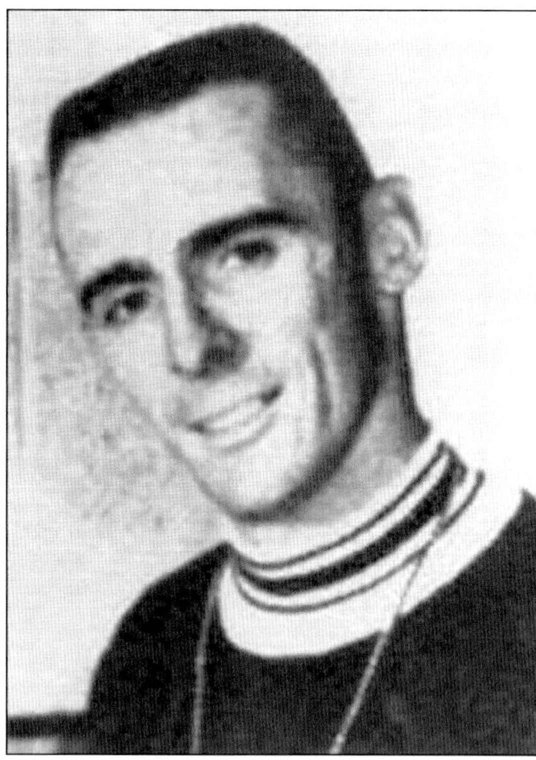

Bill Moran had many successful seasons as Reedsburg's basketball coach during the 1960s and 1970s. During his coaching career (which also included stints at LaFarge and Hillsboro), Moran compiled a 253-166 record, with two sectional titles. In 2000, Moran was inducted into the Wisconsin Basketball Coaches Association Hall of Fame. (Courtesy of Reedsburg Area High School.)

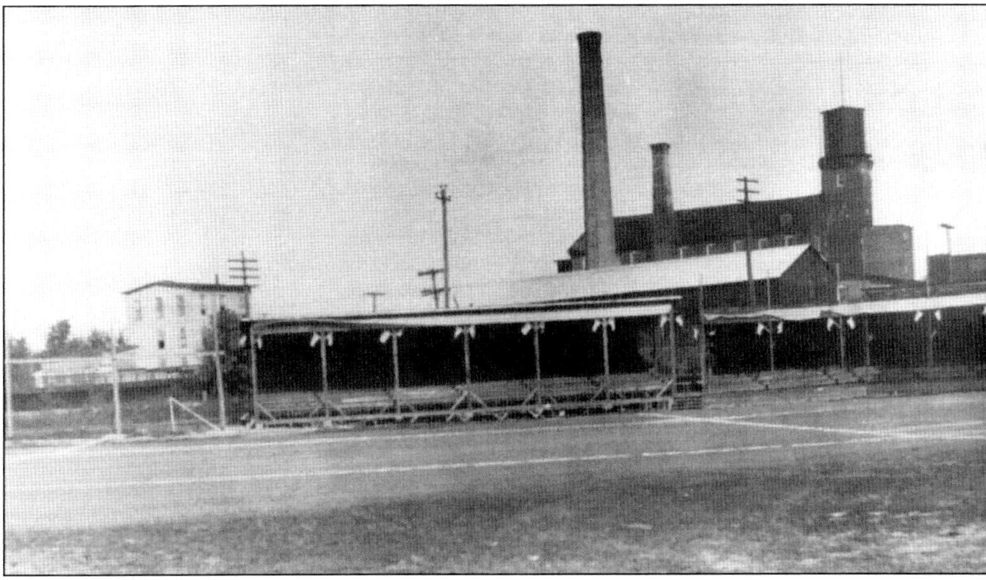

Reedsburg High School's first football and baseball fields were located by the Baraboo River. Today, this location is the site of the city dump. (Both, courtesy of Reedsburg Public Library.)

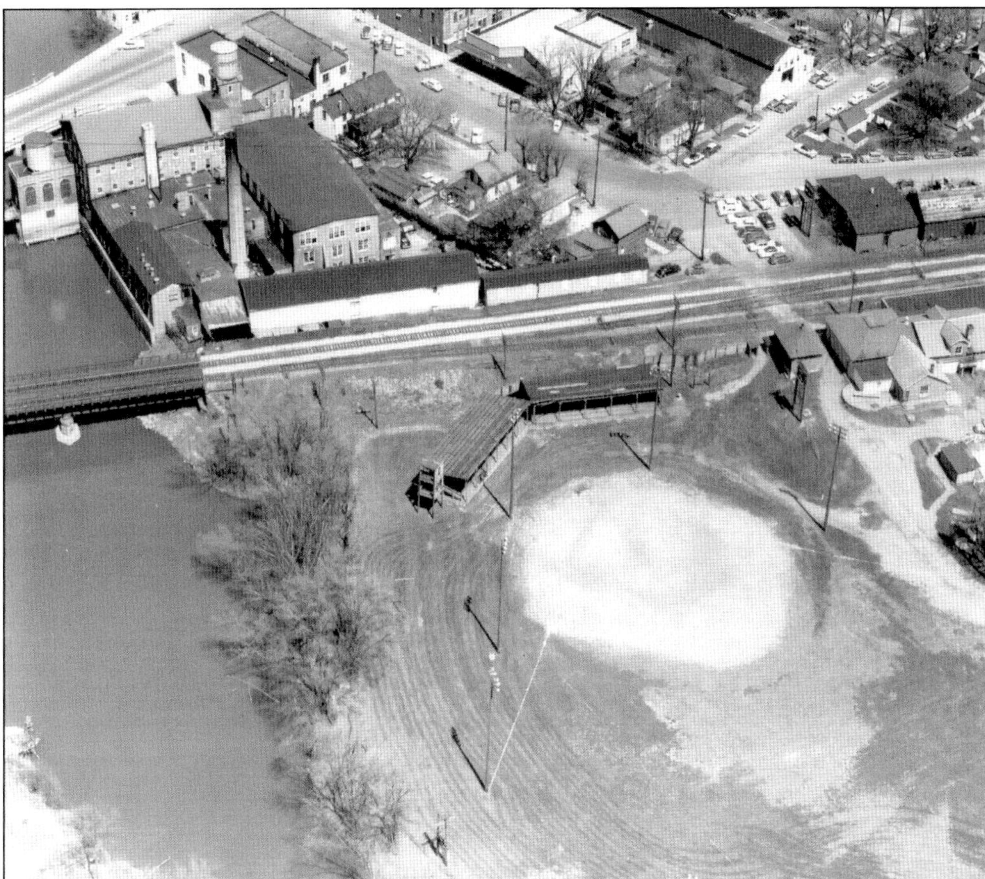

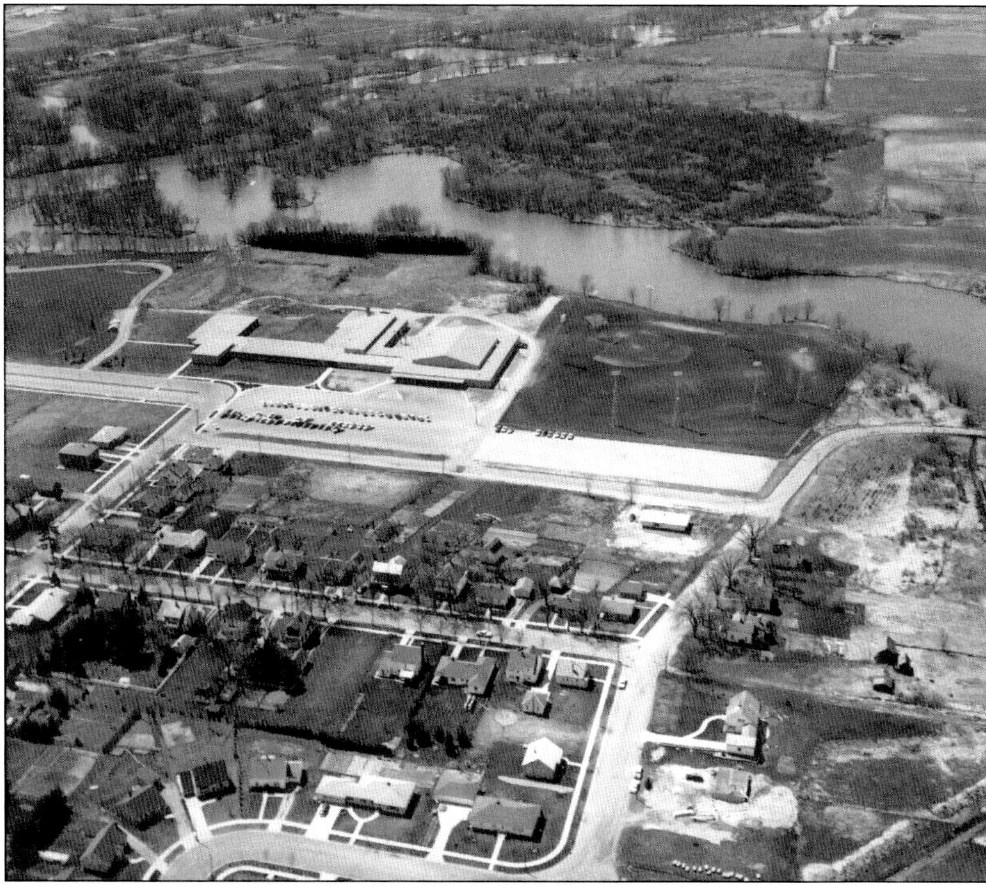

After the high school was moved to Webb, Webb Field was created next to the school. The football team played at Webb Field until Millennium Field was built. The Reedsburg High School junior varsity baseball team still plays at Webb. In addition, Webb Field is home to Reedsburg's youth football teams. (Above, courtesy of Reedsburg Public Library; below, courtesy of Noah Hofrichter.)

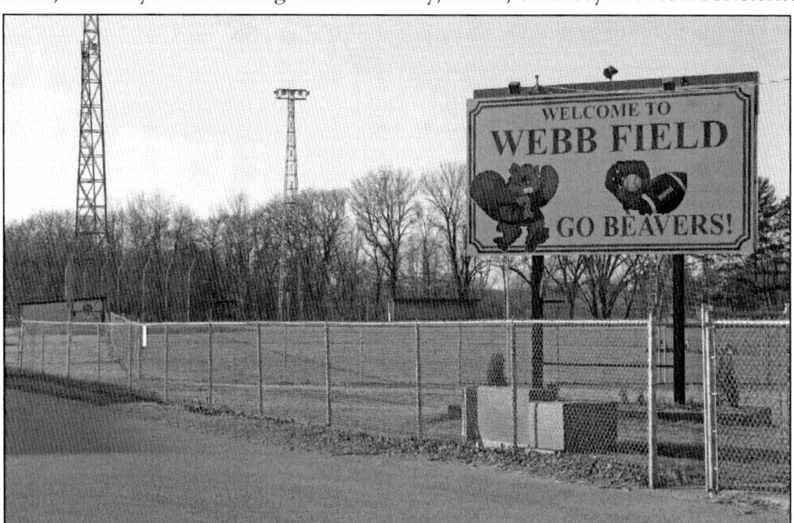

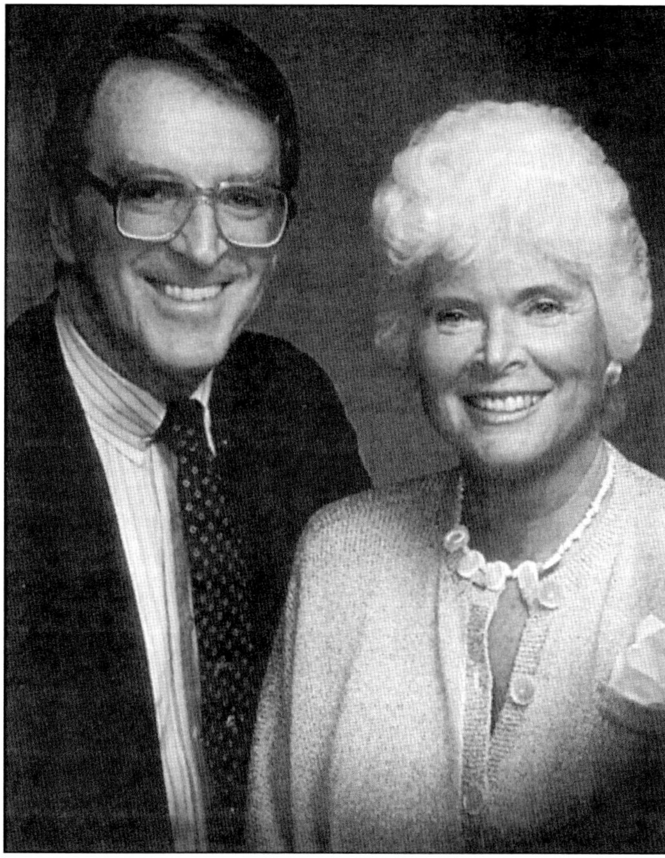

Nancy and Bill Goessel (right) donated money to build the new Millennium Field, located next to Reedsburg Area High School. Reedsburg's football and track-and-field teams compete at Millennium Field. (Right, courtesy of Jeff Seering; below, courtesy of Noah Hofrichter.)

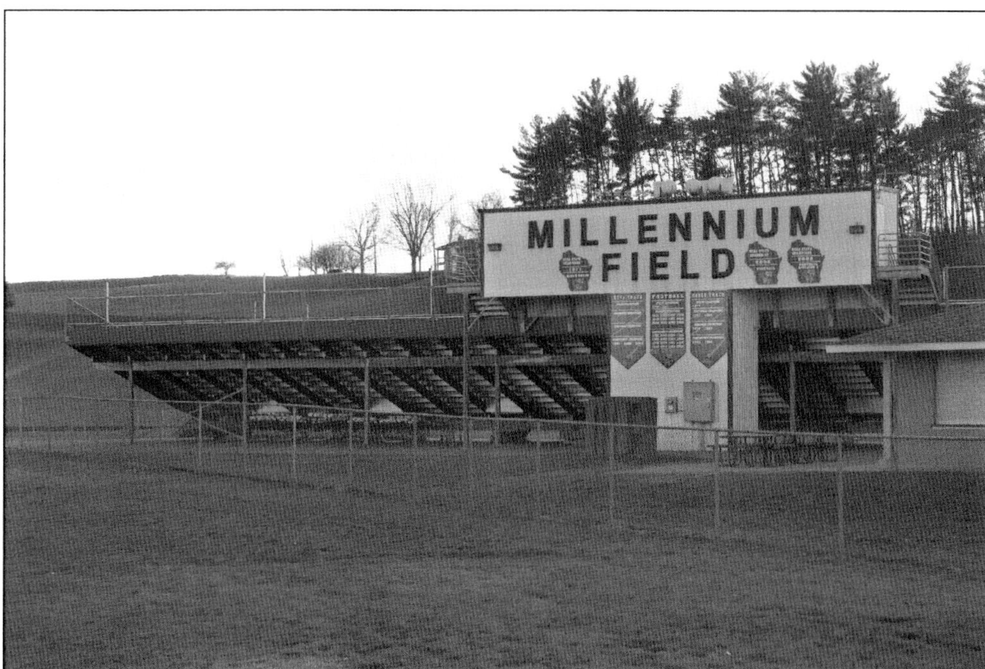

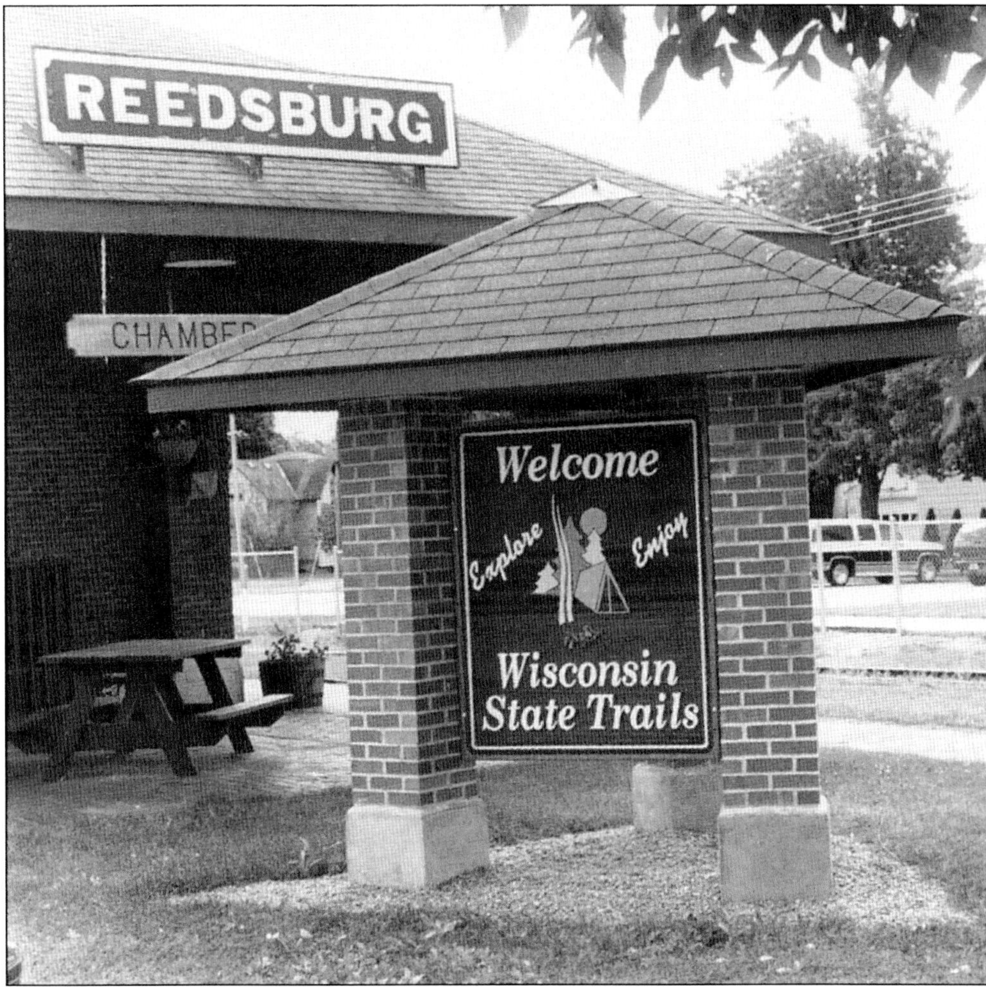

In June 1993, the 400 Trail was opened. The 22-mile trail, which extends from Elroy to Reedsburg, got its name from the Chicago-Northwestern passenger train that ran on the old rail bed and covered the distance between Chicago and the Minneapolis/St. Paul area in 400 minutes. The trail goes by the Baraboo River and passes though the villages of La Valle, Wonewoc, and Union Center. The old train station, currently the chamber of commerce building, is the headquarters for the 400 Trail. (Courtesy of Reedsburg Area Historical Society.)

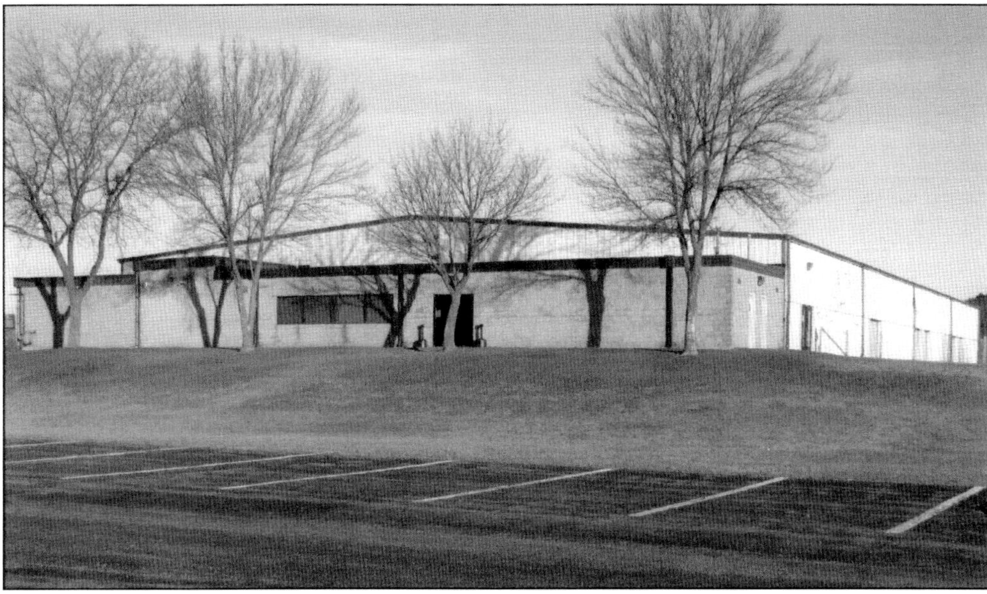

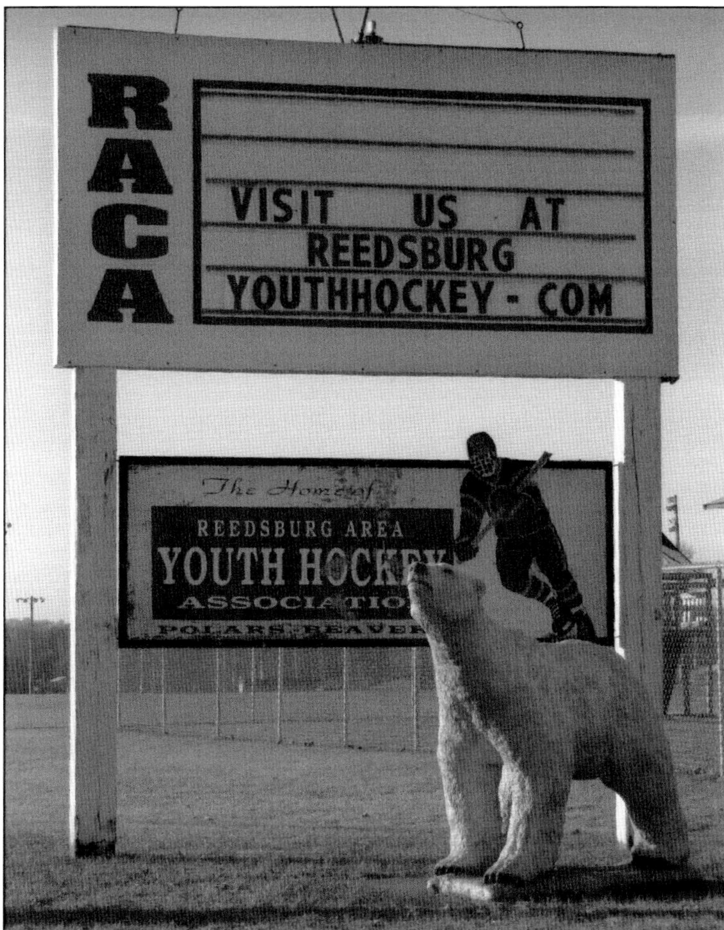

The Reedsburg Area Community Arena (RACA) is part of Nishan Park. RACA is where the Reedsburg Youth Hockey teams and the Reedsburg High School teams play. The building cost over $100,000 to construct. Before 1995, the floor was flooded during the winter to allow teams to skate on it, but in 1995, the floor was cemented and freezing coils were installed. (Both, courtesy of Steve Braunschweig.)

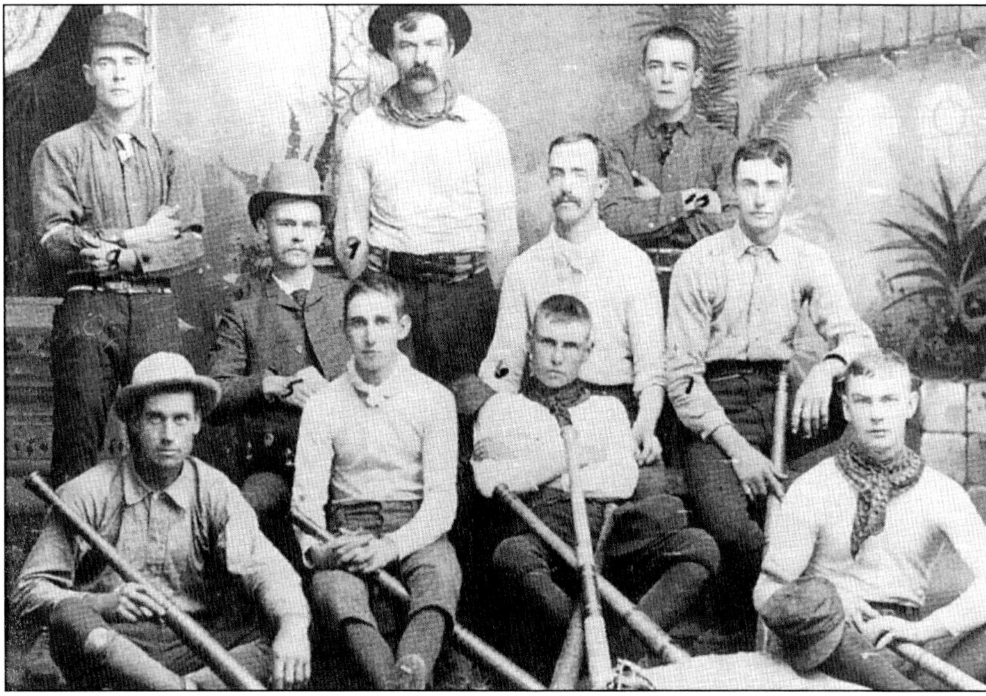

Youth baseball in Reedsburg began in 1951, with the establishment of Wisconsin's first little league. The person most responsible for creating the little league program in Reedsburg was Ed Quinlan. Little league baseball is played at most parks and schools around town, but its primary location is Nishan Park. Pictured above is an early baseball team in Reedsburg. (Above, courtesy of Reedsburg Area Historical Society; below, courtesy of Craig Braunschweig.)

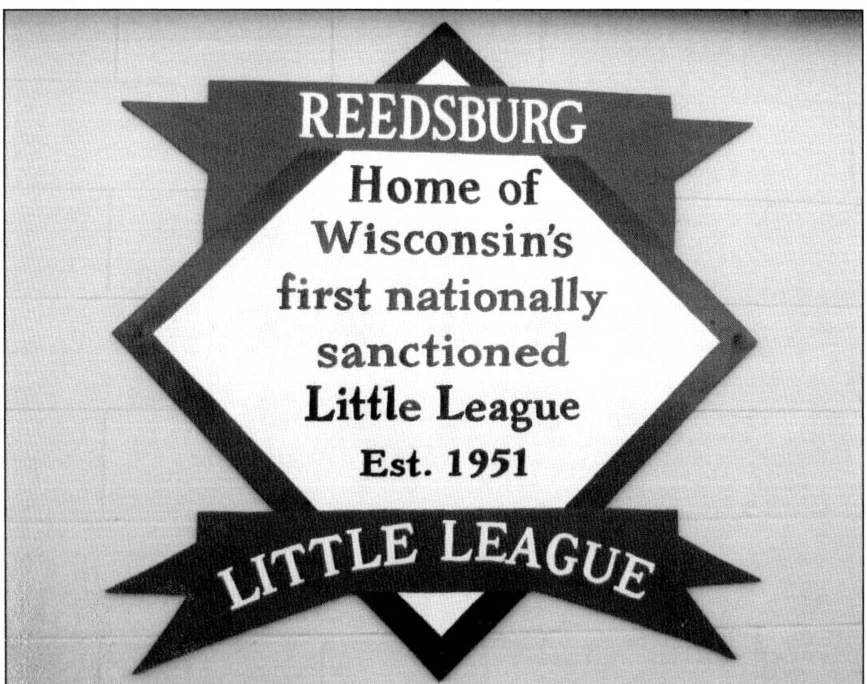

CONTRIBUTING ORGANIZATIONS

A special thank-you goes out to the Reedsburg Area Historical Society. It can be contacted at:

Reedsburg Area Historical Society
P.O. Box 405, Reedsburg, WI 53959
Email: PioneerLogVillage@Yahoo.Com
Webpage: PioneerLogVillage.WordPress.com

Reedsburg Pioneer Log Village was only a dream in 1965, the product of a brainstorming session in a downtown barber shop. The ideals of this like-minded group became a reality with the purchase of 52 wooded acres in 1966 and the addition of an old log cabin, moved intact from the North Freedom area, in 1967. Local families began donating precious mementos, artifacts from their ancestors, and old log cabins to the village, wishing them to be shared and preserved for the education of future generations. From this beginning, the rest became history.

Today, the Pioneer Log Village consists of eight log cabins, representing family homes, a general store, a post office, a church, and a one-room schoolhouse. Three large museum buildings are filled with keepsakes and memories of the area's past. The village is a place to experience days gone by, imagine what life was like then, and learn from those who came before. See you at the village.

Thanks also go to the Reedsburg Public Library. Without its resources, the authors would not have many of the photos for this book. The library can be contacted at:

Reedsburg Public Library
370 Vine Street, Reedsburg WI, 53959
Phone: 608-768-READ (7323)
Fax: 608-524-9024
Email: rplstf@scls.lib.wi.us

Discover Thousands of Local History Books Featuring Millions of Vintage Images

Arcadia Publishing, the leading local history publisher in the United States, is committed to making history accessible and meaningful through publishing books that celebrate and preserve the heritage of America's people and places.

Find more books like this at
www.arcadiapublishing.com

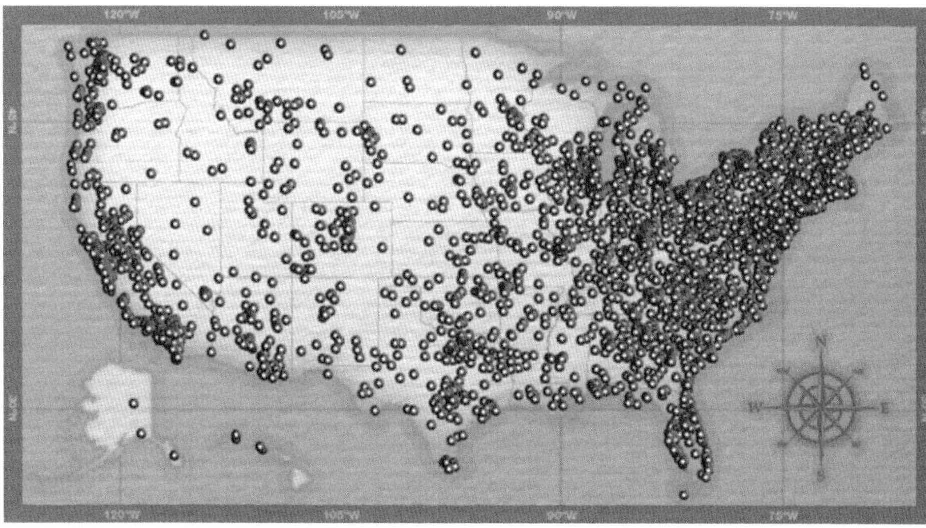

Search for your hometown history, your old stomping grounds, and even your favorite sports team.

Consistent with our mission to preserve history on a local level, this book was printed in South Carolina on American-made paper and manufactured entirely in the United States. Products carrying the accredited Forest Stewardship Council (FSC) label are printed on 100 percent FSC-certified paper.

MADE IN THE USA